Children's
BUSY
BOOK

The Children's BUSY BOOK

Trish Kuffner

m Meadowbrook Press

Distributed by Simon & Schuster
New York

Library of Congress Cataloging-in-Publication Data
Kuffner, Trish.
    The children's busy book / Trish Kuffner; [illustrations, Laurel Aiello].
        p. cm.
    Includes bibliographical references and index.
    ISBN 978-0-88166-405-8 (Meadowbrook) ISBN 978-1-476-70207-0 (Simon & Schuster)
        1. Creative activities and seat work. 2. Education, Primary—Activity programs. I. Title.
    LB1537 .K94 2001
    372.13—dc21

                                                                        2001044047

Editorial Director: Christine Zuchora-Walske
Copyeditor: Kathleen Martin-James
Proofreader: Megan McGinnis
Desktop Publishing: Danielle White
Production Manager: Paul Woods
Cover Photography: © Laura Doss/Corbis
Cover Illustration: Dorothy Stott
Interior Illustrations: Laurel Aiello

Published by
Meadowbrook Press
6110 Blue Circle Drive, Suite 237
Minnetonka, MN 55343

www.meadowbrookpress.com

BOOK TRADE DISTRIBUTION by
Simon and Schuster, a division of Simon and Schuster, Inc.
1230 Avenue of the Americas
New York, NY 10020

20 19 18 17 16 15 14 13   10 9 8 7 6 5 4 3 2 1

Printed in the United States of America

Acknowledgments

Years ago I had no idea that writing books would become a regular part of my life. Now that it has, I know it wouldn't be possible without the support of a very special group of people.

God is awesome, and I know that without His love, grace, mercy, and guidance I couldn't accomplish all that He's set out for me to do in this life.

My family is amazing. Their sacrifice makes it possible for me to write. Thank you for going out of your way many times and in many ways to help when help was needed.

I have a great group of friends with whom I can laugh, cry, hope, dream, whine, complain, and otherwise share the adventure of parenting. My heartfelt thanks to all of you. I couldn't have made it through the tough times without your wisdom, encouragement, and comfort.

My family was blessed for a time with the help of a cheerful, dependable, capable young woman named Corine Opliger. Her desire to see Canada and improve her English became our good fortune when she traveled from Switzerland to stay with us for several months. I couldn't have met my writing deadline without her. Thanks, Corine; we miss you.

I am very fortunate to have the Meadowbrook Press publishing team behind me: Bruce Lansky; my excellent editor, Christine Zuchora-Walske; and everyone else who's helped get this book from my head to the store shelves. I sincerely appreciate all your contributions—seen and unseen—that have made *The Children's Busy Book* a reality.

Dedication

This book is dedicated to the people with whom I spent my childhood: my parents, Jack and Irene McGeorge; and my three sisters, Linda Young, Carol Hannah, and Marlene Ciaburri.

Here's to memories of riding bikes, flying kites, baseball games, the neighborhood gang, snow forts, water fights, skipping, pet mice, Whiskers and Angel, Betsy, long road trips, summers on the farm, the red-coated vulture, Peep and Willie, and much, much more.

Bishop Desmond Tutu said, "You don't choose your family. They are God's gift to you, as you are to them." I love you all.

Contents

Introduction

Children are the hands by which we take hold of heaven.
—Henry Ward Beecher

I'm not a person who likes change, or at least not too much change. When things are going smoothly, when all my kids are in stages I like, I sometimes wish that time would just freeze and I could hold on to the golden moments forever. The first time I experienced that feeling was the day I came home from the hospital with my first-born daughter. I knew I would never again experience that special joy of becoming a mother for the first time. Never again would I feel the same surge of pride and happiness I felt when my parents held their first grandchild for the very first time.

But to be truly alive is to change. As Natalie Babbitt writes in *Tuck Everlasting*, "You can't pick out the pieces you like and leave the rest." Without change, Babbitt writes, "We just *are*, we just *be*, like rocks beside the road."

Life with children is certainly about change. When your first child was born, your life changed. When he first slept through the night, your life changed. When he began walking and talking, your life changed. When your needy toddler grew into an autonomous preschooler, your life changed. And when your child entered school for the first time, your life changed again.

Did you think it would ever happen? After years of sticky fingers, runny noses, diapers, spilled milk, teething, endless days, sleepless nights, and all the other joys of life with babies and toddlers, did you think your child would ever turn into the independent little person who now boards the school bus or walks to school with the neighborhood gang each morning? Perhaps now you're able to return to work or have some time to pursue your own hobbies or interests. Or perhaps you still have little ones at home, and it seems like it'll take forever before they'll all be in school! Or maybe your family, like ours, has chosen to home-school, and school is no farther than the kitchen table. Whatever your situation, the arrival of the school years means change of one form or another.

Many people breathe a sigh of relief when their children begin school. Finally, they think, they'll have some time to themselves. (And after five or more years with babies, toddlers, and preschoolers, this can be a very pleasant thought.) Others, like Marguerite Kelly and Elia Parsons, weep when their children begin school, "not because of the child we're losing, but because of the chances we've lost. So much is left undone."

Like Kelly and Parsons, you may have a lot left undone, but life isn't over yet! Although your school-age child may have a full schedule and a busy little social life, he'll still have some free time. And what will you encourage him to do in that free time? Watch TV? Play computer games? Or is there something better for him to do? Something that will encourage him to think, be creative, or interact with others?

The purpose of *The Children's Busy Book* is to help you make the most of your child's free time. The 365 games and activities in this book will challenge your child's creativity, imagination, thinking skills, social skills, and more. You can use this book to plan activities for after-school hours, for a summer afternoon when you're taking a break from the heat, or to fill a winter weekend. The games and activities you set in motion will encourage your child to be creative, to think, and to interact with others, which most computer games, DVDs, and TV programs won't do.

While the ideas in *The Children's Busy Book* are most suitable for children between the ages of six and ten, older children and adults will also enjoy many of them. On the other hand, you may find the ideas in this book too advanced for your six-year-old, an indication of nothing more than the fact that he is completely different from every other six-year-old in the world. The ideas in *The Preschooler's Busy Book* might better suit your child's present interests and abilities. Don't hesitate to come back to *The Children's Busy Book* in several months or a year.

I've tried to organize this book in what I think is the most logical way, but many ideas easily fit into two or more categories. For example, pencil-and-paper games are great for traveling, but they're also ideal for rainy days and they definitely help develop language and math skills. Many indoor games can easily be played outdoors in the summer, while some outdoor games are adaptable for indoors when the weather won't cooperate. Arts-and-crafts projects are great for rainy days and holidays, too, so be sure to "think outside the box" when it comes to selecting activities from each chapter.

I hope you find this book helpful. If you do, or if you have questions or comments about any of the books I've written, you can write to me in care of Meadowbrook Press. I'd love to hear from you.

Trish Kuffner

P.S. In recognition of the fact that children do indeed come in both sexes, and in an effort to represent each, the use of masculine and feminine pronouns will alternate with each chapter.

CHAPTER 1
The Basics

Parents are often so busy with the physical rearing of children that they miss the glory of parenthood, just as the grandeur of the trees is lost when raking leaves.

—Marcelene Cox

Congratulations! You survived!

You survived the newborn stage, when you were afraid to let anyone hold your child for fear she'd be dropped. The stage when going to the mall with a baby, a car seat, a stroller, and a diaper bag seemed an insurmountable task. The stage when you couldn't go anywhere in case your baby woke up and *had to nurse!*

You survived your child's infancy, when you couldn't wait to see what was going to happen next: She smiled! She laughed! She rolled over (back to tummy)! She rolled over (tummy to back)! She sat up! She ate baby cereal! She cut a tooth! The stage when your baby's cry would wake you in the dead of night, and your body felt like stone as it refused to get out of bed one more time.

You survived your child's toddlerhood, when you realized that your child possessed absolutely no social skills: If I like it, it's mine. If it's in my hands, it's mine. If I can take it from you, it's mine. If I had it a week ago, it's mine. If it looks just like mine, it's mine. If I think it's mine, it's mine. If it's near me, it's mine. (If it's broccoli, it's yours.)

And you survived your child's preschool years, when her determination, energy, and curiosity combined to create some truly memorable events: the haircut she inflicted on herself, the time she called 911 by accident, the day she decided to change the baby's dirty diaper all by herself, and her unforgettable early morning refrigerator raid.

You survived it all, and now you get to enjoy a brief respite before your child's adolescence begins!

Children of all ages bring their parents joy, and children between the ages of six and ten can be a true delight. Kids at this age have a newfound ability to take part in fun, interesting, and creative activities that even adults enjoy. A child of this age can easily learn a new card game, begin a stamp collection, read a novel, write a story, play marbles, learn to bake, and much more. Perhaps she can ski, swim, bike, or hike with the rest of her family. She can learn to sew, build, paint, garden, or share in the interests of the significant adults in her life.

Another thing that six-to-ten-year-old children usually do is go to school. Most children thrive as they learn many things from the new adults in their lives. A child of this age seeks acceptance from her peers and may develop a wide circle of friends with whom she loves to play. She certainly develops a sense of independence from her parents as she heads off to her classroom each day.

On the downside, the arrival of the school years means that a child has far less time for creative and spontaneous play and for spending time with her family. Going to school and after-school lessons, sports, and clubs; playing with friends; and doing other activities usually leave little time for a child to use her imagination, to think, to dream. Finding the time to play a game or take a walk, make crafts or bake, or even read and talk together is a challenge for a family with a school-age child. During the preschool years, the days seemed to have too many hours in them. Now, suddenly, the days aren't long enough.

There are, however, wonderful lulls in a school-age child's busy routine: weekends and holidays. These provide much-needed downtime for children, their teachers, and their families; time when children can pursue interests and hobbies; time when parents and children can reconnect; time when families can relax and enjoy playing games, reading, talking, walking, or just being together. Read on to discover ways in which you can make the most of your child's school-free time, whether it's a half-hour in the car, a rainy weekend afternoon, or your family's two-week summer vacation.

PLANNING YOUR ACTIVITIES

You've probably heard it said that failing to plan is planning to fail. When my children were young, I learned that this axiom applies not only to big things like saving for your child's education, but also to little things like reading a new book together, starting a stamp collection, or playing a game of cards with your child. Schools plan curricula very carefully to ensure that children have a variety of experiences, cover specific material, and learn or practice certain skills each day. Parents at home can be a lot less formal, but planning is still important. A book like this one is only valuable if you use the ideas it contains. If you don't do a little planning, chances are that this book will sit on your shelf and gather dust.

Here are some guidelines to help you plan activities for your child:

1. Browse this book from cover to cover and make a list of activities you'd like your child to do alone, with you, or with your whole family.
2. Create a weekly plan from your list of activities. Be realistic—you likely won't be able to do something every day. Choose just one or two activities for the week. Then choose an alternate activity or two for bad weather days or for days when what you've planned just won't work.
3. If any of the activities you've chosen need special supplies, make a list of the items you'll need and assemble or purchase them beforehand.
4. Make a list of anything you need to do ahead of time, such as mix paint, make a batch of modeling clay, and so on.

5. Plan special activities for your baby sitter (if you have one) and have all the necessary materials handy. This will let your sitter know that spending an afternoon or evening in front of the TV with your children is not an option.
6. Make a list of ideas that would be fun to do anytime you can fit them into your schedule. Have this list ready for when you have some unexpected free time.

STOCKING UP ON SUPPLIES

Most of the activities in this book require some basic supplies. You can easily find many of the following items around the home, but you will need to purchase some of them. Store your supplies in a cupboard in the kitchen, a shelf in the garage, a box in the basement, or in your child's playroom.

aluminum foil
art prints
art smock (or old
   T-shirt)
balloons
balls: golf, tennis,
   Ping-Pong
beads (assorted)
beanbags
bed sheets (old)
book club fliers

bottle caps
boxes
buttons
calendars (old and
   current)
camera
candles
cardboard
catalogs
ceramic tile (vari-
   ous sizes)

cereal boxes
children's dic-
   tionary and
   thesaurus
chopsticks
clay
clear acrylic spray
clear nail polish
clothes and cos-
   tume jewelry
   (for dress-up)

clothespins
coffee cans with
    lids
coins
cold-water dye
colored pencils
construction
    paper
contact paper
copper wire
corks
cotton balls
craft magnets
crayons
crepe paper
darning needle
drinking straws
dry beans
dry pasta (differ-
    ent shapes and
    sizes)
egg cartons
empty jars and
    lids
envelopes
fabric scraps
felt
film canisters

(empty)
fishing line
flannel
flashlight
funnel
gift-wrap scraps
glitter
glue
glue gun
glue sticks
glycerin
grass seeds
greeting cards
    (used)
grout
hole punch
ice cream buckets
    (empty)
index cards
iodine
jewelry clasps
jump rope
junk mail
kitchen timer or
    wind-up alarm
    clock
kite

lids from plastic
    gallon jugs, baby
    food jars, frozen
    juice cans
magazines (old)
magnifying glass
marbles
markers (dry-
    erase, perma-
    nent, and wash-
    able)
maps
matte board
metal washers
modeling com-
    pound (Fimo,
    Sculpey, or
    other)
newspapers
newsprint roll
notebooks
paint (acrylic, fab-
    ric, tempera)
paintbrushes
paper clips
paper fasteners
paper lunch bags
paper plates

paper scraps
paper towel and
toilet paper
tubes (empty)
pencils
pens
petroleum jelly
photographs of
friends and
family
pill bottles (empty)
pillowcases (old)
pine cones
pipe cleaners
plaster of Paris
plastic bowls, lids,
bottles
plastic dishpan
plastic jugs
(empty)
plastic wrap
playing cards (mis-
matched and
complete decks)
Popsicle sticks
poster board

potpourri
potting soil
ribbon
rickrack
rubber bands
ruler
sand
sandpaper
scissors
shallow box (the
kind a 24-pack of
soda comes in)
shoeboxes with
lids
socks (old)
sponges
spray bottle
stapler
stationery and
stamps
stickers of all
kinds
stones
string
Styrofoam cups
and trays

tape (transparent,
masking, col-
ored)
terra cotta pots
phone books (old)
thin elastic cord
three-ring binders
thumbtacks
tin cans (empty)
tissue paper
thread
toothbrushes (old)
toothpicks
utility knife
wine bottle
(empty)
wood scraps
wooden dowels
writing pads
yarn scraps
Ziploc bags

"BUT THERE'S NOTHING TO DO!"

No matter how busy your child is with school, music lessons, sports, friends, or other activities, there will always come a time when she's bored or restless. Children whose time is always rigidly planned for them and those who spend a lot of time with TV or computer games often find it difficult to be creative and imaginative with their free time.

When my children were young, I organized our home to help reduce episodes of boredom. If you've read either *The Toddler's Busy Book* or *The Preschooler's Busy Book,* you may recognize some of the following ideas, which have been modified for older children.

Keep a baker's box in the kitchen.

Fill a plastic crate or storage box with a collection of unbreakable kitchen tools: cake pan, cookie cutters, baking sheet, bowls, measuring cups and spoons, mixing spoons, rubber spatula, muffin pan, and so on. Store it in a spare cupboard that's low enough for your child to reach. She can use her tools for playing with play dough, modeling clay, or dry pasta or for helping you with cooking and baking projects.

Have a busy box handy.

Fill a small plastic crate or storage box with things your child can use on her own anytime. A school-age child will appreciate many craft items in her busy box: crayons, markers, coloring books, paper, tape, stickers, scissors, glue, ink pad, rubber stamps, play dough, and so on.

Set up a tickle trunk.
A tickle trunk full of dress-up clothes and props will not only foster your child's imaginative play, but it also will likely hold her interest throughout her childhood. Fill a trunk, toy box, large plastic container, or cardboard box with adult clothes, shoes, hats, scarves, gloves, and costume jewelry to use for dress-up. Old suits are great, as are Hawaiian shirts, vests, baseball hats, bridesmaid dresses, nightgowns, wigs, boots, slippers, and purses. Look for tickle trunk items at garage sales or local thrift shops, or stock up on princess gowns and animal costumes at post-Halloween sales.

Make a rainy day box.
When the weather is bad, or when your child is sick, a rainy day box full of surprises can help break the monotony. Good things to put in a rainy day box for a school-age child are:

- New art supplies (pad of paper, markers, paint box, stickers, or play dough)
- A new toy (or one that your child hasn't played with in a while)
- A new book, CD, or DVD
- Special dress-up items
- Cookie cutters and a new or favorite cookie recipe

- Supplies and directions (stored in a Ziploc bag) for a new game or craft

Don't overuse your rainy day box; your child will find it interesting only if its appearance is somewhat extraordinary. Hide your rainy day box in a safe place and bring it out only when the day seems unusually long.

Make a job jar for your family.
Instilling a sense of responsibility for household chores is something that can be started at any age. Make a job jar for your family using an empty jar, coffee can, or small box. Cut out strips of paper and print a small job that needs to be done on each one. A toddler will enjoy wiping a floor or refrigerator with a damp cloth or sponge, stacking towels in a cupboard, or picking up toys and placing them in a basket or container. A preschooler can straighten bookshelves, wash a bathroom sink, put away towels, or wash vegetables. Six-to-ten-year-olds can sweep, vacuum, dust, wipe counters, set and clear a table, load and unload a dishwasher, and so on. Older children can fold laundry, clean bathrooms, wash floors, and more. You know best which jobs your child is capable of doing with minimum supervision and assistance.

Whenever you do your household chores or your child whines one too many times about being bored, have her pick a job from the job jar. If your child is normally an unwilling helper, letting her choose her own job may reduce her reluctance.

Rotate your child's toys.

If your family is like ours, your kids have received many wonderful toys as gifts for birthdays, holidays, and other occasions. While parents appreciate the good intentions of the givers, most children have more toys than they can possibly play with. Also, even the most creative toys will fail to hold your child's interest if they're always around. If you rotate your child's toys every four to six weeks, they'll seem new to her and will be interesting and exciting all over again.

Separate your child's toys into piles. (If your child has a favorite toy, keep it out all the time.) Keep one pile in your child's room or play area and pack the others away in boxes, marking dates for when they are to be brought out. If you have friends with children the same age, why not try a toy exchange? Keep a list of what's been exchanged and be sure to agree on the terms beforehand (how long, who's responsible for breakage, and so on).

Make a crazy can.

Someone once referred to the dinner hour as "arsenic hour." Perhaps you've worked all day, driven the car pool to ballet or hockey practice, and are now faced with a tired, hungry family to feed. Or maybe you've been home all day with preschoolers and toddlers whose naps were too short. Whatever the case, the dinner hour is usually when you're busiest and your children are crankiest. In the midst of the chaos, you yearn for a distraction to keep them busy. Since you're probably not feeling at your most creative or your most patient, this isn't a great time to brainstorm activities. Planning ahead with a crazy can may be the answer.

Make a list of on-the-spot activities that require no special materials, no time-consuming preparation or cleanup, and no serious adult participation or supervision. Write these ideas down on index cards or small slips of paper and put them in an empty coffee can. If you like, cover the can with cheerful contact paper, or cover it with plain paper and have your child decorate it using paint, markers, or crayons. When things start to get crazy or when there's just nothing to do, choose a card from the can for an instant remedy. See Appendix B (page 410) for a list of activities appropriate for a school-age child's crazy can.

Bring a busy bag.
A busy bag will help prepare you for those times when your child just has to wait—at a doctor's office, hairdresser, or restaurant; in the car; on the bus; and so on. Turn a draw-string bag or backpack into a portable busy bag that can be filled with special goodies to keep your child amused. School-age children may enjoy Barbies, Legos, dolls, books, audio-tapes, CDs, Matchbox cars, puzzles, special snacks, stickers and a sticker book, paper and markers, magnets and a small metal cake pan, and so on. You can make the contents of the busy bag a surprise for your child or have her help you fill it before you go.

WHAT ABOUT TV?

TV may not have been much of an issue during your child's toddlerhood and preschool years. Maybe she has enjoyed watching several programs during the day or maybe she hasn't been interested at all. Whatever the situation, it's likely to change when your child starts school. First, her free time will be drastically reduced by the time she spends at school. Second, influence from her classmates may prompt your child to ask permission to watch more TV or to watch programs you feel are inappropriate.

The influence of television on children has been much debated over the years. As I stated in *The Preschooler's Busy Book*, the crux of the children-and-TV issue is not really what children watch, because parents can control that. I am more concerned about how parents use TV and what children do not do when they watch TV. It's easy to use TV as a baby sitter, but TV can be habit-forming for both parent and child. The little free time that school-age children have is better spent playing, reading, walking, talking, painting, and crafting.

But TV is here to stay. It's up to parents to use it in a way that will benefit their child's development and their relationship with their child. How should parents do this? First, be selective about what your children watch. Good TV programs can make learning fun and can expand your child's knowledge of the world. Look for programs or DVDs that instruct, entertain, and reinforce the values and principles you wish to develop in your child.

Second, limit your child's viewing time each day. Time spent watching TV is time that your child does not spend on other more valuable activities like playing games, reading (or being read to), or using her imagination in countless other ways. Children who spend a lot of time watching TV may be less likely to use their own imagination and creativity to entertain themselves.

Third, watch TV with your child when possible. Many programs move so quickly that it's almost impossible for children to stop and ponder what's happening. Parents can provide connections that children miss. By reminding your child of related events in her own life, you'll help her make sense of what she sees.

Finally, set an example for your child. Show her that you'd rather read a book or play a game or talk to her than watch TV. Don't expect your child to limit her viewing and choose programs wisely if you do the opposite. Remember: Children learn from our actions more than from our words.

A WORD OF ENCOURAGEMENT

Parenting is a tough job and one for which you don't often receive appreciation or praise. But as Dr. Benjamin Spock said, raising children, "seeing them grow and develop into fine people, gives most parents—despite the hard work—their greatest satisfaction in life."

Raising children also brings more than just satisfaction. As your child has grown from a newborn baby through the various stages of early childhood, you've grown, too. You've been stretched in more ways than you ever thought possible, you've made new friendships and learned new things about yourself, and you've probably developed the patience of a saint along the way!

Keep a positive outlook on life. Don't compare yourself to others unless the comparison gives you incentive to improve. Enjoy your children and accept them for who they are. Show them unconditional love. Give them lots of hugs and kisses while you can, because the "last time" may come any day: the last time you cuddle together for a bedtime story; the last time she'll let you hold her hand in the mall; the last time she'll let you pick out her clothes. Don't be influenced by what others view as success. If your children love you, if they look up to you, if they enjoy spending time with you, you're succeeding at life's biggest job.

CHAPTER 2
Rainy Day Play

Children today are tyrants. They contradict their parents, gobble their food, and tyrannize their teachers.

—Socrates

Rainy days aren't necessarily bad. In fact, I began writing books as a result of too many rainy days. The west coast of British Columbia, where we live, is often called "the wet coast." I've had more experience than I'd care to remember dealing with homebound babies, toddlers, and preschoolers. When my three oldest children were young, there were many rainy days when everyone was up at 5:00 A.M., and our entire day's worth of activities had been completed by 8:00 A.M. And there, stretching before us, were eight or nine more hours to fill until Daddy came home. The rain forced me to be creative in keeping my kids busy for all those hours, and the writing saved my sanity!

Now that the school years have arrived, our weekdays are filled with learning, sports, lessons, and other activities. Maybe we're too busy to pay attention to the weather during the week, but it sure seems that when the weekend comes, it's likely to be raining! Around here there's an oft-told joke that asks, "What follows two days of rain?" Answer? "Monday!"

But rainy days with school-age children are quite different from rainy days with preschoolers and toddlers. Most six-to-ten-year-olds don't need constant supervision and can work independently on crafts, games, hobbies, or other projects. So although our weekend plans may go out the window when the weather won't cooperate, it doesn't mean we can't have fun! It just means that we have to be a little more creative deciding how we're going to spend our time. Don't give in to the temptation to use computer or video games or TV to pass the time. A rainy afternoon can be a real blessing, reminding us how much fun it is to eat popcorn and play games, to work on a puzzle together, or to build an indoor tent with couch cushions, sheets, and clothespins.

Sometimes playing indoors together for a prolonged period results in bickering. Children who are laughing and having fun together one minute can be angry and not speaking to each other the next minute. I find that the following ideas from *101 Activities for Siblings Who Squabble* by Linda Williams Aber help relieve tension and get kids playing together again:

• Give each child an equal number of paper lunch bags. Have the children stand about six feet apart (or in a circle, if there are more than two children), blow into a bag to fill it with air, hold it tightly closed with one hand, then pop it with the other. Continue popping until laughter replaces squabbling.

- Designate one child "heads" and the other "tails," then flip a coin. The winner holds the coin and tells his side of the story. The other child may not speak while the player with the coin is talking. When the first child is finished, he passes the coin to the second child, who then tells his side of the story. The coin is passed back and forth until the children run out of things to say. They cannot repeat what they've said on a previous turn. Then they pass the coin back and forth three more times, with each child saying one nice thing about the other child on each turn.

- Give each child a supply of scrap paper and a wastebasket. Have each child stand about five feet from a basket, ball up a piece of paper, and toss it into his basket. As the children throw, let them express their anger out loud. For example, they might yell, "Take that!" Their anger will soon subside, and the children will be ready to play with each other again.

The games and activities in this chapter include ideas for children playing indoors on their own, with an adult, or with friends and siblings. Other chapters, such as "Arts and Crafts" (page 277), "Kids in the Kitchen" (page 87), "On the Move" (page 177), and "My Family and Me" (page 251), also have lots of ideas for things to do indoors. Even outdoor games like marbles (page 152) and hopscotch (page 147) can be played indoors. And if you like the indoor games and activities in this chapter, many can be adapted easily for outdoor play when the weather clears up.

ALL BY MYSELF

It's a rainy Saturday afternoon. Your active six-year-old is bored. He's called all his friends, but no one's available to play. The neighbor kids have gone out for the day. His older brother is doing homework, and his little sister, a last resort, is playing house. He has absolutely nothing to do. Sound familiar? Before you turn on the TV or a computer game, try one of the following activities. Children can do these all by themselves, but they're also fun for an adult and a child or for two or more children to do together.

Ping-Pong Pinball

Utility knife
Shallow box (from a 24-pack of soda)
Ping-Pong ball

Use a utility knife to cut three or four holes slightly larger than a Ping-Pong ball in a random pattern across the bottom of a shallow box. Have your child place a Ping-Pong ball at one end of the box, then hold the box and maneuver it so the ball reaches the other end without falling through a hole. For more challenge, cut more holes in the box or play with more than one ball at a time.

Coin Toss

Coin

How many times can your child flip a coin without dropping it? The coin must spin in the air without touching anything, and he must catch it in the palm of his hand. See if your child can beat his previous record for catches or use an egg timer to see how many catches he can make before the time is up. Have him play against a sibling or friend to see who can make the most catches or who can toss the coin the highest without dropping it.

Flashlight Fun

Scissors
Uninflated balloons (one red, one yellow, and one blue)
Flashlight
Rubber bands

Cut the rounded ends from the balloons. Stretch one balloon end over a flashlight and hold it in place with a rubber band. In a darkened room, have your child shine the flashlight on the ceiling or a wall to see the colorful light. Change colors. Layer balloons to see how mixing the colors creates new ones: yellow over blue to make green, red over yellow to make orange, and so on.

If you have three flashlights, place a different color on each. Shine two or more colors on the same spot to create a new color.

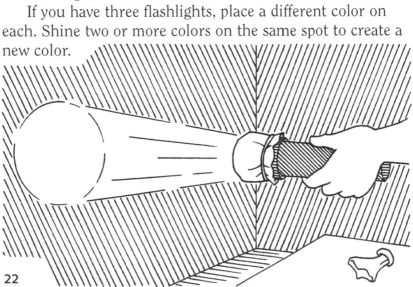

Scavenger Hunt

Grocery bag
List of things to collect

Give your child a grocery bag and a list of things to collect. The list may include things like a small toy, a Lego piece, a comb, a book, or anything else your child can find indoors. Set a time limit—perhaps twenty minutes for ten objects. (If the items are fairly obvious and easy to find, you'll need to shorten the time.) Reward your child with a small prize (for example, a pack of gum or an ice cream cone) for finding all the items on his list.

If your child isn't reading independently yet, draw pictures instead of writing a list of words.

For group play, prepare one list for each child. You can make the list of objects the same for each player or have players look for different things. The first player to find all the items on his list is the winner.

Grid Game

Large sheet of poster board or paper (at least three feet square) or old bed sheet
Pen or marker
Beanbag

On a large sheet of poster board or paper or an old bed sheet, draw a grid pattern of five columns by five rows. Across the top of the grid, label each column with an adjective like *big, small, hard, soft, round, long, short,* and so on. Down the side of the grid, label each row with a common color name like *red, green, yellow, blue, black, white,* and so on.

Lay the grid on a floor or other flat surface. Have your child stand several feet away from the grid and toss a beanbag on it. Your child must then find an object that matches the characteristics of the square into which the beanbag lands. For example, if the beanbag lands on a square in the "red" row and the "round" column, he must find something round and red like a ball, balloon, or marble.

To vary the grid, change the labels to correspond with different objects in your home. To include younger children, label the grid to correspond with stuffed animals (white cat, pink bear), toys (red Duplo piece, blue car), clothing (green sock, white T-shirt), and so on.

Library

Cataloging books is a good rainy day project for the book-worm in your family.

Paper
Pencil
Books
Notebook, index cards and recipe box, or simple computer
database
Date stamp (optional)

Compile a list of your family's books, starting with your child's bookshelf. Show your child how to write a list that includes at least the title and author of each book. If you like, your child might also include each book's subject, publisher, and year of publication.

Your child can list the books alphabetically in a notebook, note each book on an index card and keep the cards in a recipe box, or enter the information into a simple computer database so it can be sorted by author, title, or subject.

Once you've cataloged your books, open your library for loans to friends and family members. If you like, create a library card for each borrower and record the items you've loaned out. Your little librarian may enjoy using a date stamp for stamping due dates.

What's in the Bag?

Paper bag
Four or five small, hard-to-identify household objects

Fill a paper bag with four or five small household objects. *Science Wizardry for Kids* by Margaret Kenda and Phyllis S. Williams suggests hard-to-identify items, such as a small battery, a marble, a grape, an olive, an unshelled nut, and a pincushion with no pins in it. Look around your home to see what else you can come up with.

Have your child reach into the bag and try to identify the objects in it without looking. If you like, have him challenge a parent, sibling, or friend to identify the objects in the same way.

Shuffleboard

*Four or five flat, circular, unbreakable objects (lids from
   milk jugs or baby food jars, plastic hockey pucks, checkers, and so on)*
Ruler

Seat your child at the edge of a table with four or five flat,
circular, unbreakable objects in front of him. If possible, use
similar items rather than a mixture of objects. Ask your child
to try to slide the objects one at a time toward the opposite
end of table without sending them over the edge. Award
points as follows: one point for coming within six inches of
the edge, two points for coming within an inch of the edge,
three points for touching the edge, and four points for hanging over the edge. How many points can your child win in
five tries? If you like, have him play against a friend to see
who gets the most points.

27

Trick Your Fingers

This trick has a scientific twist, and most kids will think it's pretty neat.

Three bowls
Water
Ice cubes

Fill one bowl with cold water and ice cubes. Fill a second bowl with hot tap water (hot to the touch, but not hot enough to feel uncomfortable or burn your child's skin). Fill a third bowl with room-temperature water.

Put one of your child's hands in the bowl of ice water. Put the other hand in the bowl of hot water. After a minute, put both hands in the bowl of room-temperature water. Although both hands are in the same bowl, the water will feel cold to the fingers that have been in the hot water and hot to the fingers that have been in the cold water.

Cards in a Hat

Hat
Playing cards

Put the hat on the floor in the middle of a room. Have your child stand at a distance from the hat and try tossing cards one at a time into it. Keep track of how many make it in, then play again so he can try to improve his record.

For two players, separate the red and black cards. For three or four players, divide the cards by suit. Give one set to each child and have the children stand at equal distances from the hat and take turns tossing cards. Whenever a player gets a card in the hat, he gets another try. When all the cards have been tossed, the player with the most cards in the hat wins the round.

House of Cards

Building a house or castle with cards is a tricky thing to do. Using old cards with slits cut into them makes building less frustrating and more fun for young children.

Old playing cards
Scissors

Help your child cut two half-inch slits about two inches apart in each long side of each card. Show him how to fit the cards together to build a house, castle, or other structure.

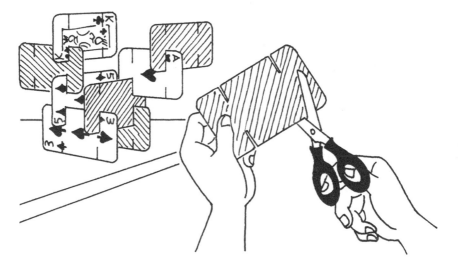

Card Toss

Playing cards (Old, incomplete, or mismatched decks are okay.)

Have your child stand several feet away from a wall and toss cards at its base. The object of the game is to get a card to lean upright against the wall instead of falling flat on the floor. When a card falls flat, it stays where it is. Whenever your child gets a card to lean, he wins all the cards lying on the floor. The game is over when he runs out of cards. See how long your child can keep this game going.

For two or more players, divide the cards equally among the players. Have the players take turns tossing their cards against the wall. Play until one player has all the cards or until you want to end the game.

31

ANOTHER KIND OF ALPHABET

Children around the world enjoy making up secret codes to communicate with each other. Your child may enjoy not only making up his own secret code, but also learning other ways of communicating with his friends using sign language, Braille, Morse code, or semaphore (a flag-based system).

American Sign Language

Most kids enjoy learning sign language—especially when they realize they can use it as a secret code. Help your child practice the manual alphabet illustrated below. Look for a poster you can hang in your child's room or a place mat that can turn mealtimes into practice times. You might also learn signs for basic words and phrases like *please, thank you, more, enough,* and so on.

Check your local library or bookstore for *Talking with Your Hands, Listening with Your Eyes* by Gabriel Grayson, Mary Beth Miller, and George Ancona and *Nursery Rhymes from Mother Goose* by Harry Bornstein and Karen Saulnier. Or look for *Beginning American Sign Language VideoCourse,* a set of fifteen DVDs produced by Sign Enhancers.

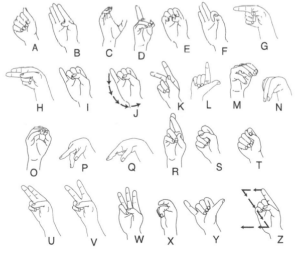

Braille

Paper and pen or pencil
Flat piece of Styrofoam

People with visual impairments use their fingers to read
Braille, a system of raised dots named after its creator, Louis
Braille. Different arrangements of six dots represent the
alphabet, numbers, punctuation marks, and so on.

Show your child how to write the Braille letters shown
below by punching holes in a sheet of paper (laid on a flat
piece of Styrofoam) with the tip of a pen or pencil. Because
Braille is read by feeling the raised dots on the reverse side of
the paper from left to right, it must be written backward—
from right to left. Begin by helping your child write his
name in Braille. With practice, he'll soon be able to write
phrases, sentences, and even entire messages.

If your child would like to learn more about Louis
Braille, you'll enjoy reading Russell Freedman's *Out of
Darkness: The Story of Louis Braille* together.

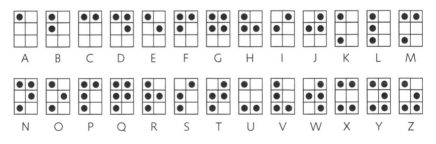

Morse Code

Morse code is a series of dots and dashes transmitted by sound or light. Developed in the 1830s by Samuel Morse, it was used by telegraph operators before the advent of the telephone. It is still used today in situations where there is no other means of communication. Although Morse code signals are commonly referred to as dots and dashes, the correct term for the short signal is *dit,* and the term for the long signal is *dah.* A *dah* is three times as long as a *dit.* Letters are separated by a signal the length of three *dits;* words are separated by a signal the length of seven *dits.*

Help your child learn Morse code (illustrated below). If you like, write each letter on an index card and use the cards to review the code. Begin by tapping out letters and having your child tell you what the letter is. As he learns, tap out names, words, and phrases. If you like, darken the room and use a flashlight to transmit the code.

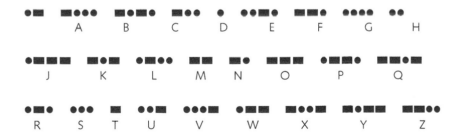

Semaphore

Semaphore is a flag-based system of communicating used by the military, pilots, sailors, and railroad workers. One flag is held in each hand; the flags are positioned in various combinations to represent letters and numbers.

Two flags

Help your child learn semaphore. Begin with the alphabet, then your child's name, common words, and so on. Your child will enjoy using semaphore to communicate with friends across the yard or street.

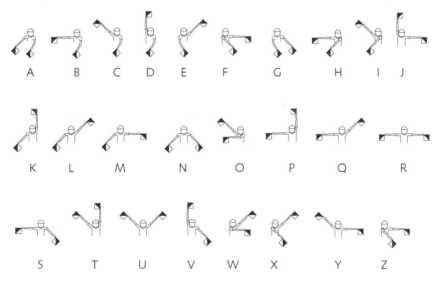

Chicken Scratch

Chicken scratch is a code in which one symbol represents each letter of the alphabet. At first you'll need a copy of the key in order to write and read chicken scratch messages. But with practice, you'll be able to write and read chicken scratch without looking at the key.

Chicken scratch key
Paper
Pencil

Have your child write a message on a sheet of paper. Help him use the key below to find the symbols that represent the letters in his message. Then have him copy his message in code on a separate sheet of paper. He can give his message and a copy of the key to a friend and challenge his friend to decipher what he's written.

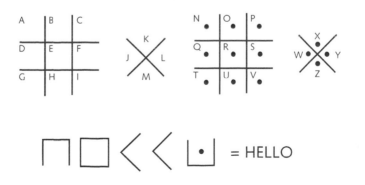

Top-Secret Code

Paper
Pencil

To create a top-secret code, your child should write the alphabet on a sheet of paper. After each letter he should write a symbol, such as a heart for *A*, a star for *B*, and so on. Once he's developed the code, make a copy of the key for a friend to whom he'd like to send secret messages.

Now have your child write a message on a sheet of paper. Next, he should rewrite the message on a separate sheet of paper, replacing the letters with code symbols. Then he can give the encoded message to his friend to decipher.

If you have a computer, codes are easy to write using fonts like Wingdings and Symbol or other alphabets like Arabic, Greek, or Hebrew. Just type your message in English, then highlight the message and change the font. I wrote the following message on my computer. Use the code to see if you can read what it says.

Here's the key:

A ♨   B ✌   C 👌   D ✋   E 👉   F 👉   G 👆   H 👇   I ✋
J ☺   K ☹   L ☹   M 💥   N ☠   O 👂   P 👈   Q ✈   R ☼
S 💧   T ❄   U ✝   V ✝   W ✠   X ✠   Y ✡   Z ☪   ! ✏

38

CARD GAMES FOR ONE PLAYER

Solitaire games are a great way to pass the long hours of a rainy afternoon, a sick day, or those inevitable times when "there's no one to play with." When I played cards by myself as a child, I knew only three ways to play solitaire. What a delight it was to discover that there are many enjoyable card games one can play alone.

The games that follow are fun to play yet simple enough for six-to-ten-year-olds. If your child enjoys playing cards—and most do—the book *101 Best Family Card Games* by Alfred Sheinwold provides games the whole family can enjoy.

Accordion

Deck of playing cards

Deal four cards faceup in a row from left to right. Compare each card with the two cards on its left (if available) to see if it matches with either card in number or suit. If so, place the card on top of its match. Moving the card creates a space in the row. Move the cards together to close up the space and check to see if new matches have appeared as a result.

Add one new card from your deck to the right of the row. Check to see if it is a match with the two cards on its left. Move the piles of cards accordingly if it is. If not, deal another card to the right of the row. Repeat.

The object of the game is to get the whole deck of cards into one pile. This is difficult to do, so ending up with five piles is a good outcome.

Aces Up

Deck of playing cards

Deal four cards faceup in a row. If two of the cards are of the same suit, discard the lower-value card. In this game, aces are the cards with the highest value. Fill the resulting empty space with a card from the deck. Continue until one card of each suit is displayed.

Deal a second row of cards on top of the first row. Compare the top cards of each pile. If two cards are of the same suit, discard the lower-value card. Fill any empty space with a card from the deck. Continue comparing and discarding until one card of each suit is displayed.

Continue dealing rows, comparing, discarding, and filling empty spaces until the entire deck of cards has been dealt. The object of the game is to discard all the cards except the aces.

Klondike

Deck of playing cards

Deal the cards facedown into seven columns of overlapping cards. The first column contains one card, the second column two cards, the third three cards, and so on. Turn the last card of each column faceup. Stack the leftover cards facedown to form a stock pile. The object of this game is to move the four aces to four foundation piles above the seven columns, then build each foundation pile up in suit from ace to king.

To play, turn three cards at a time faceup from the stock pile to form a waste pile. Only the top card of the waste pile and the last card of each column may be moved to a foundation pile. To move cards from the waste pile to the columns or to move cards among the columns (to expose new cards for play), build columns downward in sequence and alternating colors. (For example, lay a black ten on a red jack, a red nine on a black ten, and so on.) You may also move a sequence of cards together from the end of one column to the end of another. (For example, move a red five and a black four together from the end of one column to another column ending with a black six.) When a facedown card in a column is exposed, turn it faceup. An empty column may only be filled with a king. When the stock pile is empty, turn the waste pile facedown and use it as a stock pile. The game ends when either all the foundation piles are filled or when no more moves are possible.

Monte Carlo

Deck of playing cards

Deal the cards faceup into five rows of five cards each. The rows should not overlap.

Remove all pairs of adjacent cards (cards next to each other horizontally, vertically, or diagonally) that match each other in number. Then close up the holes in the layout by moving cards to the left and up, keeping the cards in the same order in which they were dealt. Deal new cards faceup to fill out the bottom row(s), so you end up with five rows of five cards each again.

Continue removing pairs, closing up holes, and dealing new cards until the entire deck has been dealt. The object of the game is to discard the entire deck in pairs.

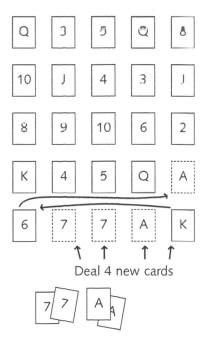

Deal 4 new cards

Thirteens

Deck of playing cards

Deal five cards faceup in a row. Remove any kings or pairs of
cards that add up to thirteen: an ace and a queen, a two and
a jack, a three and a ten, a four and a nine, a five and an
eight, or a six and a seven. Discard all the pairs, then deal a
new row of five cards on top of the first row. Discard any
pairs of top cards that add up to thirteen. Continue in this
way until the whole deck is dealt. The object of the game is
to discard the entire deck in pairs that add up to thirteen.

Fourteens

Deck of playing cards

Deal twelve cards faceup in a row. Deal three more rows
overlapping the first row, then deal the remaining four cards
as a fifth row on the first four columns. All the cards should
be visible. Remove any pairs of cards in the bottom row that
add up to fourteen: an ace and a king, a two and a queen, a
three and a jack, a four and a ten, a five and a nine, a six and
an eight, or a seven and a seven. The object of the game is to
discard the entire deck in pairs that add up to fourteen.

CARD GAMES FOR TWO OR MORE PLAYERS

Card games are fun to play as a family. They help children learn about numbers and provide practice in logical thinking for both children and adults. Card games also provide opportunities to practice appropriate winning and losing behavior. And unlike many board games that are either too complex for children or too simple for adults, well-chosen card games are enjoyable for everyone because they allow children and adults to play as equals.

If you're planning to play a new card game, make sure you have a good grasp of it before you try teaching it to your children. When you're teaching your children the game, be sure to set aside time to play it with them. After your children understand the rules, they can play it without an adult. If your children tend to bicker when they play together, explain before each game what type of behavior you expect. Rudeness, name calling, cheating, gloating, and pouting should not be tolerated.

The following games are nice alternatives to old favorites like crazy eights, old maid, go fish, concentration, and war. You might even consider sweetening each game with a treat for the winner.

Go Boom

Deck of playing cards

Two players can play this game, but it works best with three or four. Deal seven cards facedown to each player and place the remainder of the deck facedown on the table.

The first player places one of his cards faceup on the table. The player to his left must play a card that matches it in number or suit. If the player to the left cannot do so, he must draw one card at a time from the deck until he gets and plays a matching card. Play continues with the next player to the left and so on.

The game ends when one player has no cards left in his hand. If the last card in the deck is drawn before the game ends, reshuffle the played cards and continue the game until one player runs out of cards.

Variation
When the last card is drawn from the deck, the player with the fewest cards in his hand wins the game.

Pigs

Deck of playing cards

Up to thirteen players can play this game, but it works best with three to six. Assemble four cards of the same number for each player. Shuffle the cards and deal four to each player.

Each player looks at his cards to see if he has four of a kind (of the same number). If nobody does, each player passes one unwanted card facedown to the player on his left. The players look at their cards again. If nobody has four of a kind, the players pass again until someone has four of a kind. When someone has four of a kind, instead of passing a card he quietly makes a pig snout by pushing up the tip of his nose with his finger. As the other players notice the player making a pig snout, they stop passing and do the same. The last player to make a pig snout must deal the cards for the next game.

Variations

Donkey: The first player with four of a kind quietly lays his cards on the table but continues passing cards. As each player notices, he does the same. The last player to notice gets a *D.* Play until one child gets *D-O-N-K-E-Y.*

Spoons: In the middle of the table place a pile of spoons (one spoon fewer than the number of players). When one player gets four of a kind, he grabs a spoon. As the other players notice, they quickly grab spoons, too. The player left without a spoon deals the cards for the next game.

Play or Pay

Deck of playing cards
Counters (poker chips, dry beans, pennies)

Deal an equal number of cards to each player. Place any left-over cards faceup in the center. Give each player an equal number of counters.

The player to the left of the dealer begins the game by laying an ace from his hand or from the leftover cards faceup on the table. If he can't do so, he must put a counter in the kitty. The next player to the left lays down the next card of the same suit (in this case, the two) from his hand or from the leftover cards. If he can't do so, he must put a counter in the kitty. The game continues in this way until the king is played. The player who plays the king makes the first play in the next round.

The player who runs out of cards first wins the game. Every other player puts one counter in the kitty for each card left in his hand. The winner takes all the counters in the kitty.

Slapjack

Deck of playing cards

This game is best played with three or four players at a small table. Deal the cards facedown evenly among the players. Stack any extra cards in the middle of the table. Each player should stack his cards facedown in front of him.

The player to the left of the dealer turns over a card and drops it faceup on the middle stack (in a way that lets everyone see it at the same time). The next player to the left does the same. Play continues in this way until someone turns over a jack. Players slap the jack to win the pile of cards. If more than one player slaps the jack, the player whose hand is at the bottom of the pile wins. The winner places his new cards facedown under the others in his stack. Then play continues.

If a player slaps a card that isn't a jack, he must give the top card facedown from his stack to the person who played the card he slapped. If the false slapper has no cards left, he's out of the game.

When a player has turned over all his cards, he can still watch for the next jack and try to slap it to get more cards. If he misses, he's out of the game. The game ends when someone wins all the cards.

Jiggety, Joggety, Jig

Deck of playing cards

Three to thirteen players can play this game. Deal the cards facedown evenly among the players. Place any extra cards faceup in the middle of the table. Each player holds his cards so that he can see them, but no one else can.

The dealer chooses any card from his hand and lays it faceup in front of him. The player to the dealer's left checks for a card of the same number in his hand or among the left-over cards. If he finds one, he lays it down and shouts, "Jiggety!" If he doesn't, the next player to the left takes a turn.

The next player to find a match lays it down and shouts, "Joggety!" The third player to find a match lays it down and shouts, "Jig!" which ends the round. The "jigger" gets to start the next round.

The player who runs out of cards first wins the game.

Seven of a Suit

Deck of playing cards

Three to five players can play this game. For three players,
assemble three suits of seven cards each (twenty-one cards
total). For four players, assemble four suits of seven cards
each (twenty-eight cards total). For five players, assemble
three suits of nine cards each and one suit of eight cards
(thirty-five cards total). Shuffle the cards and deal seven to
each player.

The object of the game is to collect seven cards of one
suit. One at a time, each player passes a card from his hand,
facedown, to the player on his left. This should be a card that
doesn't match the suit he is trying to collect. Play continues
until a player collects seven cards of one suit.

INDOOR GARDENING

Gardening is usually considered an outdoor activity, but gardens can be grown indoors, too. Indoor gardening is fun and rewarding whether you live in an apartment with no outdoor garden space, need a class science project, or simply want to grow some seedlings to plant outdoors in the spring. An indoor garden can be grown in pots on a balcony, in containers on a windowsill, in hanging baskets, or in window boxes.

One of the best guides for indoor gardening projects is *Gardening Wizardry for Kids* by L. Patricia Kite. It provides many easy-to-read, easy-to-do indoor plant projects and experiments for children and explains gardening history, folklore, games, crafts, and more. Best of all, the projects don't need a lot of space, time, money, or parental involvement.

The following activities are simple and fun and will introduce your child to the wonderful world of gardening.

Herb Garden

Because growing requirements vary among herbs, be sure to read each seed packet before you begin.

Marker
Popsicle sticks
Empty coffee cans or other leakproof containers
Potting soil
Herb seeds, such as basil, thyme, rosemary, parsley, sage, marjoram, oregano, dill, cilantro, mint, or chives
Spray bottle full of water

Help your child write the name of each herb on a Popsicle stick. Fill each container two-thirds full of potting soil. Plant the seeds according to the instructions on the packets, using a different container for each herb. Mark each container with the appropriate Popsicle stick. Spray each container with water until the surface of the soil is completely damp. Place the containers by a sunny window.

Spray the containers regularly to keep the soil damp but not wet. Seedlings will appear in two to four weeks, depending on the herb. Let the plants grow for several weeks. Use the leaves for cooking and freeze or dry any surplus. You can freeze herbs by chopping them, mixing them with a bit of water, and freezing them in ice cube trays. To dry herbs, see the instructions on page 58.

Green Onions

Green onions, or scallions, are easy to grow indoors from seed and are a nice addition to salads and other dishes.

*Leakproof container, such as a large yogurt or cottage
    cheese tub or a small coffee can
Potting soil
Green onion seeds
Spray bottle full of water*

Have your child fill a container about two-thirds full of pot-ting soil. Sprinkle the seeds on top of the soil and cover them lightly with more soil. Spray the surface of the soil with water until it's completely damp. Place the container in an artificially lit or partially sunny place.

Spray the containers regularly to keep the soil damp but not wet. Seedlings will appear in two weeks. When the plants are about three inches tall, thin them so the remaining plants are about an inch apart. When the stems are as thick as a pencil, the onions are ready to be picked.

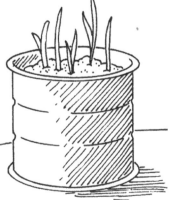

Peanuts

*Glass or plastic container (about six inches wide and four
    inches deep)*
Potting soil or earth without lumps
Sand
Fresh, unroasted peanuts in the shell
Water

Have your child fill a container about two-thirds full of potting soil or earth without lumps. Mix a little sand with the
soil. Remove the shells from five peanuts and place the nuts
on top of the soil in your container. If you are using a clear
container, place the nuts near the edge so you can see them
grow. Cover the peanuts with one inch of soil. Place the container in a warm, sunny spot and keep the soil damp.

In about two weeks, round leaves will begin to sprout.
When the tallest plant is about five inches high, remove the
other plants from the container and throw them away. When
the plant is about a foot tall, it will have yellow flowers on it
that will fall off. Smaller flowers that form on each stalk will
develop fruit that will start bending toward the soil. The fruit
will push its way into the soil, and a peanut will form at each
tip. You can dig up the peanuts when the leaves begin to
turn yellow.

Fruit and Veggie Plants

Lemon, orange, grapefruit,
   and/or potato
Knife
Leakproof containers
Water

Potting soil or earth
   without lumps
Plastic wrap and rubber band
Large bucket

Lemon, Orange, or Grapefruit Plant

Soak the seeds in water overnight. Have your child fill a container about halfway with soil or earth. Poke the seeds about a half-inch into the soil. Cover the container with plastic wrap secured with a rubber band. Place the container on top of your refrigerator. In about three weeks, plants will sprout.

Potato Plant

Have your child fill a large bucket about halfway with soil or earth. Lay two small potatoes on the soil and cover them with about one more inch of soil. Water the soil until it's slightly damp, then place the bucket in a warm, sunny place. Leaves will sprout in a week or so, then purple flowers, then maybe even tiny potatoes beneath the soil. (Caution: Potato plants can be poisonous if handled improperly. Keep your plant away from small children and animals. Keep your potatoes away from light by covering them with plenty of dirt and storing them in a dark place. Never eat a potato with green spots.)

Seedlings

Your child should grow seedlings indoors about one month
before he wants to plant them outside.

Styrofoam cups
Potting soil
Seeds
Pen
Tray
Spray bottle full of water
Plastic wrap

Fill Styrofoam cups with potting soil. Plant the seeds according to the instructions on the seed packets, then label each
cup with the name of the plant in it. Put the cups on a tray
and spray them with water until the soil is damp. Cover the
tray with plastic wrap and place it on top of your refrigerator.
Don't put the tray in a sunny spot.
   Every day, lift the plastic from the cups for an hour.
Water the plants when the surface of the soil looks dry. When
green sprouts appear, remove the plastic wrap and place the
tray in a sunny spot. When the plants are four inches tall,
you can transplant them. Help the plants adjust by putting the
seedlings outside for a few hours each day before you transplant them. After a week, they'll be ready for planting in your
garden.

Dried Flowers

Drying flowers is a wonderful way for your child to enjoy their beauty all year long.

Variety of flowers   *Florist's foam (optional)*
Rubber bands or string   *Vase or pot*
Coat hangers

Choose a variety of flowers to dry. Some flowers that dry well are baby's breath, thistles, roses, strawflowers, statice, dahlias, black-eyed Susans, and poppies. Use rubber bands or string to tie flower stems together in groups of five. Tie the bunches by their stems to coat hangers. Be sure the bunches don't touch each other. Hang the coat hangers in a closet or in a dark, dry, well-ventilated room. The dark-ness prevents the flowers from fading, and the dryness and ventilation prevent the growth of mildew. After about two weeks, the flowers should be dry. If you like, place a piece of florist's foam in a vase or pot to help hold the flowers in place. Arrange the flowers however you wish.

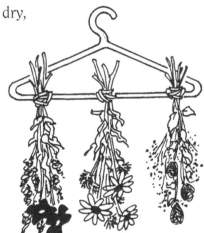

COLLECTOR'S CORNER

Kids love to collect things. When I think of all the things my kids have collected over the years, I recall that their interest in fad items waned quickly. Collections of coins, stamps, and sports cards, however, stand the test of time and have long been enjoyed by both children and adults.

Collecting is a valuable hobby for children. Collections can teach children about other cultures, history, art, sports, animals, nature, and more. Collecting requires children to be observant, encourages skills like sorting and classifying, and gives children the opportunity to interact with fellow collectors of all ages. Children appreciate receiving additions to their collections as gifts, and organizing a collection is a wonderful way to pass the hours of a rainy afternoon.

Most collections require a minimal amount of special equipment to get started. Look for books on the subject of your child's collection at your local bookstore, library, or online. Ask friends and relatives to be on the lookout for interesting and unusual coins, stamps, rocks, and so on, and to add to your child's collection at birthdays and holidays. Encourage togetherness by starting a collection as a family. Collecting can be enjoyed by all ages, and collections can be worked on and expanded as time and money permit.

Coins

Coins have been a popular item to collect for hundreds of years. They tell fascinating stories about kings and queens, gods and goddesses, history, nature, and more. Beginning a coin collection is easy—just start with the money you have in your pocket or lying around the house. My family's interest in coins was sparked by a special series of "millennium" quarters circulated by the Royal Canadian Mint in 1999 and 2000. My children have continued to pay special attention to the coins they see, and one of our daughters has taken over a collection of international coins that I began as a child.

Be sure to let your family and friends know that your child has begun a coin collection. Most people have at least a few interesting coins around the house, and they'll probably be happy to share them with someone who will appreciate them. Special uncirculated (or mint) sets are fairly affordable and make wonderful gifts.

For additional information on collecting coins, check your local bookstore or library for a book like *A Kid's Guide to Collecting Coins* by Arlyn G. Sieber. Mints publish colorful catalogs several times each year and will, on request, put you on their mailing list. In the United States, call 800-USA-MINT (872-6468) or order online at www.usmint.gov. In Canada, call 800-267-1871 or order online at www.mint.ca.

Stamps

Stamp collectors require some special equipment, but your child may begin his collection simply by saving the stamps that come in your mailbox each day. Ask friends and relatives to save interesting stamps, too, and you'll be surprised at how quickly your child's collection grows. If you want to kick-start his collection, you can buy bags of stamps from around the world at a hobby shop, stamp dealer, stamp show, or online for as little as five dollars for five hundred stamps.

Look online for information on stamp collecting from national philatelic organizations and the postal service. In the United States, kids can join clubs such as the Young Stamp Collectors of America and the All Star Stamp Club by visiting The American Philatelic Society's web site at: www.stamps.org/Young-Philatelists.

In Canada, the Canada Post Corporation has a stamp collecting club kids can join called The Stamp Quest Club. To find out more, visit www.canadapost.ca or call 800-565-CLUB (2582).

Rocks

Some people like to collect old things—and rocks are the oldest things one can collect. They date back to the beginning of time! Collecting rocks is a great way to learn about the natural world. Rock collectors hunt for specimens, carry out experiments, and learn how rocks, minerals, and fossils are formed. Clubs and societies allow members to share their information and provide information on mail-order dealers, rock shops, and good places to look for specimens.

Whether your child wants to become a true rock collector or just display some interesting specimens he finds, a book like *The National Audubon Society Pocket Guide to Familiar Rocks and Minerals* will provide your child with basic information about rocks and help him identify the specimens he finds.

For more information on rocks, minerals, and fossils, go to www.usgs.gov/ask/index.php or write to U.S. Geological Survey National Center, 12201 Sunrise Valley Drive, Reston, VA 20192 or call 888-ASK-USGS. Or contact the American Museum of Natural History at Central Park West at 79th Street, New York, NY 10024-5192 or 212-769-5100. You can also visit the web sites of many organizations, institutions, and rock lovers around the world.

Sports Cards

The most popular types of sports cards are baseball cards, followed by football, basketball, and hockey cards. Cards are also made and sold for other sports, such as golf, boxing, lacrosse, soccer, tennis, wrestling, and so on. Kids who play amateur sports often have the opportunity to have cards of themselves made when their team photo is taken.

Collecting sports cards is a fun hobby for sports-loving kids. It's also a great way for them to learn more about the people and events associated with a sport they enjoy. Help your child decide what cards to collect. He may want to focus on a certain sport, team, or year or collect only rookie cards, superstar cards, or cards with mistakes on them.

A number of web sites have information on sports cards, such as Beckett Media (www.beckett.com) and Sports Card Forum (www.sportscardforum.com). Your child will also enjoy visiting a sports cards store and may want to join a sports cards club or subscribe to a sports cards magazine. (Ask at a sports card store for a list of magazines.)

Leaves

Leaves
Paper towel
Newspaper
Cardboard
Heavy book

Wax paper
Iron
Thin paper
Crayons
Tree identification book

Have your child collect a variety of fresh leaves. Gently dry wet ones with a paper towel. Preserve them by pressing, waxing, or rubbing.

To press the leaves, place them between two sheets of newspaper. The leaves shouldn't touch each other. Place the newspaper between two pieces of cardboard. Set a heavy book on the cardboard and let it sit for three weeks.

To wax the leaves, place them between two sheets of wax paper with the waxy sides of the sheets touching the leaves. Cover the wax paper with a sheet of newspaper and press it with a medium-hot iron for about thirty seconds. Then separate the waxed leaves from the paper.

To make leaf rubbings, place fresh leaves under a sheet of thin paper and rub the paper with the side of a crayon.

Identify your leaves with the help of a book like Diane Iverson's *My Favorite Tree: Terrific Trees of North America.*

Sand

Legend says that if you bring home sand from a beach, you'll visit that beach again. Whether that's true, collecting sand is a fun way to remember your visits to the beach and to see how sand differs from beach to beach.

Small containers (pill bottles, film canisters, and so on)
Labels
Pen
Camera
Magnifying glass

The next time you go to a beach, have your child fill a small container with sand (or bring home extra sand in a larger container to use for an arts-and-crafts project). Label the container with the name of the beach and the date. Help your child take a photo of the beach, too.

Look at the sand with a magnifying glass. Compare it with other samples in your collection. Notice the different colors, textures, and grain sizes. Store the sand collection on a shelf in your child's room. Every time he looks at it, he'll remember all the fun of his visits to the beach!

INDOOR OLYMPICS

The following games are quite physical and are great for using up excess energy on a rainy afternoon. Most are fun for one child playing alone and can also be played as contests among multiple children. If you like, award a small prize like a bite-size chocolate bar or small pack of gum to the winner of each game or hand out homemade medals (foil-covered cardboard circles stapled to ribbon). Don't forget to write the names of the record holders in your Family Book of Records (page 267). And if your children like these games, encourage them to think up other silly sports that they can play indoors.

Long Jump

String or tape
One marker (plastic jug lid, bingo chip, or labeled slip of
  paper) per player

Mark a starting line with string or tape. Have your child
stand at the starting line and jump forward. Place a marker
where he lands. Have him jump again. If his second jump is
farther than his first, move the marker to the second landing
spot; otherwise, leave the marker where it is. Have your child
jump five times. Leave his marker at his farthest landing
spot.

Let each child have a turn jumping as described above.
The child who jumps the farthest wins.

Discus Throw

String or tape
Paper plates

Mark a square at one end of a room with string or tape. Have your child stand back several feet and try to throw paper plates into the square. A child playing alone can see how many plates land in the square in a designated time. Two or more children can take turns throwing plates to see who has more successful throws. You may want to color-code each child's plates or label them with the child's name.

Javelin Throw

Tape or string
Toothpicks

Mark two lines ten feet apart on the floor with tape or string. Give each player five toothpicks. Have the players take turns standing behind one of the lines and throwing their tooth-picks, one at a time, toward the second line. Award points for toothpicks that cross or touch the line. The child with the most points wins.

Shot Put

Tape or string
Balloons
Ribbon or medal

Mark two lines several feet apart on the floor with tape or string. Give each player a balloon. Have the players take turns standing behind one of the lines and throwing their balloons, one at a time, toward the second line. Balloons won't travel far, so any player whose balloon crosses or touches the line deserves a ribbon or a medal!

Newspaper Golf

Newspaper   *Masking tape, paper, or empty tin cans*
Tape   *One golf or tennis ball per player*

Make a "golf club" for each player by rolling up several sheets of newspaper and taping them securely. Mark several "holes" on the floor with masking tape, sheets of paper, or empty cans lying on their sides. Have your child use his club to try to roll the ball into the holes.

Beanbag Throw

Tape or string
Beanbags (at least one per player)
Laundry basket or cardboard box (optional)

Mark two lines six feet apart on the floor with tape or string. Have the players take turns standing at one line and throwing a beanbag toward the other line. The winner is the player whose beanbag comes closest to the line without crossing it.

If you like, have the players aim for a laundry basket or cardboard box instead. Have the players take turns throwing all the beanbags one at a time toward the basket or box. The winner is the player who gets the most beanbags into the basket or box. If there's a tie, have a play-off round to determine the winner.

Ring Toss

Scissors
Small paper plates
Wine bottle, candlestick, or other tall, steady object

Cut the center out of each paper plate, leaving a one-inch-wide ring. Set a wine bottle, candlestick, or other tall, steady object on the floor. Have your child stand back several feet and try to throw the rings so that they land encircling the bottle or candlestick.

A child playing alone can see how many rings he tosses successfully in a designated time. Two or more children can take turns tossing rings to see who has more successful tosses. You may want to color-code each child's rings or label them with the child's name.

Beanbag Race

Tape or string
One beanbag per player

Mark two lines ten feet apart on the floor with tape or string. Give each player a beanbag and have the players stand at the starting line. Announce, "Ready, set, go!" and have the players race toward the finish line in one of the following ways:

- Crawling, while balancing beanbags on their backs
- Running, while squeezing beanbags between their knees

A player is disqualified if his beanbag falls before he reaches the finish line.

A child playing alone can race against the clock and try to cross the finish line within a designated time. He'll have fun trying to better his time with each try.

Cross the Creek

Rope or string

Mark two lines two feet apart on the floor with rope or string to make a "creek." Have each player take a turn jumping across the creek. Widen the creek by moving the ropes apart another three or four inches. Have the players jump again. Keep widening the creek and having the players jump until they fail to make it across. The winner is the player who's able to cross the widest creek.

Pillowcase Race

Tape or string
One pillowcase per player

Mark two lines ten feet apart on the floor with tape or string. Have each player stand inside a pillowcase, holding its top, at the starting line. At your signal, have the players jump to the finish line in their pillowcases. The winner is the first to reach the finish line.

Hide the Clock

This game works well with mixed age groups.

Clock or timer that ticks loudly

Have all the kids leave the room while you hide the clock or timer. At your signal, the kids return and search for the clock. The winner is the first player to find the clock.

Penny Hunt

Pennies
One cup or dish per player

Have all the kids leave the room while you hide pennies every-where—under cushions, in drawers, behind curtains, on top of books, and so on. Have all the kids return and give each a cup or dish. At your signal, have the players start searching for pennies. After five minutes, call off the hunt and have the players count their pennies. The player with the most pennies wins. Let the kids keep the pennies they find.

Blind Penny Hunt

One blindfold per player
Pennies
One paper bag per player

Use a large, open room for this game. Remove any objects that may be dangerous if children crawl into them or knock them over. Blindfold each player, then scatter pennies on the floor. Give each player a paper bag. At your signal, have the players crawl on their hands and knees, feeling for pennies. After five minutes, call off the hunt and have the players count their pennies. The player with the most pennies wins. Let the kids keep the pennies they find.

Dress-Up Relay

This funny game requires four or more players. It's great for families, as children think it's hilarious when adults play along.

Two suitcases or boxes
Dress-up clothes (hats, scarves, jackets, skirts, pants, boots, and so on)

Fill two suitcases or boxes with equal amounts of clothing. The clothes must be big enough to fit all the players. Place the suitcases or boxes at one end of the room.

Divide the players into two equal teams. If there's an odd number of players, one player on the team with fewer players takes two turns. Have the teams form two lines at the end of the room opposite the suitcases.

At the word *go,* the first player from each team runs to one of the suitcases or boxes and dons all the clothes in it over the clothes he's already wearing. Decide ahead of time whether buttons, zippers, and so on must be fastened. When a player is completely dressed, he then quickly removes all the dress-up clothes, puts them back in the suitcase or box, and runs to the end of his team's line. The next player then takes a turn and so on until everyone on the team has had a turn. The first team to finish wins.

Indoor Obstacle Course

As you design your obstacle course, keep in mind the ages, abilities, and number of children involved as well as the space you have. Make the course simple at first and change the stations as they're mastered. If you like, time the kids to see who can complete the course fastest. Below are a few ideas to get you started. Ten stations is a good number for most kids.

- Crawl under or over a row of chairs.
- Crawl under a string stretched between two chair legs.
- Jump into and out of a Hula-Hoop five times.
- Walk on a balance board.
- Throw a beanbag into a laundry basket.
- Run while balancing a beanbag on your head.
- Do a ring toss. (See page 71.)
- Play one hole of Newspaper Golf. (See page 69.)
- Ride a tricycle along a predetermined route.
- Somersault from one point to another.
- Do a handstand.
- Skip in place while reciting a jump rope rhyme. (See pages 160–163.)
- Do ten jumping jacks.

INDOOR GAMES FOR TWO OR MORE

Most of these games require two or more players, but some can be modified for a child playing alone.

What's Different?

This game requires at least two players. Stand in front of your child and tell him to study you. Leave the room and change something about your appearance. For example, you might turn a baseball cap backward or remove a sweatshirt. Return to your child and challenge him to tell what's different about you.

Table Hockey

Blocks or hardcover books
Popsicle sticks
Wad of paper

Create a rectangular "rink" on a large table or the floor by lining up blocks or hardcover books to make walls. Leave an opening at each end of the rink to make goals.

The players use Popsicle sticks to shoot a wad of paper (the "puck") toward each other's goals and to guard their own goals. Let the kids play hockey-style (each player tries to gain possession of the puck and then score) or penalty shot–style (the players take turns trying to score).

Cork Drop

Glass or bowl of water
Towel, old sheet, or plastic tablecloth (optional)
Ten corks

Place a glass or bowl full of water on the floor. If you like, place a towel, old sheet, or plastic tablecloth under it to catch splashes.

Have the players take turns. Standing over the bowl or glass with his arm extended at shoulder level, each player drops the corks one at a time into the water. Award points for successful drops. The player with the most points after each player has dropped ten corks is the winner. A child playing alone can see how many corks he drops successfully in a designated time.

Observation

Fifteen to twenty small household objects (key, bottle cap,
*   paper clip, safety pin, coin, and so on)*
Tray or tabletop
Towel or sheet
Paper
Pencils

Place fifteen to twenty small household objects on a tray or
tabletop. Cover the objects with a towel or sheet. Have the
players stand around the tray or table so each has a good
view. Remove the sheet or towel and let the players look at
the objects for one to two minutes. Then cover the objects
again. Give each player a sheet of paper and a pencil.
Challenge the players to write down as many objects as they
can recall. The winner is the player who correctly recalls the
most objects.

   If a young child who can't write is playing, pair him with
an older child or adult. After the younger child has viewed
the objects, have him dictate what he recalls to his partner,
who writes it down.

Charades

Choose a player to start the game. The player thinks of a book title, a famous person's name, a saying, a movie title, or a song title to pantomime. He should choose something with which the others will be familiar. If you like, designate a category like sports or Disney. The player then pantomimes the word or phrase he's chosen to the other players. Here are some common clues used in charades:

- To indicate a book, pretend to read a book.
- To indicate a song, pretend to sing.
- To indicate a movie, pretend to crank an old movie camera.
- To indicate the number of words, hold up that many fingers. (Then hold up one finger before pantomiming the first word, two fingers before the second, and so on.)
- To pantomime a word that rhymes with the word you want players to guess, first tug on your ear to say "sounds like."

The first person to guess the word or phrase gets a point.

If you like, divide into teams before playing. Players from each team take turns pantomiming for their teammates. The first team to guess the word or phrase gets a point.

Keep track of the points earned by each player or team. The one with the most points at the end of the game wins.

3-D Tick-Tack-Toe

Tape or string　　　　　*Markers like plastic lids, blocks,*
At least two　　　　　　　*or index cards (optional)*
　beanbags　　　　　　　*Pen (optional)*

This game requires two players. Mark a large tick-tack-toe
grid on the floor with tape or string. Give each player five
beanbags of a color different from the other player's beanbags. If you don't have ten beanbags, give each player one
beanbag and five markers labeled with his name.

　　The first player stands several feet away from the grid and
tosses his beanbag into any square. If he has five beanbags,
he leaves the tossed one where it landed. If he has only one
beanbag, he places one of his markers in the square where
the beanbag landed, then removes his beanbag. The second
player takes a turn. Play continues until one player has three
beanbags or markers in a horizontal, vertical, or diagonal
row. The other player begins the next round.

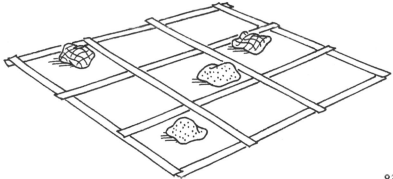

Tossup Topics

The more players in this game, the better! Before you play, learn the Tossup Topics jingle and its rhythmic accompaniment:

(slap knees)	(clap hands)	(snap left hand)	(snap right hand)
Toss-	up	Top-	ics
Arctic	to the	trop-	ics
Tossup	Topics	now	begins
Starting	with the	top-	ics.

The players sit in a circle on the floor. To begin, they recite the jingle together while slapping, clapping, and snapping as shown above. All the players continue to slap, clap, and snap as the first player declares a topic: for example, birthdays. The player to his left then must name something related to birthdays: for example, cake. Play continues around the circle. Each player must name something related to the topic during one *slap-clap-snap-snap* pattern. If a player is stumped or names something that's already been said, he must drop out. To resume the game, the remaining players recite the jingle again and declare a new topic. The last player remaining after all the others have dropped out is the winner.

Swap Meet

Occasionally the kids in our neighborhood have an informal swap meet. They dig through their closets and drawers for tradable treasures, then spend hours (and sometimes days!) pondering the treasures and bartering with each other. It's a great way for kids to recycle their belongings and get new things without spending money.

Items to trade (books, toys, sports cards, DVDs, CDs, stickers, knickknacks, and so on)

Each child chooses the items he's ready to part with. He should also label his items with his name and have his parents okay his choices. You can hold the swap meet in two different ways:

• The children meet in a central area and barter directly with each other for items they'd like to trade.
• Each child has a turn to display his items and entertain trade offers from other children.

Trades can be temporary or permanent. If trades are temporary, be sure to agree on the term of each trade. If trades are permanent, give the children a two- or three-day trade-back period in case they change their minds.

CHAPTER 3
Kids in the Kitchen

You know children are growing up when they start asking questions that have answers.

—John J. Plomp

For children, the kitchen is a tantalizing place full of wonderful things to see, hear, smell, touch, and taste. Toddlers love to play with pots and pans, preschoolers love to "help," and older children are often eager to learn to cook and bake on their own.

Kitchen activities are valuable for children. They help develop hand-eye coordination, small motor skills, and reading and math skills. Learning to prepare food will give your child practical skills she can use all her life, and being able to cook and bake for others will boost her self-esteem. Most of all, working in the kitchen is a fun and constructive way to spend time together.

If your child is interested in learning cooking and baking basics, do everything you can to encourage her. Let her work alongside you and teach her as you work. Buy a good kids' cookbook like Betty Crocker's *Kids Cook!* or one of the books in the Company's Coming series by Jean Paré. Let your child cook or bake for friends or make family desserts. Make or buy your child her own recipe box and copy her favorite recipes using simple words (or pictures and symbols for nonreaders). Start with simple no-cook recipes that she can make with little supervision and add more complex recipes as she learns.

The kitchen is indeed a stimulating environment, but it can also be a hazardous place for unsupervised children. Always be safety conscious. Make sure dangerous objects are well out of reach and be sure to supervise use of sharp utensils and hot appliances. Better yet: Until you're sure of your child's abilities, tell her that only an adult can use such things.

The recipes in this section provide some tasty and fairly easy things you and your child can make together. Before you begin cooking, read through the recipe with your child and explain any unfamiliar ingredients or terms. Assemble all your supplies and premeasure the ingredients. (This will make it easier for your child to follow the recipe.) Always emphasize health and safety considerations like washing hands before touching food, holding sharp utensils by the handles, turning saucepan handles inward on the stove, and so on.

With a bit of effort and patience, you can make your kitchen a wonderful place to interact with your child as you teach her how to measure, mix, cut, sift, and more to produce edible creations the whole family can enjoy.

MAIN COURSE

Your child can use the following recipes to make delicious, nutritious main-course dishes. She may need your help at first, but she'll need you less and less as she gains cooking experience. How proud you'll both be when she cooks a family meal all by herself!

Hawaiian Toast

Your family will adore this exotic alternative to French toast.

4 eggs
One 8-ounce can crushed pineapple
¼ cup milk
1 tablespoon maple syrup
1 tablespoon sour cream
1 tablespoon sugar
8 slices bread, crusts removed
¼ cup butter (optional)
Powdered sugar
Shredded coconut

1. In a blender, combine the eggs, pineapple, milk, syrup, sour cream, and sugar until the mixture is smooth.
2. Put the bread slices in a shallow dish. Pour the egg mixture over them, then turn them to coat both sides with egg.
3. Heat a nonstick griddle over medium heat (or melt 1 tablespoon of butter in a frying pan).
4. Put 2 bread slices on the griddle and cook them until they're brown. Turn them to cook the other sides.
5. Repeat with the remaining bread slices.
6. Dust the bread with powdered sugar and sprinkle it with coconut before serving.

Oatmeal Pancakes

½ cup all-purpose flour
½ cup quick-cooking oats
¾ cup buttermilk (or 1 cup
milk plus 1¾ tablespoons
cream of tartar)
¼ cup milk

1 tablespoon sugar
2 tablespoons vegetable oil
1 teaspoon baking powder
½ teaspoon baking soda
½ teaspoon salt
1 egg

1. Beat all the ingredients until the batter is smooth.
2. For each pancake, pour ¼ cup of batter onto a hot non-stick griddle or frying pan. Fry the pancakes until they bubble and their edges are dry. Flip the pancakes and cook the other sides until they're golden brown.
3. Serve the pancakes with butter and syrup, applesauce, or jam. This recipe makes 10–12 pancakes.

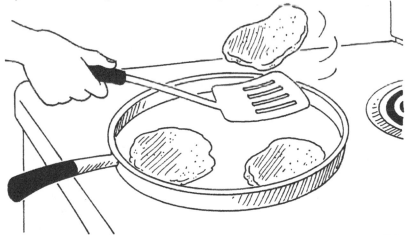

Veggie Frittata

If your child likes omelets, she'll love this frittata. It looks and tastes fancy, but it's very easy to make.

½ medium-size yellow onion, chopped
1 garlic clove, minced or pressed
2 tablespoons olive or vegetable oil
1 cup any chopped, cooked vegetable(s)
4 eggs, lightly beaten
¾ cup grated cheese
¼ teaspoon dried marjoram (or oregano)
1 teaspoon dried basil
½ teaspoon salt
¼ teaspoon black pepper

1. Preheat your broiler.
2. In a medium-size iron skillet, sauté the onion and garlic in the oil until the onion is soft (about 5 minutes). Add the vegetable(s) and sauté for one more minute.
3. Mix the eggs, cheese, herbs, salt, and pepper in a small bowl. Pour the egg mixture over the vegetables in the skillet, reduce the heat to low, and cook the mixture uncovered until the eggs are almost set (about 7 minutes).
4. Place the skillet under the broiler until the frittata is lightly browned (2–3 minutes). Cut the frittata into 4 wedges to serve it.

Chicken Pasta Casserole

Everyone in our family loves this casserole. It's a great busy-day meal because it's assembled the night before.

One 10-ounce can cream of mushroom soup
One 10-ounce can cream of celery soup
2½ cups water
2 cups grated Cheddar
2 cups diced cooked chicken (or two 6½ ounce cans chicken, drained)
2 cups uncooked macaroni
1 cup diced onion
1 teaspoon salt
1 cup shoestring potatoes (or crumbled potato chips)

1. Mix all the ingredients except the potatoes in a bowl, then spread the mixture in an ungreased casserole dish. Cover the dish and refrigerate overnight.
2. Preheat your oven to 350°F. Remove the lid from the casserole and sprinkle the shoestring potatoes over the top.
3. Bake the casserole uncovered for 1 hour or until the macaroni is tender. This recipe makes 6–8 servings.

Teriyaki Chicken

½ cup soy sauce
½ cup sugar
1½ tablespoons red wine
  vinegar
2 teaspoons vegetable oil

1 garlic clove, minced
¾ teaspoon ground ginger
1 pound boneless, skinless
  chicken breasts

1. Preheat your oven to 350°F.
2. Mix the soy sauce, sugar, vinegar, oil, garlic, and ginger to make the marinade.
3. Place the chicken breasts in a baking pan. Pour the marinade over the chicken. (Or freeze the chicken breasts in the marinade, then thaw them later for a quick, tasty meal.)
4. Bake the chicken for 35 minutes, then serve it over rice. This recipe makes 4 servings.

Baked Fish

For a complete meal, serve this dish with a vegetable and rice or a loaf of crusty bread.

8 fillets of any white fish
2 cups breadcrumbs
1 cup grated Parmesan
½ cup butter
2 tomatoes

1. Preheat your oven to 375°F.
2. Wash the fish in cold water, then pat it dry and cut it into ½-inch-square pieces. Spread the pieces in a 9-by-13-inch baking pan or any shallow ovenproof dish.
3. Mix the breadcrumbs and cheese in a small bowl. Rub in the butter by hand until the mixture is crumbly. Sprinkle the mixture evenly over the fish to completely cover it.
4. Slice the tomatoes thinly and place them on top of the breadcrumbs.
5. Bake the fish for 15 minutes. This recipe serves 6–8 people.

Macaroni and Cheese

This macaroni and cheese is far tastier than the boxed kind!

2 cups uncooked macaroni
2 tablespoons butter
1 small onion, minced (optional)
1 tablespoon all-purpose flour
1 teaspoon salt
¼ teaspoon dry mustard
Dash of pepper
1½ cups milk
2 cups shredded Cheddar

1. Preheat your oven to 350°F. Grease a 2-quart casserole dish. Cook and drain the macaroni, then put it in the dish.
2. Melt the butter in a saucepan over medium heat. Sauté the onion until it's tender.
3. Stir in the flour, salt, mustard, and pepper. Slowly stir in the milk. Cook the mixture, stirring constantly, until it's smooth and slightly thickened. Take the pan off the heat and add the cheese. Stir the mixture until the cheese melts.
4. Pour the cheese mixture over the macaroni and stir.
5. Bake the macaroni until it's bubbly (about 20 minutes). This recipe makes 4 servings as a main dish or 6 servings as a side dish.

Cheesy Spinach Lasagna

Lasagna is delicious, nutritious, and great for company. This recipe is easy because the noodles needn't be cooked first.

10 ounces ricotta or tofu
10 ounces frozen chopped spinach, thawed and drained
½ cup grated Parmesan
3 eggs
½ teaspoon salt
3½ cups spaghetti sauce
12 uncooked lasagna noodles
3 cups grated mozzarella
3 cups grated Muenster

1. Preheat your oven to 350°F.
2. In a medium bowl, mix the ricotta or tofu, spinach, Parmesan, eggs, and salt with a fork.
3. Spread ½ cup of the spaghetti sauce in a 9-by-13-inch pan.
4. Place a layer of 4 noodles on top of the sauce, then spread ⅓ of the spinach mixture over the noodles, 1 cup of spaghetti sauce over the spinach, 1 cup of mozzarella over the sauce, and 1 cup of Muenster over the mozzarella. Repeat this layering process 2 more times.
5. Cover the lasagna with aluminum foil and bake it for 40 minutes. Remove the foil and bake the lasagna another 10 minutes or until the cheese turns golden brown. Let the lasagna cool for 10 minutes before serving it.

Bird's Nest Pie

8 ounces uncooked
  spaghetti noodles
2 eggs, beaten
⅓ cup grated Parmesan
  paste
½ cup finely chopped onion
2 tablespoons butter

1 cup sour cream
1 pound bulk Italian sausage
  or ground beef
One 6-ounce can tomato

1 cup water
1 cup grated mozzarella

1. Preheat your oven to 350°F. Grease the bottom and sides of a 10-inch pie plate.
2. Break the noodles in half. Cook and drain them, then mix them with the eggs and Parmesan. Press the mixture into the bottom and sides of the pie plate.
3. Sauté the onions in the butter for 5 minutes. Mix in the sour cream, then spread the mixture over the spaghetti "crust."
4. Brown and drain the meat. Stir in the tomato paste and water and bring the mixture to a boil. Reduce the heat and simmer the mixture uncovered for 10 minutes, stirring occasionally. Add it to the pie.
5. Bake the pie for 25 minutes. Then sprinkle it with mozzarella. Bake it again until the cheese melts. This recipe makes 8 servings.

Cozy Split Pea Soup

1 cup dried split peas
½ teaspoon dried basil
1 bay leaf
2 cups water
2 cups vegetable broth

2 cups chopped onion
½ teaspoon ground cumin
3 tablespoons olive oil
Salt and pepper

1. Put the peas, basil, bay leaf, water, and broth in a large saucepan and simmer the mixture, partially covered, until the peas turn mushy (about 45 minutes).
2. While the peas are cooking, sauté the onion and cumin in the oil in a skillet over medium-high heat until the onions are golden brown.
3. Discard the bay leaf. Stir the onion mixture into the peas and season the soup with salt and pepper to taste. This recipe makes about 4 cups of soup.

Easy Bean Burritos

One 8-ounce can refried beans
6 flour tortillas
¾ cup grated Monterey Jack
Chopped lettuce, tomato, and/or green pepper (optional)
Salsa
Sour cream

1. Cook the beans, stirring occasionally, in a small saucepan over medium heat until they're warm (about 5 minutes).
2. Spread about 3 tablespoons of beans on 1 side of each tortilla.
3. Sprinkle the cheese evenly over the beans, then add chopped lettuce, tomato, and/or green pepper, if you like.
4. Fold the bottom of each tortilla up over the filling, then fold the right and left sides in. Fold the top over so that the tortilla looks like an envelope. Turn the burrito over.
5. Cut each burrito in half and serve it with salsa and sour cream.

COOKIES, MUFFINS, AND MORE

Baking is a wonderful activity for a rainy afternoon or a cold winter evening. Your child will enjoy making dessert for the family, treats for her lunch box, or delicious edible gifts for friends, neighbors, and relatives.

Baked Apple Crisp

4 cups thinly sliced apples (about 6 medium apples)
¾ cup all-purpose flour
¾ cup packed brown sugar
½ cup quick-cooking oats
⅓ cup chopped walnuts
1½ teaspoons cinnamon
½ cup butter, softened

1. Preheat your oven to 375°F.
2. Spread the apple slices in an ungreased 8-inch-square cake pan.
3. In a small bowl, mix the flour, sugar, oats, nuts, cinnamon, and butter with a fork until the mixture is crumbly. Sprinkle it over the apple slices.
4. Bake the apple crisp uncovered until the topping is golden brown and the apples are tender (about 30 minutes). This recipe makes about 6 servings.

Chocolate Banana Bread

Wake up your family's taste buds by putting a new spin on a familiar treat.

½ cup butter, softened
1 cup sugar
2 large eggs
1 teaspoon vanilla extract
1 cup mashed banana
  (about 3 medium
  bananas)

¼ cup milk
1½ cups all-purpose flour
¼ cup powdered cocoa
1½ teaspoons baking powder
½ teaspoon baking soda
¼ teaspoon salt
½ cup chopped walnuts

1. Preheat your oven to 350°F. Grease a 9-by-5-inch loaf pan.
2. Beat the butter, sugar, eggs, and vanilla until the sugar is moistened.
3. Add the banana and milk and beat the mixture on low speed until it's blended.
4. Add the flour, cocoa, baking powder, baking soda, and salt. Beat the mixture on low speed until the dry ingredients are moistened.
5. Stir in the walnuts with a spoon.
6. Pour the batter into the pan and bake it for 50–60 minutes. The bread is done when a toothpick inserted in the center of the loaf comes out clean and dry.

Applesauce-Oatmeal Muffins

These tasty, nutritious muffins disappear quickly, so I always double the recipe.

½ cup margarine
¾ cup lightly packed
  brown sugar
1 egg
1 cup flour
½ teaspoon cinnamon
1 teaspoon baking powder

¼ teaspoon baking soda
¼ teaspoon salt
¾ cup applesauce
½ cup raisins
1 cup quick-cooking oats
½ cup chopped nuts

1. Preheat your oven to 350°F. Grease a 12-cup muffin pan.
2. Cream the margarine and sugar in a medium bowl. Beat in the egg.
3. Sift the flour, cinnamon, baking powder, baking soda, and salt. Stir the sifted mixture and the applesauce alternately into the margarine-sugar mixture.
4. Stir in the raisins, oats, and nuts.
5. Fill each muffin cup ¾ full. Bake the muffins for 25–30 minutes.

Alphabet Cookies

These cookies are fun for kids to make because the dough handles like modeling clay.

*4½ cups unsifted
  all-purpose flour
1½ cups butter
3 hard-boiled egg yolks*

*¾ cup sugar
3 raw egg yolks
1½ teaspoons vanilla extract*

1. Preheat your oven to 300°F.
2. Measure the flour into a large bowl. Cut the butter into small pieces and add it to the flour. Mix the butter and flour with your fingers until they form fine crumbs.
3. Mash the hard-boiled egg yolks and sugar together and stir them into the flour mixture.
4. Beat the raw egg yolks with the vanilla and stir this mixture into the flour mixture.
5. Press the dough into a firm ball. Work with the dough at room temperature or cover and refrigerate it if you plan to shape and bake it later.
6. Roll out the dough. Cut it into strips 3 or 4 inches long and roll them between your palms to make ropes.
7. Shape the ropes into letters. Flatten them slightly so they are about ¼ inch thick. If you like, decorate the letters with colored sugar or chocolate chips.
8. Place the letters on a baking sheet and bake them for 25–30 minutes.

Best Chocolate Chip Cookies in the World

This recipe makes truly great chocolate chip cookies. My kids are always trying other recipes, but we haven't yet found one we like as much as this. Double the batch and freeze half of the dough for instant, no-mess baking fun on a rainy day.

½ cup margarine, room
   temperature
½ cup unsalted butter,
   room temperature
1 cup packed dark
   brown sugar
1 cup granulated sugar
2 eggs, lightly beaten
2 tablespoons milk
2 teaspoons vanilla extract

2 cups sifted all-purpose flour
1 teaspoon baking powder
1 teaspoon baking soda
1 teaspoon salt
2 cups quick-cooking oats
1 cup (or more) chocolate
   chips
1 cup coarsely chopped
   walnuts

1. Cream the margarine, butter, and sugars in a large bowl until the mixture is light and fluffy.
2. Beat in the eggs, milk, and vanilla.
3. Sift the flour, baking powder, baking soda, and salt and stir them into the dough until it's just blended.
4. Stir in the oats. Fold in the chocolate chips and walnuts.

5. Cover the dough and refrigerate it for at least 1 hour. (Don't skip this step; it makes a difference!)
6. Preheat your oven to 350°F. Grease the baking sheets.
7. Shape the dough into balls using a rounded teaspoon for small cookies or a scant tablespoon for large ones. Flatten the balls slightly and place them 2 inches apart on baking sheets.
8. Bake the cookies until their edges are slightly browned but the cookies are mostly still white (8–10 minutes). Don't overbake the cookies; they'll set as they cool. Remove the cookies from the oven and let them cool for 5 minutes. Transfer them to wire racks to finish cooling. This recipe makes about 5 dozen small cookies.

Easy Double-Chocolate Cookies

These decadent cookies are surprisingly easy to make.

1 large egg
3 tablespoons water
5 tablespoons vegetable oil
1 package chocolate fudge cake mix
1½ cups chocolate chips
1½ cups chopped walnuts (optional)

1. Preheat your oven to 350°F.
2. Mix the egg, water, oil, and cake mix in a bowl.
3. Add the chocolate chips (and walnuts, if desired) and stir the dough until it's blended.
4. Grease the baking sheets.
5. Drop the cookie dough by rounded spoonfuls onto the baking sheets. Use a teaspoon for small cookies or a tablespoon for larger ones.
6. Bake small cookies for 10–12 minutes or large cookies for 15–20 minutes.
7. Remove the cookies from the oven and let them cool for 10–20 minutes. Transfer them to wire racks to finish cooling. This recipe makes about 4 dozen small cookies.

Fudge Brownies

¼ cup butter
1½ cup chocolate chips
¾ cup sugar
⅔ cup all-purpose flour
½ teaspoon vanilla extract
¼ teaspoon baking powder
¼ teaspoon salt
2 eggs
½ cup chopped nuts (optional)

1. Preheat your oven to 350°F. Grease the bottom of an 8-inch-square cake pan.
2. Melt the butter and 1 cup of chocolate chips in a saucepan over low heat, stirring constantly. Remove the pan from the heat.
3. Stir in the sugar, flour, vanilla, baking powder, salt, and eggs until the batter is smooth.
4. Stir in the remaining chocolate chips (and nuts, if desired). Spread the batter in the cake pan.
5. Bake the brownies until a toothpick inserted in the center comes out clean and dry (about 30 minutes).
6. Let the brownies cool completely before you cut them. This recipe makes about 20 brownies.

Fiddle Diddles

½ cup butter
2 cups sugar
½ cup milk
6 tablespoons powdered
   cocoa

3 cups quick-cooking oats
½ cup shredded coconut
½ cup chopped walnuts
Pinch of salt
1 teaspoon vanilla extract

1. Heat the butter, sugar, and milk in a saucepan over medium heat, stirring constantly, until the mixture comes to a boil. Remove it from the heat.
2. Stir in the cocoa, oats, coconut, walnuts, salt, and vanilla. Drop the batter by rounded teaspoonfuls onto wax paper. Wait until the cookies cool completely before sampling them.
3. Store the cookies in an airtight container with wax paper between layers. This recipe makes about 40 cookies.

Blueberry Dessert Cake

Your child will enjoy making and eating this easy, delicious dessert.

One 20-ounce can crushed pineapple
One 16-ounce can blueberry (or cherry) pie filling
1 package yellow 2-layer cake mix
1 tablespoon sugar
½ teaspoon cinnamon
1 cup butter or margarine
¾ cup chopped walnuts (optional)

1. Preheat your oven to 350°F. Grease a 9-by-13-inch baking pan.
2. Spread the crushed pineapple and its juice in the pan. Spoon the pie filling over the pineapple. Sprinkle the cake mix over the pie filling.
3. Mix the sugar and cinnamon in a small cup and sprinkle the mixture over the cake mix.
4. Thinly slice the butter and place it on top of the cake mix. Then sprinkle the cake with the walnuts.
5. Bake the cake for 45–55 minutes. Remove it from the oven and place it on a wire rack to cool.
6. Cut the cake into squares and serve it warm or cold with ice cream or whipped cream.

Icebox Cake

The name of this recipe suggests it's been around for many decades. As children, my sisters and I loved making this treat as much as eating it.

½ cup sugar
2 tablespoons powdered
  cocoa
1 egg, beaten
½ cup margarine

1¼ cups graham cracker
  crumbs
¾ cup walnuts
½ teaspoon vanilla extract

1. Grease an 8-inch-square cake pan.
2. Mix the sugar and cocoa in a small bowl. Stir in the egg.
3. Melt the margarine in a medium saucepan. Add the sugar mixture, stirring constantly until the mixture boils. Let it boil for 1 minute, then take it off the heat.
4. Stir in the graham cracker crumbs, walnuts, and vanilla, then press the mixture into the cake pan.
5. Chill the cake until it's firm, then frost it with canned frosting or homemade Fudgy Frosting. (See below.)
6. To make Fudgy Frosting, mix 1 tablespoon of melted margarine with 1 tablespoon of cocoa. Blend in 1 tablespoon of milk and 1 cup of powdered sugar until the frosting is smooth. If necessary, add more powdered sugar until the frosting is spreadable.

Snails

My mom has been making these treats since I was little. We called them snails because they look like snail shells. There are no exact quantities for this recipe—just use whatever you have on hand.

Pastry scraps (or premade pie shell, bread or biscuit dough,
*   or refrigerated bread sticks)*
Margarine, softened
Brown sugar
Cinnamon

1. Preheat your oven to 350°F.
2. Roll the pastry into a rectangular shape about ⅛ inch thick. (Roll bread or biscuit dough slightly thicker.) The sides of the rectangle should be at least 6 inches long. If you are using refrigerated bread sticks, simply unroll and separate them.
3. Spread a thin layer of margarine on the dough. Sprinkle brown sugar and cinnamon over the margarine.
5. Starting at a long side of the rectangle, roll up the dough. Cut the roll into ½-inch slices. If you're using bread sticks, roll each one to resemble a snail shell.
6. Lay the snails flat on a baking sheet, 1 inch apart, and bake them for 10–15 minutes.
7. Transfer the snails to a wire rack to cool before you eat them.

Cheese Pretzels

1 cup flour
2 tablespoons grated Parmesan
½ teaspoon salt
½ cup butter or margarine
1 cup grated Cheddar
2–3 tablespoons cold water

1. Preheat your oven to 375°F.
2. Mix the flour, Parmesan, and salt in a large bowl. Cut in the butter with a pastry blender or 2 knives until the mixture resembles fine crumbs. Stir in the Cheddar.
3. Sprinkle the water over the mixture 1 tablespoon at a time, stirring lightly with a fork, until the dough holds together.
4. Shape the dough into a ball. Cut it in half, then cut each half into 12 pieces. Put each piece on a lightly floured surface and roll it back and forth with your palms to make a rope. Shape the ropes into pretzels and place them on an ungreased baking sheet.
5. Bake the pretzels for 12 minutes. This recipe makes 24 small pretzels.

NO COOKING REQUIRED

These recipes are quick and easy to make and produce a tasty variety of snacks. Although none requires an oven or stove, some call for a sharp knife, a grater, hot water, a blender, or toaster. For safety's sake, adults should always supervise children while they make these recipes.

Fresh-Squeezed Lemonade

If your kids are like mine, they think lemonade comes from a can. Help them make a batch of fresh-squeezed lemonade as a refreshing treat on a hot summer day.

½ cup sugar
1 teaspoon finely grated lemon peel
½ cup very hot water
3 lemons (or enough to make ½ cup lemon juice)
Cold water or club soda

1. In a 2-cup jar with a tight lid, shake the sugar, lemon peel, and the hot water until the sugar dissolves.
2. Squeeze the lemons to make ½ cup lemon juice. Add the juice to the sugar water. Refrigerate the mixture for at least 2 hours or up to 1 week.
3. To make lemonade, pour ¼ cup of the lemon mixture in a glass. Stir in ¾ cup of cold water or club soda. This recipe makes about five 1-cup servings.

Variation
If you don't have lemons, make No-Lemon Lemonade by mixing 8 cups of water with 12 tablespoons of lemon juice, 1 teaspoon of salt, and 1½ cups of sugar.

Vanilla Milk Shake

2 rounded scoops vanilla ice cream
¾ cup cold milk
1 tablespoon vanilla pudding powder (optional)
½ teaspoon vanilla extract

1. Place all the ingredients in a blender and blend them until they're smooth and frothy (about 20 seconds).
2. Pour the mixture into 2 glasses and add a drinking straw to each. This recipe makes about 2 cups.

Variation
To make a chocolate milk shake, leave out the vanilla extract and add 2 tablespoons of chocolate syrup instead.

Fruity Pops

1 package Kool-Aid powder   *¾ cup hot water*
1 package Jell-O powder   *¾ cup cold water*
1¼ cups sugar

1. Mix the dry ingredients thoroughly in a bowl.
2. Measure 6 tablespoons of the dry ingredients into another bowl, then stir in the hot and cold water.
3. Pour the mixture into Popsicle-type molds and freeze the treats.
4. Store the remaining dry ingredients in an airtight container for future use.

Fruit Dip

½ cup yogurt, any flavor
½ cup frozen whipped topping, thawed
Fruit slices, such as apple, orange, banana, pear, or melon

1. Thoroughly mix the yogurt and whipped topping in a small bowl.
2. Dunk the fruit pieces in the dip. Enjoy!
3. Refrigerate any leftover dip and use it within a couple of days.

Carrot-Raisin Salad

3 carrots, peeled
½ cup raisins
½ cup crushed pineapple,
  drained

⅓ cup salad dressing
  or mayonnaise
2 teaspoons white vinegar
2 teaspoons sugar

1. Grate the carrots into a medium bowl. Stir in the raisins and pineapple.
2. Thoroughly mix the salad dressing, vinegar, and sugar. Stir this mixture into the carrot mixture. This recipe makes about 2 cups of salad.

Trail Mix

Dried fruit
Chocolate chips or M&M's

Peanuts
Granola (optional)

1. Mix all the ingredients in a bowl. Use whatever amounts you like or try ½ cup each of fruit, chocolate chips or M&M's, and nuts with 1 cup of granola.
2. Store the trail mix in an airtight container or in small Ziploc bags that can be packed in lunches or enjoyed as after-school snacks.

Waffle Sandwich

2 frozen waffles
Peanut butter

Jam, jelly, or honey
4–6 banana slices

1. Toast the waffles in a toaster.
2. Spread peanut butter and jam, jelly, or honey on 1 waffle and top it with banana slices and the other waffle.

S'mores

Graham crackers
Chocolate squares or chocolate chips
Large marshmallows

1. For each s'more, place a graham cracker on a plate or a paper towel. Top the cracker with a chocolate square or several chocolate chips and 1 marshmallow.
2. Microwave the s'more on high for 20 seconds or until the marshmallow starts to puff up. Remove it from the microwave, top it with another cracker, and enjoy!

Finger Gelatin

3 packets unflavored gelatin
One 12-ounce can frozen juice concentrate, thawed
1½ cups water

1. Mix the gelatin and the juice. Bring the water to a boil in a medium saucepan.
2. Stir the juice-gelatin mixture into the boiling water until the gelatin dissolves.
3. Pour the mixture into a lightly greased shallow pan and refrigerate it until it sets (about 2 hours).
4. Cut the gelatin with cookie cutters or a knife.

CHAPTER 4
Fun Outdoors

The best inheritance a parent can give his children is a few minutes of his time each day.

—O. A. Battista

Parents of young children know that toddlers and preschoolers need to be outdoors every day to use up some of their seemingly endless energy, to help them develop their large motor skills, and to pass the long hours of difficult days. As children grow and enter school, they still need to play outdoors, but their daily free time is drastically reduced. For some children, free time virtually disappears when they start first grade: Lessons, practices, and other activities fill after-school hours, and at night, homework and chores leave little or no time for playing outside.

Adults, too, often need to be pushed outdoors. A hectic lifestyle can make simple pleasures like taking a walk and playing in the yard seem frivolous. As a busy home-schooling mom with a writing schedule to keep, I often feel I don't have the time to go outside. How can I justify a leisurely walk with my toddler when my fourth-grader needs help with his math, the bills haven't been paid, and I haven't a clue what we'll eat for dinner?

If you see your child or yourself or your whole family in this routine, perhaps it's time to reevaluate the pace of your lives. Make downtime a priority. Write it on your to-do list. Set aside a little time each day or at least several times a week for some outdoor fun—whether it's a family walk in the rain or a game of hopscotch or marbles with the neighborhood kids. The best memories aren't made by folding laundry; they're made by spending time with your children. Go out-side with your kids and have fun!

OUT AND ABOUT

The following activities are perfect to do with your child(ren) in your own neighborhood or yard.

Left or Right

Quarter or other coin

The next time you and your child embark on a walk in your neighborhood, take a quarter with you. When you reach the sidewalk or road in front of your home, flip the quarter. If it comes up "heads," turn left. If it comes up "tails," turn right. Walk until you get to the next intersection, then flip your quarter again to see which way you should turn.

Fly a Kite

Kite

On a fine, breezy day, head out to an area that's free of trees and telephone poles. Bring along a store-bought or home-made kite. Gently launch your kite in the air, give it plenty of string, and run! If two or more children are flying kites, have a contest to see who can keep his kite in the air the longest, whose kite flies the highest, and so on.

Nature Hunt

One paper bag per player
One list of natural objects to collect per player

Give each player a paper bag and a list of natural objects (a
bird's feather, a leaf, a smooth rock, a pine cone, a wildflower,
and so on) to collect. You can give the same list to all the
players or have each player look for a different group of
objects. Challenge the players to find all the objects on their
lists. Set a time limit: perhaps twenty minutes to find ten
objects. The first player to find all the items on his list is
the winner.

A child may play this game alone or with others. For a
group of children, pair up nonreaders with readers.

Volcano

Dirt or wet sand
Small shovel or spoon
Two teaspoons baking soda
White vinegar

Build a mound of dirt ten inches high. Dig a deep hole in the middle of the mound with a small shovel. Put two teaspoons of baking soda in the hole. Then slowly pour in vinegar and watch your volcano erupt!

Stargazing

Blanket
Astronomy book (optional)
Flashlight (optional)
Snack (optional)

Let your kids stay up later than usual on a clear summer evening. When it's really dark, go outside and look at the stars. If you live in a city, the city lights may make it hard to see the starlight, so drive to the country if you can. Bring a blanket, lie on your backs, and look at the constellations. If you like, bring an astronomy book, a flashlight, and a snack as well.

Water Fun

Sprinkler
Garden hose with spray nozzle

- If you have a swing set, set up a fan-style sprinkler close to it so your children can swing into the spray.
- Have children stand in a circle around a rotating sprinkler and jump over the stream of water as it comes around. The children can compete to see who'll be the last to miss a jump and get wet. A child playing alone can see how many jumps he can make before getting wet.
- Play limbo with a garden hose. Have one player hold the hose so that the water sprays horizontally. Begin with the stream of water at chin level and have each child walk under the stream. Lower the stream a bit and have the children walk under it again. Continue lowering the stream so that players have to crouch, crawl, and perhaps even slither to get under it to avoid getting wet. Players are out once they get wet. The player who stays dry the longest is the winner.
- Play tag with a garden hose. The player who's it chases the other players and tries to tag them with the stream of water. Define a safe zone to which players can run to avoid being tagged. The first player to be tagged is it for the next game.

Penny Toss

Dishpan, baby bathtub, or kiddie pool
Water
Open plastic container
Pennies

Fill a dishpan, baby bathtub, or kiddie pool halfway with
water. Place an open plastic container carefully on top of the
water so that it floats. Have each player stand three feet from
the dishpan, tub, or pool. Give each player the same number
of pennies. Have the players take turns tossing pennies at the
floating container. Award a point for each penny that lands in
the container. The player with the most points after all the
pennies have been tossed is the winner. A child playing alone
can keep track of how many pennies land in the container in
a row.

Breakfast in the Park

Our family often has picnic lunches and dinners at the
beach, but I hadn't thought of having breakfast in the park
until a friend suggested it. What a great idea for early ris-
ers—and you'll definitely beat the crowds!

Breakfast foods
Blanket or tablecloth
Sweatshirts
Hot cocoa

The night before your outing, pack up everything you'll
need. Your meal may be as simple as cereal, milk, and juice
or may include pancakes or bacon and eggs. Bring a plastic
tablecloth if you plan to sit at a picnic table or a blanket if
you'll be sitting on the ground. Mornings are often cool, so
don't forget to bring sweatshirts and hot cocoa, too.

If planning a breakfast at the park requires more energy
than you've got, how about inviting another family to your
place for breakfast?

BUBBLE, BUBBLE

Children of all ages enjoy bubbles. Babies like to watch other people blow bubbles, and toddlers and preschoolers can learn to blow bubbles. Older children enjoy making homemade bubble solution and trying bubble tricks. And parents can tolerate the mess by remembering that blowing bubbles is a scientific activity—honest!

Bubble Solution

The following three recipes come from Science World in Vancouver, British Columbia. According to Science World, glycerin helps soap bubbles hold water, which helps keep the bubbles from popping. Try a tablespoon or two of glycerin for a small batch of solution. Glycerin can be purchased at most pharmacies.

All-Purpose Bubble Solution

This solution works for most bubble tricks, experiments, and activities.

7–10 parts water
1 part dish detergent
Glycerin
Bowl

Mix the water, detergent, and glycerin in a bowl.

Thick Bubble Solution

This is a very thick, goopy solution that forms bubbles strong enough to withstand a small puff of air. This solution is great for blowing bubbles inside of bubbles. (See page 136.)

2½–3 parts water
1 part dish detergent
Glycerin
Bowl

Combine the water, detergent, and glycerin in a bowl.

Bouncy Bubble Solution

This fun solution makes bubbles you can bounce off your clothes.

2 packages unflavored gelatin
4 cups hot water (just boiled)
3–5 tablespoons glycerin
3 tablespoons dish detergent

Dissolve the gelatin in the hot water. Add the glycerin and detergent. This solution will jell, so you'll need to reheat it whenever you use it.

Giant Bubble

String
Two drinking straws
Bubble solution
Large, flat baking pan

Thread a length of string through two straws. Tie the ends together to make a loop. Leave as much slack string between the straws as you like, depending on the size of bubble you want.

Pour bubble solution into a large, shallow baking pan. Hold one straw in each hand, leaving the string hanging slack between them. Dip the straw-and-string loop into the bubble solution, then lift it out slowly, taking care not to break the film of bubble solution. Pull the straws apart until the string is taut, then hold the bubble film in front of a fan or the wind and watch a giant bubble take shape!

Bubble Fun

Try these ideas for blowing some neat bubbles.

Drinking straws
Bubble solution
Scissors
Tape
Funnel
Tea strainer
Set of plastic rings from beverage six-pack

- Dip one end of a straw into bubble solution. Blow through the other end of the straw to make bubbles.
- Cut each of two straws in half. Tape the four short straws together in a bunch. Dip one end of the bunch into bubble solution and blow through the other end.
- Wet part of a tabletop with bubble solution. Dip a drinking straw into the solution. Blow a large dome-shaped bubble on the tabletop. Release the bubble, then insert your straw in it and blow into the straw to form a smaller bubble inside the big one.
- Dip the wide end of a funnel into bubble solution. Blow through the narrow end to form interesting bubble shapes.
- Dip a set of plastic rings from a beverage six-pack in bubble solution and wave it through the air.

Bubble Contest

Nothing to do on a summer afternoon? Organize a bubble-blowing contest! Mix up some bubble solution, assemble some tools for blowing, and you're set. These contest ideas come from the book *Science Wizardry for Kids* by Margaret Kenda and Phyllis S. Williams.

Bubble solution
Bubble-blowing tools: drinking straws, funnels, wire loops,
   and so on
Marble or other small toy

Give each contestant a supply of bubble solution and some bubble-blowing tools. Wet the tabletop with bubble solution and have the kids get blowing.

* Who can blow the biggest bubble?
* Who can create the biggest pile of bubbles in thirty seconds?
* Whose bubble lasts the longest?
* Whose bubble is the prettiest?
* Who can blow a bubble within a bubble?
* Who can get a marble or other small toy inside a bubble?

Bubble Doughnut

Length of wire (large paper clip, thin-wire coat hanger)
Bubble solution
Length of thread shorter than wire

Shape the wire into a circle about two inches in diameter. Dip the wire loop into the bubble solution and blow bubbles through it.

Dip the thread in the bubble solution and roll the ends together between your fingers to form a loop. Dip the wire loop into the bubble solution again, but don't blow bubbles this time. Instead, place the thread loop gently on top of the film inside the wire loop.

Break the film inside the thread loop. This should give you a doughnut-shaped film between the thread loop and the wire loop. Tilt the wire loop from side to side and watch the doughnut change shape.

FAIR-WEATHER GAMES

The following games are fun for children to play on their own or in groups. If your child is playing alone, he can race against a clock. Many of these games can be adapted for indoor play on rainy or cold days.

Three-Legged Race

*Scarves or fabric strips long enough for tying legs together
(one for each pair of children)*
Two ropes

Divide children into pairs, matching children of similar
height and build. Have each player stand next to his partner
and put his arm around his partner's waist. The partners'
inside legs (the right leg of the partner on the left and the
left leg of the partner on the right) should be touching. Tie
the partners' inside legs together so each pair of children has
three legs rather than four.

Use two ropes to mark a starting line and a finish line.
Have the players line up at the starting line. At your signal,
have players walk or run as fast as they can to the finish line.
It sounds easy, but it takes practice to make two legs work as
one! The winners are the pair of children who cross the finish line first.

Catch the Rings

Construction paper
Scissors
Glue or stapler
One basket or bucket per player

Make at least thirty construction paper rings. Cut strips of construction paper about two inches wide and nine inches long. Glue or staple the ends of each strip together to make a ring.

Give each player a basket or bucket. Choose one child (or an adult) to be the leader. As the leader throws the rings into the air one at a time, the other players try to catch the rings in their baskets or buckets. The player who catches the most rings is the winner.

If there are only two players, they can take turns throwing the rings and catching them. The players can compete against each other, or each player can simply try to better his own score with each turn.

Hit the Ball

Hammer or large bucket of sand
Broomstick with a flat end
Chalk, a stick, or a rope
Ping-Pong ball
Five beanbags or sponges

Hammer one end of a broomstick into the ground or set the broomstick upright in a large bucket of sand. Make sure the flat end of the broomstick is pointing up. If you're playing on pavement, use chalk to draw a circle three feet in diameter around the broomstick. If you're playing on dirt, use a stick to draw the circle; if you're playing on grass, mark the circle with a rope.

Balance a Ping-Pong ball on the end of the broomstick. One at a time, each child stands five feet from the broomstick and tries to knock the Ping-Pong ball off the broomstick by throwing the beanbags or sponges at it.

If the ball falls within the circle, the player scores one point. If the ball falls outside the circle, the player scores two points. The child with the highest score after five throws wins.

If one child is playing alone, he can test his skill by trying to attain a perfect score of ten points after five throws.

Sack Race

Two ropes
One burlap sack or old pillowcase per player

Use two ropes to mark a starting line and a finish line. Give each player a sack or pillowcase. Have the children line up at the starting line and stand in their sacks or pillowcases while holding up the ends with their hands. At your signal, have the players hop to the finish line. The first child to cross the finish line is the winner.

Horseshoes

Shovel
Empty, clean tin can
Paint in as many colors as there are players
Four 2-inch metal washers per player
Paper and pencil

Dig a hole in the ground and place the can in it so the top of the can is flush with the ground. Using spray paint (or acrylic or tempera paints finished with clear acrylic spray), paint four washers (horseshoes) with each color.

Give four horseshoes to each player. One player stands about six feet away from the can and tries to throw his horseshoes into the can. Each player takes a turn. When all the horseshoes have been thrown, retrieve them from the can and record each player's score. A horseshoe that lands in the can scores two points, and each player's horseshoe nearest the can scores one point. (This way, every player always scores at least one point.) Set a time limit. The player with the most points when time runs out is the winner.

A child playing alone can try to accumulate a certain number of points within a given time period.

Golf

Shovel
Empty, clean tin can
Golf putter (or child's golf club, narrow length of wood, or
 heavy cardboard rolled and taped into a "club")
Several golf balls
Paper and pencil

Dig a hole in the ground and place the can in it so the top of the can is flush with the ground. Mark a spot about ten feet away from the can. This will be the point from which players will putt.

Give the balls to the first player and challenge him to putt them into the can. When he has putted all the balls, retrieve them from the can and record his score. A ball that lands in the can scores two points, and the ball nearest the can scores one point. (This way, every player always scores at least one point.) Each player takes a turn. Set a time limit. The player with the most points when time runs out is the winner.

A child playing alone can try to accumulate a certain number of points within a given time period.

Jug Catch

Utility knife
One gallon-size plastic jug per player
Duct tape (optional)
One tennis ball or beanbag per player

Use a utility knife to cut a one-gallon plastic jug in half horizontally. Recycle the bottom half of the jug, but save the top half (the half with the handle). If you like, cover the cut edge of the jug with duct tape.

Two or more children playing together can use the jugs to toss a tennis ball or beanbag back and forth without touching it with their hands. A child playing alone can toss a ball or beanbag in the air and catch it in his jug, seeing how many successful catches he can make in a row.

HOPSCOTCH GAMES

Hopscotch is a traditional game that has been played by children around the world for hundreds of years. As a child, I played hopscotch for hours on end by myself and with my sisters and friends.

Hopscotch is usually played outdoors on a court drawn with chalk on a sidewalk or other flat, paved surface. Many school playgrounds have painted courts, making them great places to play on evenings, weekends, or during the summer. For indoor fun on a rainy day, draw a hopscotch court with a permanent marker on an old sheet. To play, lay the sheet flat on a carpet or other nonslip surface.

There are many different kinds of hopscotch courts. A basic court is made up of ten numbered rectangles in a column with a semicircle at the end labeled *out*. A snail court has spaces arranged in a spiral. Another traditional court is the airplane, with eight numbered squares plus "home" and "out" arranged in an airplane shape.

Some hopscotch games require markers. When I was a child, my favorite markers were small chains. They're easy to toss, don't roll, and don't hurt if they hit someone.

There are hundreds of different hopscotch games. The following games are fairly common and provide a good introduction to hopscotch for beginners. Once you and your child are familiar with these games, you'll enjoy learning others and making up your own. If you want to learn more hopscotch games, read *Hopscotch around the World* by Mary Lankford.

Basic Hopscotch

Chalk

Use chalk to draw any kind of hopscotch court.

The first player hops up the court and back again, hopping in each space both up and back. On the first trip, he hops on his right foot. On the second trip, he hops on his left foot. On his third trip, he hops on alternating feet. On the fourth trip, he hops with his feet together. The player hops in this sequence until he makes a mistake like hopping on a line, putting both feet down when he's supposed to be hopping on one foot, or hopping on the wrong foot, at which point he fouls out. The other players take turns hopping in the same way.

When it's the first player's turn again, he starts hopping from where he fouled out on his last turn. The winner is the first player to finish the entire sequence of hops.

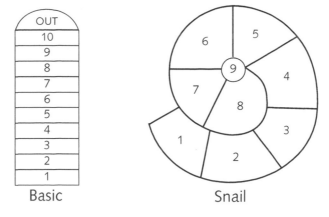

Basic

Snail

Ten and Out

Chalk
One marker (small chain, coin, or stone)
  per player

Use chalk to draw the hopscotch court shown
at right.

Ten and Out

The first player stands in front of space one. He tosses
his marker into that space, then hops on one foot into the
space, bends over and picks up his marker, and hops up the
court and back again on one foot, hopping in each space
both up and back. He then tosses his marker into the next
space, hops to that space, picks up his marker, and hops up
the court and back again. He continues hopping in this way
until he fouls out (hops on a line, puts both feet down, or
misses his target when tossing his marker).

The players take turns tossing and hopping in the same
way. When it's the first player's turn again, he starts hopping
from where he fouled out on his last turn. The winner is the
first player to finish the entire sequence of tosses and hops,
including the space labeled *out.*

Ten Spaces

Chalk
One marker (small chain, coin, or stone) per player

Play Ten and Out, but when a player fouls out, he leaves his marker in the last space he played successfully. Players must hop over other players' markers and skip tossing their markers into spaces where others' markers rest.

Names Hopscotch

Chalk

Use chalk to draw any kind of hopscotch court. The first player hops up the court and back again on one foot, hopping in each space both up and back. If he does this without fouling out (hopping on a line or putting both feet down), he can claim any one space by writing his name on it with chalk. If he fouls out, his turn ends.

The players take turns hopping and claiming spaces in the same way. A player must hop over spaces claimed by others, but he may hop with both feet in his own space. Play continues when all the spaces have been claimed, but at this point anyone who fouls out is out of the game. The game ends when only one player—the winner—remains.

Eight and Back

Chalk
One marker (small chain, coin, or stone)
  per player

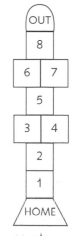

Airplane

Use chalk to draw an airplane hopscotch court. One player stands in the home space. He tosses his marker into space one, hops on one foot over space one and into space two, hops in spaces three and four at the same time, hops on one foot in space five, hops in spaces six and seven at the same time, and hops on one foot into space eight. He turns around and hops back in the same way to space two, where he picks up his marker. Then he hops into space one and the home space. He turns around and tosses his marker into space two and hops in the same way until he fouls out (hops on a line, puts both feet down when he's supposed to be hopping on one foot, or misses his target when tossing his marker).

The players take turns tossing and hopping in the same way. When a player takes a new turn, he starts hopping from where he fouled out on his last turn. The first player to finish the entire sequence of tosses and hops through space eight is the winner.

MARBLE GAMES

Marbles and marble games have been around for ages. Glass marbles have been used for about six hundred years, and clay marbles were found in the tombs of Egyptian Pharaohs buried more than six thousand years ago.

Today's marbles are made from a variety of materials. The most common marbles are glass, but marbles are also made of agate (a hard stone), alabaster (a soft stone related to marble), clay, and metal. Although most marbles are made by machine, some are works of art handmade by glass blowers.

The standard method of shooting a marble is called knuckling down. The shooter kneels and places the knuckles of his shooting hand on the ground. He sets a marble in the curve of his index finger, resting the marble on his thumb, which is behind the marble. He shoots the marble toward the target by flicking his thumb forward.

If your child finds knuckling down difficult, he can shoot marbles by bowling or flicking them. To bowl a marble, he holds it in the palm of his hand and rolls it toward the target. To flick a marble, he places it on the shooting surface with the tip of his thumb behind it, curls his index finger or middle finger to the first joint of his thumb, then flicks his finger to shoot the marble toward the target.

Marble games often require drawing circles and lines on the ground. Drawing straight lines is fairly easy, but drawing circles freehand is tough. Here's an easy way to draw a perfect circle on the ground: First, cut a length of string a little over half as long as the diameter of the circle you want to draw. For example, if you need a circle ten feet in diameter, your string should be slightly longer than five feet. Tie one end of the string to a pencil and the other end to a piece of chalk, measuring carefully so that the distance between the chalk and the pencil is exactly five feet. Have someone hold one end of the pencil tightly against the ground while someone else pulls the string taut—and keeps it taut—while drawing a perfect circle around the pencil with the chalk.

A traditional aspect of playing marbles is keeping your opponents' marbles when you win a game. Be sure players agree on whether they are playing for keeps before they begin a game. This will help prevent arguments and hurt feelings.

If you like the following games and want to know more about marbles and marble games, try the book *Marble Mania* by Stanley Block. It provides information on marble makers, games, and clubs.

Target

Metal cake pan
Marbles

Set out a small metal cake pan as a target. The first player crouches ten feet from the pan and tries to flick his marbles one at a time into the pan. If he hits the target, he continues to shoot. If he misses, his turn ends. Players take turns shooting in this way. The winner is the first player to land five marbles in the pan.

If children have difficulty flicking their marbles, you can draw a target with chalk and have the kids roll their marbles toward the target. The winner is the first player to land five marbles inside the target.

A child playing alone can try to land five marbles in the target within a certain amount of time or count how many marbles he must shoot before he lands five in the target.

Bowling

Chalk or string
Marbles

This game requires two players. Use chalk or string to mark a line behind which players must stand when they shoot their marbles.

The first player stands behind the line and shoots a marble any distance. This marble becomes the target marble, which the second player tries to hit by shooting a marble toward it. If the second player's marble lands within a hand span of the target marble, he wins the target marble. If the second player's marble doesn't land within a hand span of the target marble, the first player wins the second player's marble.

Have the players take turns shooting the target marble and trying to hit it.

Bombers

Marbles

This game requires two players. The first player shoots a marble any distance. This marble becomes the target marble. The second player stands over the target marble. Holding a marble at eye level, he tries to drop his marble onto the target marble. If he hits it, he wins the target marble. If he misses it, the first player wins the second player's marble. Have the players take turns shooting the target marble and tryingto hit it.

Rebound

Marbles

This game requires two or more players and a flat surface near a smooth wall. Each player throws one marble against the wall so that it bounces off and lands on the flat surface. These marbles become the target marbles. Players take turns shooting marbles one at a time against the wall, trying to rebound each marble to hit a target marble. A marble that doesn't hit a target marble becomes another target marble. The first player to hit any target marble wins all the target marbles.

Marble Arcade

This game can be played indoors or outdoors.

Scissors
Shoebox
Marker
Heavy object, such as large book or shoe
Marbles

Cut five or six holes of different sizes and shapes (semicircle, triangle, rectangle, and so on) in one long side of a shoebox. Each hole should be wide enough for a marble to pass through.

Write a number between one and ten above each hole. Give easier (bigger) holes lower numbers and harder (smaller) holes higher numbers. Set the box upside down on a flat surface and put a heavy object on the box to hold it in place.

Have the players take turns shooting their marbles one at a time through the holes from a designated spot. If a marble misses the holes, it stays where it lands. If a marble goes through a hole, its owner retrieves it and collects the designated number of marbles from the playing area. For example, if a marble goes through a hole marked with the number five, its owner collects five marbles from the playing area. If there aren't enough marbles in the playing area, have each player put one or two marbles into a kitty, from which the shooter is paid.

Bounce Eye

Chalk
Marbles

This game requires two or more players. Draw a circle about one foot in diameter. Have each player scatter an equal number of marbles inside the circle.

The first player stands outside the circle. Holding a marble with an outstretched arm at eye level, he drops it into the circle. If his marble knocks any marbles out of the circle, his marble plus the marbles he knocked out belong to him. If he fails to knock any marbles out of the circle, his marble stays with the other marbles inside the circle.

Players take turns trying to knock marbles out of the circle until there are no marbles left in the circle. At that point, the player with the most marbles is the winner.

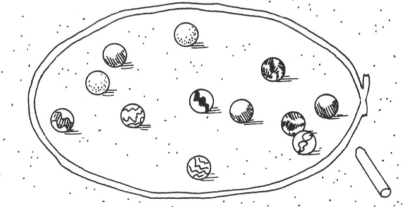

JUMP ROPE

Jump rope is a classic children's activity. Over the past hundred years or so, jump rope changed from a competitive individual sport for boys to a cooperative game for girls. Girls began the practice of jumping in groups, and girls were also responsible for adding rhymes that help jumpers keep their rhythm.

Jump rope was a favorite pastime for children of my generation, but its popularity has declined in recent years. In our community, several mothers have banded together to revive the lost art of jump rope by volunteering to teach it to students at their local school at lunch time.

Jump rope combines exercise with mild competition. Children with their own ropes enjoy seeing who can jump the fastest or the most times without tripping. A child jumping alone can see how many jumps he can do in a minute or before tripping. And a group of children can share one long rope as they take turns twirling the rope and jumping. Group jump rope helps children learn to cooperate with others while having fun.

You may enjoy teaching traditional jump rope rhymes and routines to your children and their friends. The rhymes on the following pages are ones to which many generations of North American children have jumped rope. For more rhymes, chants, songs, and techniques, check out Joanna Cole's book *Anna Banana*.

Straight Jumping

These rhymes can be used by individual jumpers and by children jumping in groups.

I love coffee.
I love tea.
I love the boys (girls),
And the boys (girls) love me.

Postman, postman,
Do your duty.
Send this letter
To an American beauty.
Don't you stop and don't delay.
Get it to her right away.

Mother, mother, I am ill.
Call for the doctor over the hill.
In came the doctor.
In came the nurse.
In came the lady
With the alligator purse.
"Measles," said the doctor.
"Mumps," said the nurse.
"Nothing," said the lady
With the alligator purse.

To get the jumping started for group jump rope, say the following rhyme while swinging the rope back-and-forth along the ground as shown. Make a full turn of the rope on the word *over,* then begin a new rhyme.

(back)	(forward)	(back)	(forward and over)
Bluebells,	cockle shells,	eevy, ivy,	over!

Counting Jumps

These rhymes can be used by individual jumpers and by children jumping in groups to see how many times a jumper can jump without tripping.

Candy, candy in the dish.
How many pieces do you wish?
One, two, three, four, five...

Mother made a chocolate cake.
How many eggs did it take?
One, two, three, four, five...

Cinderella, dressed in yellow,
Went downstairs to kiss her fellow.
How many kisses did she give?
One, two, three, four, five...

Speed Jumping

These rhymes can be used by individual jumpers and by children jumping in groups. Twirl the rope very fast after saying the word *pepper* and count to see how many fast jumps the jumper can make before he trips.

Mabel, Mabel, set the table
Just as fast as you are able.
Don't forget the salt, sugar,
Vinegar, mustard, red hot *pepper!*
One, two, three, four, five...

Mother sent me to the store.
This is what she sent me for:
Coffee, tea, and red hot *pepper!*
One, two, three, four, five...

Question-Answer Jumping

These rhymes can be used by individual jumpers and by children jumping in groups. Each rhyme asks a question that's followed by a series of possible answers. The answer is determined by the word on which the jumper trips.

If the punching in this rhyme bothers you, say, "My ma stepped on your ma's toes" instead.

My ma and your ma were hanging out clothes.
My ma gave your ma a punch in the nose.
Did it hurt her?
Yes, no, maybe so, yes, no, maybe so…

For the next rhyme, the jumper names something that starts with the letter on which he trips.

ABCs and vegetable goop.
What will I find in the alphabet soup?
A, B, C, D, E, F, G…

In this last rhyme, the letter on which the jumper trips predicts the name of the jumper's future sweetheart.

Strawberry shortcake, cream on top.
Tell me the name of my sweetheart.
A, B, C, D, E, F, G…

Action Jumping

Each of these rhymes is meant for group jump rope. As everyone chants the rhyme, the jumper jumps while dramatizing the actions.

I'm a little Dutch girl dressed in blue.
Here are the things I like to do:
Salute to the captain, bow to the queen,
Turn my back on the submarine.
I can do the tap dance, I can do the splits.
I can do the hokey pokey just like this.

Spanish dancer, do the splits.
Spanish dancer, give a kick.
Spanish dancer, turn around.
Spanish dancer, get out of town. (Jumper runs out.)

Benjamin Franklin went to France
To teach the ladies how to dance.
First the heel and then the toe;
Spin around, and out you go.

GARDENING

Most kids are drawn to working with earth—observe any child making mud pies! What begins as play can develop into a life-long love of gardening.

Gardening is a valuable activity for kids. It not only teaches them about science and nature, it also requires planning and patience, encourages experimentation and observation, provides fresh air and exercise, and produces tangible results. You can grow fruits, vegetables, herbs, or flowers, and you can eat your harvest fresh-picked, freeze it, dry it, cook or bake with it, use it to decorate your home, give it away, sell it for profit, or make crafts with it.

Don't worry if you haven't much space. You can grow a garden in pots on a balcony or windowsill, in hanging baskets or window boxes, or in any small strip of land. Your neighborhood may even have a community garden.

A kids' gardening book plus a pair of gloves, a small set of tools, and a few seed packets make great gifts for a beginning gardener. Two books we like are Karyn Morris's *The Kids Can Press Jumbo Book of Gardening* and L. Patricia Kite's *Gardening Wizardry for Kids.*

Use the following activities to introduce your child to gardening. You'll learn as you grow, so don't get frustrated. Gardening takes patience, flexibility, and a willingness to learn from mistakes. Always use good soil and choose plants that you like and that match your garden's growing conditions. Be creative, take your time, and have fun!

Homemade Composter

The key to a healthy garden is good soil, and good soil is full of nutrients and organic matter. The best way to improve your soil is to add compost. You can buy compost or make it yourself in a store-bought or homemade composter.

Large plastic garbage can with lid
Utility knife
Hammer
Nail

Cut the bottom out of the garbage can with a utility knife. Help your child use a hammer and nail to punch holes about eight inches apart in three parallel circles around the top, middle, and bottom of the can.

Compost

Composter
Soil
Fresh kitchen scraps
(vegetable matter only)
and/or grass clippings

Dry material like sawdust,
dead leaves, and dry grass
clippings
Shovel

Place your composter in a sunny spot with at least twelve inches of space around it so air can circulate.

Have your child put a four-inch layer of soil in the bottom of the composter. Add a four-inch layer of fresh kitchen scraps and/or grass clippings. Add a four-inch layer of dry material. Keep alternating layers of fresh and dry materials.

When you're done, place the lid on your composter. When the compost is dark brown and smells like earth, it's ready to use in your garden.

Compost Tea

Compost
Cheesecloth or burlap bag
String
Pail
Water

Have your child place about one cup of compost on a piece of cheesecloth or burlap. Tie the cheesecloth or burlap shut with string. Fill a pail with water and hang the compost bag inside the pail. Cover the pail and let it sit for a week or so. Water your plants with compost tea every few weeks to help them thrive.

Pumpkins

Pumpkins need about four months to grow, so plant the seeds three to four weeks after the last spring frost.

Soil and compost
Pumpkin seeds
Compost tea
Leaves or grass clippings
Newspapers or straw mulch

Choose a sunny area for your pumpkin patch. Help your child use soil and compost to make a hill. If you have a large garden, make three or four hills spaced about three feet apart. Plant three or four pumpkin seeds in each hill.

Water the hill(s) each week and watch for seedlings to appear. When they do, pull out the weaker looking ones to leave one strong seedling growing in each hill. When blossoms appear, remove all but three from each plant. Each blossom will become a pumpkin.

Water your plant(s) with warm water every week and with compost tea every few weeks. Spread compost, leaves, or grass clippings on top of the soil around the growing pumpkins. Make sure the grass clippings don't touch the stem(s) of your plant(s). To ensure that the pumpkins won't rot on the moist soil, place newspapers or straw mulch under the pumpkins as they grow. Turn them frequently so they ripen on all sides.

Potatoes

Potatoes

Cut each potato into four pieces with at least two eyes per piece. Have your child plant each piece eyes-up about four inches deep. Water the plants regularly. As the potatoes grow, mound soil around them to keep them covered. Dig up your potatoes in the fall after the stems and leaves die. See page 56 for more information.

Sunflowers

Sunflower seeds
Compost tea
Compost
Stakes (optional)

Have your child plant sunflower seeds early in the growing season, after all danger of frost has passed, about one inch deep and three feet apart. If you're planting sunflowers in a garden, plant them where they won't shade shorter plants. Water the plants regularly with water and every three weeks with compost tea. When seedlings appear, put compost around the base of each plant, making sure the compost doesn't touch the stem. Taller plants may need stakes for support.

Strawberries

Strawberries are easy to grow and delicious to eat. Best of all, the plants bear fruit year after year.

Strawberry seedlings
Compost
Straw mulch

Help your child plant strawberry seedlings about one foot apart in a sunny area with well-drained soil. Plant multiple rows about two feet apart.

Water the plants regularly. For the first three months after you plant them, remove the blossoms from each plant. During the first two growing seasons, remove all the runners from the plants. These techniques help the plants grow sturdy.

You won't get any berries in the first growing season, but you will get berries in the second growing season. When cold weather arrives and the ground freezes, cover your plants with straw. Remove the straw the following spring.

Starting in the third growing season, let the runners grow. These will form new rows of strawberry plants. Remove the older plants in the fall.

Tomatoes

Plant tomatoes early in the growing season, about two or three weeks after the last frost. Some varieties produce only one crop of tomatoes (a good choice for containers), while others keep producing until the first frost.

Tomato seedlings
Tomato cages
Compost
Compost tea

Help your child plant tomato seedlings about two feet apart in a sunny area, with their bottom leaves at soil level. Place a cage around each plant. Spread compost around the plants, making sure it doesn't touch the stems. Water the plants regularly with water and with compost tea every three weeks. Wind the stems through the cages as they grow.

FUN IN THE SNOW

I've lived most of my life in an area that doesn't get much snow. Any snow that falls usually melts in a day or two, giving us barely enough time to make a few snow angels and a snowman. But if you live in a place that gets lots of snow during the winter, snow angels and snowmen probably just aren't enough. Here are a few games and activities to add some fun and variety to your snow play.

Fox and Geese

This game requires four or more players and a large, open area of unspoiled snow. Stomp a big circle in the snow and two intersecting paths through the middle of the circle. Where the paths meet, stomp out a small safe zone. The figure should look like this: ⊗. Choose one person to be the fox; all other players are geese. The fox chases the geese and tries to tag one of them. All players must run only on the paths, and geese can't be tagged when they're standing in the safe zone. As soon as the fox catches a goose, that goose becomes the new fox.

Snow Bricks

Loaf pan

Pack snow into a loaf pan. (If the snow is powdery, sprinkle a little water on it before packing it into the pan.) Turn the pan upside down and tap the bottom lightly to release the brick. Use snow bricks to build a fort. Bricks laid with their long sides together will make a sturdy structure. Pack snow in the gaps between the bricks as you lay them.

Target Practice

Scissors
Old sheet or blanket
Clothespins
Clothesline or rope
Snowballs
Needle and thread (optional)

Cut three or four holes, each about twelve inches in diameter, in an old sheet or blanket. Fasten this target with lots of clothespins to a clothesline or a rope strung between two trees or posts. Have each child stand about ten feet away and throw snowballs at the holes. Score one point for each snowball that goes through a hole. The first person to score a certain number of points is the winner. A child playing alone can see how many snowballs it takes to score a certain number of points.

To make a sturdy target that won't flap in the wind, sew casings along its long sides. (Fold each long side over an inch or two and sew it down to create a tube.) Thread one rope through the top casing and another through the bottom one, then tie the ropes to two trees or posts.

You can also play this game in the summertime, using balls instead of snowballs.

Ice Sculptures

*Molds (buckets, ice cube
    trays, plastic containers,
    milk cartons, and so on)*

*Bucket of warm water
Mittens or gloves
Spray bottle full of water*

Fill the molds with water and set them outdoors overnight to freeze. Dip each mold in warm water for a few seconds to loosen the ice. Turn the mold upside down to slide the ice out. (Be sure to wear mittens or gloves.) Let your child build an ice sculpture. To stick two shapes together, spray water on the surfaces you want to join and hold them together for about ten seconds.

Snow Painting

*Spray bottle full of water
Food coloring or liquid
    tempera paint*

*Paintbrushes
Small containers*

Add a few drops of food coloring or a spoonful or two of tempera paint to a spray bottle full of water. Let your child paint the snow by spraying it or brushing on undiluted tempera paint poured into small containers.

Button, Button

Snow
Snowballs
Colored button

This game requires four or more players. Make a number of snowballs one fewer than number of players you have. Hide a brightly colored button inside one of the snowballs.

Choose one player to be it. The other players stand in a circle around him and pass the snowballs quickly around the circle until he tells them to stop. He must then guess which player has the snowball with the button inside. The players break open their snowballs to see if he has guessed correctly. If not, he's it again for the next round; if so, the player holding the button becomes it. Make some more snowballs and play again.

CHAPTER 5
On the Move

Children seldom misquote you. In fact, they usually repeat
word for word what you shouldn't have said.

—*Anonymous*

Traveling with young children can be frustrating—filled with
bickering, boredom, and the inevitable refrain *Are we there*
yet? But with a little creativity and planning, you can make
the time you spend in the car—or on the bus, train, plane, or
ferry—treasured family time. After all, when you're traveling,
there are no chores to do or meals to make. There's no telephone interrupting your conversation and no computer or TV
luring your attention away.

Some of the games on the following pages can be played
by a solitary child, but most require two or more players. The
games in this chapter are all simple and compact, which makes
them perfect for traveling—but don't forget that they're also a
valuable source of entertainment in waiting rooms or on bad-
weather days.

PENCIL-AND-PAPER GAMES

These games require two or more players. All you need to play them is a pencil and a sheet of paper for each player. If you like, you can prepare a supply of grids and other figures for the various games by making photocopies or by creating them on a computer and printing many copies.

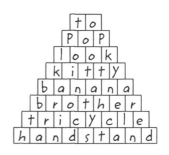

Word Pyramid

This game is good for kids with basic printing and spelling skills.

One pencil per player
One sheet of paper per player

Have each player draw a pyramid on a sheet of paper. The pyramid should be made up of squares, with two squares in the top row, three squares in the second row, and so on to the last row, which should have nine squares. At your signal, each player fills each row of her pyramid with one word, placing one letter in each square. The winner is the first to complete her pyramid. You decide how accurate spelling must be. For beginning readers, it's best to accept honest tries, such as words from which vowels are missing or in which letters that sound alike (such as *c* and *k*) are used interchangeably.

Cooperative Drawing

One pencil per player
Paper
Crayons, colored pencils, or markers

One player draws a line or shape on paper. The next player adds a line or shape, then the next player, and so on. The players face each other so they get different perspectives on the drawing. When the players finish drawing, they color it in the same way with crayons, colored pencils, or markers.

Word Hunt

One pencil per player
One sheet of paper per player

Write a long word like *concentration* or *spaghetti* at the top of each child's paper. At your signal, have the children write as many two-, three-, and four-letter words as they can using only the letters that appear in the long word you've chosen. (Let the children use proper nouns, plurals, slang, acronyms, and so on.) Stop the game after five minutes. The child who has written the most words is the winner. A child playing alone can simply race the clock and try to beat her previous record.

Reverse Tick-Tack-Toe

One pencil per player
Paper

This game requires two players. One plays *X*s; the other plays
*O*s. Draw a tick-tack-toe grid (two vertical lines intersected by
two horizontal lines to form nine equal spaces) on paper. The
object of the game is to avoid claiming three spaces in a row.
To start the game, one player writes her letter in the center
space. The other player then writes her letter in any empty
space. The players take turns claiming spaces in this way until
one player (the loser) claims three spaces in any vertical, horizontal, or diagonal row.

Gomuku

One pencil per player
Paper

This game, a Japanese version of tick-tack-toe, requires two
players. One plays *X*s; the other plays *O*s. Draw a grid of nineteen vertical and nineteen horizontal lines on paper. The players take turns claiming the intersections of the lines rather
than the spaces. The first player to claim five intersections in
a vertical, horizontal, or diagonal row wins.

Hangman

If the imagery in this traditional game bothers you, call it "Spider" instead. Replace the nine parts of a human body with nine parts of a spider (a body and eight legs) and replace the noose with a length of spider silk.

One pencil per player
Paper

Draw an upside down *L* (the gallows) at the top of a sheet of paper. Write the alphabet at the bottom of the paper.

This game requires two players. One thinks of a word and draws a blank for each letter in the word. (For beginning readers, use only four- or five-letter words.)

The other player (the guesser) calls out one letter at a time. The first player crosses out that letter at the bottom of the page. If the letter appears anywhere in the word she chose, she fills in the appropriate blank(s). If the letter doesn't appear in the word she chose, she adds a body part under the arm of the gallows. (Use nine body parts in this order: head, neck, body, arms, hands, legs, feet, nose, eyes-mouth-ears.) The tenth and final addition to the gallows is a noose. The guesser must guess the word before the noose is drawn. If she does, she's the winner and gets to think of a word for the next game. If she doesn't, she must be the guesser again in the next game.

Battleships

One pencil per player
Four sheets of paper

On each sheet of paper draw a grid ten columns by ten rows. Across the top of the grid, label the columns with the letters *A* through *J*, one letter per column. Down the left side of the grid, label the rows with the numbers one through ten, one number per row. This game requires two players. Each uses two grids— one to mark her own battleships and one to record her guesses as she searches for her opponent's battleships.

Each player positions eight battleships (one ship five squares long, two ships each four squares long, three ships each three squares long, and two ships each two squares long) on a grid by marking squares. Each player should make sure her opponent can't see her grid.

Before playing, decide whether a battleship can be sunk by one hit or must be hit in each space to be sunk. One player starts the game by guessing a location where she thinks one of her opponent's battleships may be (for example, D-five). If the opponent has a ship at that location, the opponent says, "Hit." If no ship is there, the opponent says, "Miss." A player records her guess on her second grid by marking the location with an *H* (hit) or *M* (miss). The players take turns guessing in this way. The first player to sink all her opponent's battleships wins.

Squares

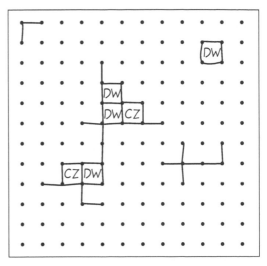

One pencil per player
Paper

On a sheet of paper draw a grid of dots composed of twelve to fifteen rows of twelve to fifteen dots each. Space the dots about a half-inch apart.

This game requires two or more players. The first player draws a line from any dot to any vertically or horizontally adjacent dot. The next player does the same, and the players continue to take turns drawing lines in this way. The object of the game is to form a square by joining four dots. When a player draws a line that closes a square, she writes her initials inside the square and gets a bonus turn.

When all possible lines have been drawn, the player with the most initialed squares is the winner.

Wordgrams

One pencil per player
One sheet of paper per player
Children's dictionary (optional)

On each sheet of paper draw a grid ten columns by ten rows.
   This game requires two or more players. Give each player a grid and have her write ten words horizontally, vertically, and diagonally on her grid using one letter per square. Words may intersect and may be written forward or backward. If you like, have the players make theme wordgrams using only birthday party words, vacation words, or whatever. If a player is not a strong speller, encourage her to use a dictionary. Once each player has written ten words on her grid, she can fill in the remaining squares with random letters. If you like, have each player list the hidden words at the bottom of her wordgram.
   When the wordgrams are finished, have each player give her wordgram to another player. Each player then tries to find all the words hidden in the wordgram she's received.

NO PROPS REQUIRED

For the following games, all you need is two or more players and some free time! For more games like these, check out "Fun with Words" (page 200).

Twenty Questions

Designate one player (the thinker) to think of a person, animal, or thing familiar to all the players. The other players (guessers) take turns asking yes-or-no questions to help them guess the person, animal, or thing.

The thinker must keep track of the number of questions asked. If you like, distribute twenty counters (pennies, beans, or paper clips) evenly among the guessers. As each guesser asks a question, she gives a counter to the thinker. When the guessers run out of counters, the game is over.

Any guesser may try to guess the person, animal, or thing on her turn. If she's right, she's the thinker for the next game. If she's wrong, the guess counts as one question, and the game continues until someone guesses right or until twenty questions have been asked. If no one guesses right within twenty questions, the thinker reveals the person, animal, or thing and starts a new game by thinking of a different person, animal, or thing.

Is it an animal?

Yes.

Is it hairy?

Yes.

Does it have four legs?

No.

Reverse Twenty Questions

Designate one player (the guesser) to cover her ears while the other players (thinkers) think of a person, animal, or thing familiar to all the players. The guesser then uncovers her ears and asks yes-or-no questions to help her guess what the thinkers are thinking of.

Choose one thinker to keep track of the number of questions asked. If you like, give the guesser twenty counters (pennies, beans, or paper clips). Each time the guesser asks a question, she gives a counter to the thinker. When the guesser runs out of counters, the game is over.

The guesser may try to guess the person, animal, or thing at any time. If she's right, she remains the guesser for the next game. If she's wrong, the guess counts as one question, and the game continues until she guesses right or until she has asked twenty questions. If she doesn't guess right within twenty questions, the thinkers reveal the person, animal, or thing, and a different player gets to be the guesser for the next game.

Grandmother's Trunk

To begin the game, one player says, "I went to my grandmother's trunk, and I found a (coat)." The next player says,
"I went to my Grandmother's trunk, and I found a (coat and
hat)." The players continue to take turns, on each turn
repeating the words already mentioned and adding a new
word to the list. Start a new game when the list becomes too
hard to remember.

If you'd like to reinforce alphabet skills and make the list
easier to remember, require the players to add words in
alphabetical order (*antique, book, coat,* and so on).

Word Race

This game is fun for talkative kids. Choose a song, poem, or
nursery rhyme familiar to all the players. At your signal,
have the first player sing or recite the song, poem, or rhyme
as fast as she can. Time her by using a clock or a watch or by
counting "one Mississippi, two Mississippi, three
Mississippi...." Let each player take a turn. Remember each
player's time and see who's the fastest yakker. If you like,
record the results in a Family Book of Records (page 267).

Brainstorming

According to Susan K. Perry in *Playing Smart,* the more a child uses brainstorming skills, the more creative a thinker she will be. Brainstorming is thinking up as many answers to a question as possible. Below are some ideas to get you started. After you've brainstormed for a while, brainstorm some new brainstorming topics!

- Think up far-fetched excuses for why something was or wasn't done, for example: *I didn't have a bath because the tub was full of piranhas.*
- Ask the question *Must you _____ to _____?* For example: *Must you go to school to be smart?*
- Make up a ten-ways-not-to list, for example: *Ten Ways Not to Get Good Grades: Sleep during class. Don't do your homework....*
- Fill in the blanks in the following sentence: *It was so _____ that _____.* For example: *It was so hot outside that my lemonade boiled.*
- Make up a 101-uses-for list, for example: *101 Uses for Paper Clips: Holding papers together. Picking locks. Making necklaces. Playing with magnets....*
- Think up as many oxymorons (figures of speech that seem to contradict themselves) as you can, for example: *an honest thief* or *tears of joy.* Just for fun, you might think up oxymorons that are particular to your family. In our house, *quiet boy* and *sleeping baby* are oxymorons!

Cooperative Story

One player makes up the beginning of a story. For example, she might say, "One day a little girl was walking down the street when...." She stops telling the story at any exciting or suspenseful moment, and the next player adds to the story in the same way. The players take turns adding to the story, which will likely take some hilarious twists and turns. End the story when the players tire of it.

Name That Rhythm

One player claps the rhythm of a familiar song or nursery rhyme, such as "Three Blind Mice" or "Twinkle, Twinkle, Little Star." The other players must guess what song she's clapping by listening to the rhythm. The player who correctly guesses the song gets to be the next clapper.

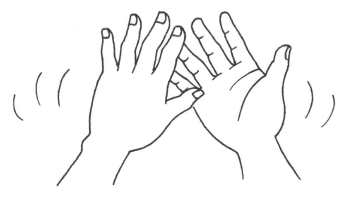

GAMES WITH PROPS

The following games require a little advance preparation. For some, all you need is a supply of marbles; for others, you'll have to make the game ahead of time. All the games require two or more players.

Who Wants to Be a Genius?

Start your trip with this game and award prizes that will give your children something to do while you travel.

Five index cards per player
Pen or pencil
Children's trivia games and schoolbooks (optional)
Supply of prizes like coins, marbles, playing cards, small
*   toys, markers, books, and/or snacks*

Before your trip, write a question that your children should be able to answer on each index card. Good sources of questions are the Parker Brothers game Trivial Pursuit Junior, the Brain Quest games by Workman Publishing Company, and your children's schoolbooks.

During your trip, choose the first contestant, then choose an index card and ask her the question on it. If she answers correctly, she wins one prize, and her stakes jump to two prizes for the second question. Add another prize to the stakes for each question she answers correctly. Ask her a total of five questions, then choose another contestant and ask questions and award prizes in the same way.

After each child has had a turn as a contestant, end the game and let your kids enjoy their prizes. You'll need a maximum of fifteen prizes per player.

How Big?

Six household objects　　*One pencil and one sheet of*
Lunch bag　　　　　　　　*paper per player*

Before your trip, collect six household objects that come in standard sizes (for example, a playing card, key, quarter, new pencil, fork, and spoon) and put them in a lunch bag.

　　During your trip, give each player a pencil and a sheet of paper. Ask each player to draw the objects you've collected without looking at them. Compare the drawings with the objects to see which drawing is closest to each object's actual size. The player with the greatest number of most accurate drawings is the winner.

Eggs in the Bush

Ten marbles or pennies per player

Each player takes a turn hiding one to five marbles or pennies in her hands. The other players guess how many items she's holding. (Each player must guess a different number.) The player who guesses correctly gets the hidden items. Each player who guesses incorrectly pays the hider in items the difference between the number of hidden items and the number guessed.

Travel Flannel Board

Scissors
Large piece of flannel
Cardboard
Glue gun
Felt
Magazine pictures

Family photos
Words written on index cards
Clear contact paper
Strips of Velcro, sandpaper, or
   flannel

Before your trip, cut a piece of flannel a few inches larger all around than the cardboard. Lay the cardboard in the center of the wrong (smooth) side of the flannel, fold the edges of the flannel over the cardboard, and glue the edges down. Cut out felt shapes that can be used to make a design or tell a story. Cut out magazine pictures, gather family photos, and write a wide variety of words on index cards. (To make a matching game for beginning readers, make an index-card label for each picture and photo.) Cover these with clear contact paper and use a glue gun to attach a strip of Velcro, sandpaper, or flannel to the back of each picture and card.

During your trip, encourage your kids to use the pictures and words to create a story on the flannel board. If you've made a matching game, challenge the kids to match each picture and photo with its label.

Travel Bingo

One sheet of heavy paper or cardboard per player
Markers (or magazine pictures and glue)
Clear contact paper or plastic page protectors
One dry-erase marker per child

Before your trip, make simple bingo cards by drawing a grid four squares by four squares on each sheet of heavy paper or cardboard. In each square, write words that represent things you may see as you drive, for example: *parking lot, cow, flag,* and so on. For nonreaders, draw pictures or glue on pictures cut from magazines instead. Cover the completed bingo cards with clear contact paper or slip them into plastic page protectors.

During your trip, give each player a bingo card and a dry-erase marker. Each time a player sees something described on her bingo card, she marks an *X* in that square. The first player to mark four squares in a horizontal, vertical, or diagonal row is the winner.

Odd or Even?

Ten marbles or pennies per player

Each player takes a turn hiding one to five marbles or pennies in her hands. The other players guess whether she's holding an odd or even number of items. After all the players have guessed, the hider shows them the items in her hand. Players who guessed incorrectly pay the hider one marble each; players who guessed correctly are paid one marble each by the hider.

Wave If You're Famous

This activity may seem silly, but kids love it!

Dark, wide-tip marker
Sheet of heavy paper or cardboard

Use a dark, wide-tip marker to write a sentence like *Wave if you're famous!* or *Wave if it's your birthday!* or *Wave if you love cats!* on a sheet of heavy paper or cardboard. As you drive along, let your children take turns holding up the sign to passing cars. They'll love the various reactions they get.

Magazine Scavenger Hunt

One old magazine per player
One sheet of paper per player
One pencil per player

Before your trip, leaf through each magazine. For each magazine, make a list of fifteen objects pictured in it. Each list should be on a separate sheet of paper.

During your trip, give each player a magazine and its corresponding list. Each player must look through her magazine, hunt for the objects on her list, and write down the numbers of the pages on which the objects are found. To determine a winner, you can either time the game for fifteen minutes and see who finds the most objects within that time or simply declare the first player who finds all her objects the winner.

This game is great for players of different ages and abilities, because the lists can be tailored to the players. A younger player may want to mark the pages on which she finds objects by turning down their corners. Very young players can search for colors rather than objects.

CHAPTER 6
Homework Helpers

Education commences at the mother's knee, and every word spoken within the hearing of little children tends toward the formation of character.

—Hosea Ballou

From the day your child was born, you've been his most important teacher. And when your child starts school, your help is still important. To help your child learn, make sure he eats healthy meals and gets enough rest, free time, fresh air, and quiet time for homework and reading. Limit passive activities like watching TV. Read to him each day and let him see you reading for pleasure.

You can also do activities that help your child develop basic learning skills. For example, word games strengthen memory, spelling, and vocabulary. Journaling develops writing and organizational skills. Laundry and cooking develop skills like sorting, estimating, and measuring. Have fun with these activities! Kids won't be thrilled about doing extra "school," but they'll enjoy doubling a cookie recipe or blowing giant bubbles. As former U.S. Secretary of Education Lamar Alexander said, "The first teachers are the parents, both by example and conversation. But don't think of it as teaching. Think of it as fun."

FUN WITH WORDS

Word games can be played almost anywhere, anytime—while you're traveling, doing chores, waiting in a doctor's office, taking a walk, and so on. They don't require any special equipment, although pencil and paper may come in handy.

These activities help strengthen your child's auditory memory and spelling, reading, and vocabulary skills, but remember to approach them as games. Keep them fun for your child, or he won't want to play.

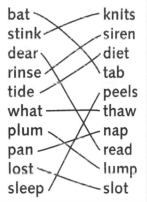

Anagrams

Anagrams are pairs or groups of words that use exactly the same letters in different order, for example: *pills/spill* and *eat/tea*. The following games are fun ways to play with anagrams. They may be tough for beginning readers, but independent readers will enjoy them.

- Grab a pencil and paper and brainstorm a list of anagrams with your child.
- Write a list of words on a sheet of paper. Challenge your child to write an anagram for each. Or if you like, list the words and their anagrams in two separate columns and in different order, then ask your child to match the anagrams by drawing a line between each pair. Here are some anagrams to get you started: *lemon/melon, rats/star, cloud/could, flow/wolf, dice/iced, race/care, bread/beard, but/tub, stop/post, step/pest.*

bat	knits
stink	siren
dear	diet
rinse	tab
tide	peels
what	thaw
plum	nap
pan	read
lost	lump
sleep	slot

- After playing with anagrams a bit, you'll enjoy making up anagram riddles like *Q: What do you call a bothersome thing on the stairs? A: A step pest.*

Which Is Different?

Think of a category, such as animals, food, or household objects. Name four objects within the chosen category, three of which begin with the same sound. For example, if the category is food, you could say, "Chocolate, cheese, apple, chips." Challenge your child to tell you which word begins with a different sound from the other three. Trade places and let your child think of four words for you.

Rhyme Time

- Ask your child simple rhyming riddles like *Q: What month rhymes with spoon? A: June.*
- Challenge your child to think of as many rhymes as he can for a particular word. If multiple children are playing, have them write their answers down and see who can think of the most words within a certain time.
- Write a word like *hat* on a sheet of paper. Ask your child how many new words he can make by changing the first letter, for example: *bat, cat, fat,* and so on.
- Make up riddles that have rhyming words as answers, such as *Q: What's a large hog? A: A big pig.*

Word Chain

This game requires two or more players. Think of a category, such as animals. The first player says a word that fits the category, such as *cat*. The next player says another animal name that begins with the last letter of the first player's word, such as *tiger*. The next word would then begin with *r*, and so on. End the game when players begin to repeat words.

Word Scramble

Pencil and paper

Scramble up some common words and challenge your child to unscramble them. For beginning readers, use three- and four-letter words and provide a definition for each scrambled word. For example, you might tell your child that *rac* is something you drive or *dirb* is something that flies. For independent readers, scramble longer words and/or skip the definitions. If you like, scramble words in categories, such as animals, musical instruments, fruits, and so on.

For two or more players, make a list of scrambled words and give a copy to each player. See who can unscramble all the words first.

Homophone Fun

Learning about language doesn't have to be boring. Playing games with homophones is a fun way to strengthen your child's vocabulary skills. Homophones are pairs or groups of words that sound alike but have different meanings, for example: *heir/air* and *nose/knows*. Homophones may be spelled differently or alike, so the words *fast* (quick) and *fast* (abstain from eating) are also homophones.

Pencils and paper (optional)

- Ask your child to tell you any homophones he can think of. Ask him to tell you their meanings, too. He might, for ex-ample, say, "A board is a piece of wood, and bored is how you feel when there's nothing to do." If two or more children are playing, have them write down their homophones on paper.
- Make up riddles that have homophones as answers, such as *Q: What do you call a teddy with no clothes? A: A bare bear.*

Nym-ble Noggin

Exercise your brains with the synonym and antonym games described below. Synonyms are pairs or groups of words with the same or similar meanings, for example: *nice/kind* and *big/large*. Antonyms are pairs or groups of words with opposite meanings, for example: *hot/cold* and *tall/short*.

Pencil and paper
Children's thesaurus

* Brainstorm the synonyms of various words. (Adjectives— words, such as *pretty,* that describe people, places, and things—are the easiest words to use.) For example, synonyms of *pretty* include *gorgeous, beautiful, lovely, attractive,* and *cute.*
* Think of a word, give your child a pencil and a sheet of paper, and challenge him to write down as many synonyms for the chosen word as he can.
* Brainstorm the antonyms of various words. (Verbs—action words, such as *stop*—and adjectives are the easiest words to use.) For example, antonyms of *stop* include *go* and *start;* antonyms of *pretty* include *ugly, hideous,* and *unattractive.*
* If you like, show your child how to use a thesaurus (a book of synonyms). A children's thesaurus is very handy when your child is doing creative writing.

Funny Sayings

Every culture has sayings that, taken literally, are very silly or make no sense at all. We rarely stop to question the meanings of such sayings, and children who hear them usually understand them just by the context in which they're used.

Think of some funny sayings your child knows, like *Two heads are better than one* or *It's raining cats and dogs.* Perhaps your family has its own funny sayings that are meaningless to outsiders but loaded with significance to you. Or perhaps a saying has crept into your family's vocabulary after read- ing a certain book. For example, when one can't find an item in our house, it's a sure thing that the Borrowers have taken it. Talk with your child about what these sayings mean, both literally and figuratively, and discuss whether they're true. If you'd like to read more about American English sayings, read *What Your First Grader Needs to Know* and *What Your Second Grader Needs to Know* by E. D. Hirsch, Jr.

Backwords

My daughter Andria "made up" this game when she was about five years old. (It has surely been played by many other families, but I'll always think of it as Andria's game.)

Choose a word, then challenge your child to reverse the letters of the word (in his head or on paper) and say it backward. For example, *tree* becomes *eert*, *car* becomes *rac*, and so on. If you like, start with simple one-syllable words. As your child becomes more skilled at this game, challenge him to reverse words with digraphs (pairs of letters, such as *sh*, that each represent a single sound), words with silent letters, multisyllabic words, and complete sentences.

Palindromes

A palindrome is a word, phrase, or sentence that reads the same backward and forward, such as *dad, evil olive,* and *Madam, I'm Adam.* How many palindromes can you and your child think of? If you like, make up riddles with palindromes as answers, for example: *Q: What do you say when something amazes you? A: Wow!*

READING AND WRITING

My daughter Andria was about six years old when she began reading fluently. One day, when my sister complimented her on her reading, Andria replied with a sigh, "Yes, it's opened up a whole new world to me!" My sister thought this statement was hilarious coming from a child, but I recognized it as one of the carrots I'd dangled before Andria as encouragement. And it's true! When parents help their children learn to read, they help open the door to a new world. A child's world is forever expanded and enriched when he becomes a reader.

The home environment powerfully influences a child's reading development. Children who read well come from homes where there are plenty of books, magazines, and newspapers and where everyone reads. Children who read well have parents who encourage reading and make time for it—who read aloud to them, talk to them about their ideas and experiences, take them places, limit their TV viewing, and take an interest in their reading progress.

Games and activities like those that follow will help develop your child's reading and writing skills, but remember that there's no better way to help your child succeed as a reader than reading aloud together. Take the time to read to your child every day. Even fluent readers enjoy and benefit from hearing good books read aloud.

World of Words

The following ideas are adapted from the U.S. Department of Education booklet *Helping Your Child Become a Reader*.

- Point out letters and challenge your child to find and name specific letters in signs, billboards, posters, product packaging, books, and magazines.
- On each page of a blank notebook or scrapbook, have your child draw or glue a picture representing one letter of the alphabet. Help him label each picture with the appropriate letter.
- Let your child decorate a box or shelf to hold his books. Help him arrange his books in any order he likes.
- Ask your child to act out a line or two of his favorite poem, rhyme, or song.
- Make a travel journal with your child. Each evening, write in a blank notebook or scrapbook about the day's special event. Later, glue in photos.
- Hang a message board in your kitchen. Leave simple notes there for your child and encourage him to leave notes there, too.

Notes and Lists

Pencil and paper

To help your child practice his writing skills and be more observant and organized, try these activities:

- Encourage your child to take notes describing what he sees on trips and outings.
- Encourage your child take to notes on a TV program, then write and illustrate a paragraph about it.
- Encourage your child to make lists of his belongings, items he'd like to buy, things he'd like to do, homework assignments, test dates, and social events.

Label the Fable

Book of fables, such as Aesop's Fables

A fable is a story that teaches a lesson. Read a fable to your child, then do the activities below to exercise your child's comprehension, reasoning, and critical thinking skills.

- Have your child explain the moral of the story in his own words. Or if you like, give your child three morals and ask him which moral matches the fable.
- Talk about situations in your child's life where the moral of the story might apply.

Crazy Captions

This activity is fun for prereaders, beginning readers, and independent readers. Adapt it to your child's ability.

Family photos or photos from old magazines or catalogs
Glue
Small notebook, sheet of poster board, or several sheets of
   plain paper plus construction paper and stapler
Pencil, pen, colored pencils, or markers

Give your child some family photos or old magazines or catalogs to look through for photos. Let him glue several photos that interest him into a small notebook or onto a sheet of poster board or several sheets of plain paper.
   Encourage your child to think of a descriptive, funny, or just plain crazy caption for each photo. Have your child write the caption below the photo. If you like, write the caption faintly in pencil and let your child trace it, or write the caption on scrap paper and let your child copy it. If you've used plain paper, assemble the pages into a booklet by adding a construction paper cover and stapling the pages together.

Word-Tracing Game

*Homemade or store-bought picture cards showing things
    that represent simple words like* hat, pig, *and* doll
Pencil
One sheet of paper per player
One marker per player

Divide the cards into as many equal sets as there are players.
For each set, print the corresponding words faintly in pencil
on a sheet of paper. Give one list to each player. Shuffle all
the cards together and put them facedown in a pile. The first
player draws a card, identifies the picture, then looks for the
word on his list. If he finds it, he traces it with a marker. If
he doesn't, he discards the card. The next player does the
same, and the players take turns until there are no more
cards in the pile. The player who has traced the most words
at this point is the winner. A child playing alone can make a
game of simply identifying the pictures, finding the words,
and tracing the words.

Variation
If all the players are independent readers, turn this into a
spelling game. For this variation, you needn't make lists.
When a player draws a card, he simply writes the word on a
sheet of paper. When there are no cards left in the pile, the
player who has spelled the most words correctly is the winner.

Just Jokes

Small notebook
Pencil, pen, colored pencils, and/or markers

Have your child write his favorite jokes and/or riddles in a small notebook. If you like, print the jokes faintly in pencil and let your child trace them, print them on scrap paper and let your child copy them, or simply print the jokes yourself. Have your child illustrate each joke.

Reading Journal

This activity is a great way for your child to practice writing and remember the books and authors he likes.

Small notebook
Pen, pencil, crayons, and/or markers

When your child finishes a book, encourage him to make an entry in his journal. He can use a separate page for each book and note its title, author, and illustrator; the date he read it; why he liked or disliked it; whether he would recommend it to others; and whether he would look for other books by that author or illustrator. Have your child illustrate the entry.

Nonsense Book

Ten or more index cards
Small notebook
Pencils, crayons, colored pencils, or markers

Divide the cards into two sets. On each card in one set, write a sentence subject like *Dad, Justin, The cat, The hat,* and so on. On each card in the other set, write a predicate like *has a bat, is tired, has a bib, is in bed,* and so on. If you like, write in one color for subjects and one for predicates.

Let your child pick a subject card and a predicate card and join them to form a sentence, for example: *The hat has a bib* or *The cat is in bed.* Have your child read the sentence aloud, or read the sentence for him. Then have your child print the sentence at the bottom of one page of the notebook (or print it for him). Let your child illustrate the sentence. Repeat this process several times to make a nonsense book.

Free Samples for Kids

Writing away for free or nearly free items gives kids valuable practice at reading and following directions, writing letters, and addressing envelopes and postcards.

Writing paper
Postcards
Ten-inch envelopes
Pencil or pen
First-class and postcard stamps
Money (optional)

Companies often offer free samples to consumers who write letters or e-mails to request them.

Check web sites such as Free Stuff 4 Kids (www.freestuff4kids.net) and Freebies (www.freebies.com) with your child to find items he'd like to request. Help him follow the intructions carefully to prevent disappointment.

Address Book

Keeping track of the addresses of friends and family members helps your child practice his writing skills, learn about alphabetical order, and learn how to write addresses correctly.

Pencil, pen, or marker
Index cards
Ruled paper
Blank address book or small notebook
Stationery and postage stamps (optional)

Tell your child that an address book organizes information alphabetically by last name. Write the names and addresses of friends and family members on index cards. Have your child organize the cards in alphabetical order.

Next, show your child the correct format for writing an address. Let him practice writing his own name and address on ruled paper.

Have your child copy the names and addresses on the index cards into a blank address book or a small notebook. If you're using a notebook, label the pages alphabetically.

Encourage your child to use his address book when sending letters, greeting cards, and thank-you cards to friends and family. If you like, give him a supply of stationery and postage stamps.

MATH

The word *math* often conjures up images of addition, subtraction, multiplication, and division problems. Those basic math skills are as necessary today as ever, but children need more than the ability to compute in order to successfully navigate their world. They need to understand various technologies, solve problems, examine relationships, and make sense of the world around them. They need realistic problem-solving practice and activities that challenge them to investigate, conjecture, and justify.

To succeed in math, a child needs good instruction and encouragement. Just as reading with your child helps build his interest in reading, doing math with him fosters his interest in math. This doesn't mean just drilling your child or doing work sheets together. Math incorporates not only numbers, but also shapes, patterns, logic, direction, time, estimation, measurement, and classification. Doing math means asking questions and playing games that encourage your child to think in these terms.

A good way to build your child's math skills is to teach him that math is a part of the real world. Shopping, traveling, gardening, meal planning, cooking, eating, and even laundry all involve math. The following activities will also help you show your child that math is fun and useful. If you're looking for even more math fun, check out *Family Math* by Jean Kerr Stanmark, Virginia Thompson, and Ruth Cossey. It's an excellent book packed with fun math activities for the whole family.

Name That Coin

This guessing game will help your child learn to recognize coins and will develop his problem-solving and higher level–thinking skills.

Variety of coins

Set out one of each kind of coin. Think of a coin and give your child hints to help him figure out which coin it is. For younger kids, give simple hints like *My coin has a man on one side and a building on the other.* For older kids, give harder hints like *Ten of these coins equal one dime.* Keep giving hints until your child guesses the coin. Take turns with your child giving hints and guessing coins.

    Once your child knows the various coins well, practice making trades. For example, you might ask your child how many pennies he'll give you for a nickel and a dime, or you might say that you'll give him twenty pennies for a quarter and ask him if that's fair.

Real-World Math

The following activities will help your child make the connection between math and the real world.

- Let your child help with the grocery shopping. Check and compare prices, weights, and quantities together. Let him use a calculator to keep track of the cost of what you've bought, to compare prices, to calculate cost per ounce, and so on.
- Point out speed limits and distances between towns. Talk about the time it takes to get from one town to another when you drive at different speeds.
- When you're gardening, have your child count the number of plants and measure the distance between them, their heights, and calculate the perimeter and/or area of the garden.
- Let your child help with the cooking by measuring ingredients and checking cooking times and temperatures.
- Keep a height and weight record for your child.
- Encourage your child to play games and do activities that involve counting, finding patterns, and solving problems. Tick-tack-toe, checkers, and chess are all good games for learning math. Doing crossword and jigsaw puzzles and playing music are also great math activities!

Treasure Hunt

This activity is adapted from the U.S. Department of Education publication *Helping Your Child Learn Math*.

Small household treasures like buttons, screws, bottle caps, and old keys
Container big enough to hold treasures

Hunt for an assortment of small household treasures. Then use them for the following math activities:

• Sort and classify the treasures. Compare their sizes and discuss how they're alike and different.

• Use the treasures to invent and solve addition, subtraction, multiplication, and division story problems. For example, if you share seventeen buttons among three people, how many buttons will each person get? Will there be any buttons left over? Or if three shirts need six buttons each, do you have enough buttons?

• Choose one type of treasure, such as screws. Lay all the screws side by side. Compare, contrast, and count the screws. For example, there may be three short screws, seven long screws, and eleven medium screws. There are four more medium screws than long ones. Older children can also use this opportunity to talk about fractions. For example, one-third of the screws are long.

Estimating

Estimating is an important everyday skill. And when a child estimates the answer to a math problem, he understands the problem better and solves it more easily. Use the following activities to help your child practice estimating.

- Fill a small jar with small treats. Challenge your child to estimate how many items are in the jar. If you like, have a weekly contest with the winner receiving the contents of the jar. Compare how many pieces of various treats fit in the same jar.
- Estimate things like how many times the refrigerator door is opened in a day, how many windows your house has, or how many cans of food are in your cupboards.
- Ask your child questions like *If I had two dimes, three nickels, and four pennies in my pocket, about how much money would I have?* or *If I buy three bottles of juice for ninety-eight cents each, about how much money will they cost me altogether?*

- Estimate things like which book you own is the heaviest, how long a line of ten paper clips is, or the difference in height between people in your household.

Guess My Number

My kids love to play this game anytime, anywhere. They don't think about the skills they're building, but asking and answering questions about numbers helps them understand the characteristics and meanings of numbers.

Let your child think of a number. Then try to guess it by asking questions. Here's a sample conversation:

Child: I'm thinking of a number between one and a hundred.
Parent: Is it odd or even?
Child: Even.
Parent: Is it more than fifty?
Child: Yes.
Parent: Is it more than seventy-five?
Child: Yes.
Parent: Can you divide this number into four equal parts?
(and so on)

After you guess the number, let your child take a turn as the guesser. For younger children, start with a lower range of numbers, such as one to twenty or one to fifty.

Variation

Limit the number of questions the guesser may ask. This will encourage your child to exercise reasoning and judgment. For example, if the number is greater than fifty, it's better to ask whether the number is greater than seventy-five than whether it's between fifty and sixty.

Just the Facts

Knowing basic arithmetic facts is crucial to math success. Only your child can memorize them, but you can help by stressing their importance and playing games with them.

- When you're playing board or card games, have each player read a math problem from a flash card and give the correct answer before taking his turn.
- Practice a fact each day. For example, repeat the fact *five plus three equals eight* whenever you can all day long. Sing it, say it in funny voices, shout it, and whisper it. Your child will have it down by bedtime!
- Look at a fact table and cross out all the ones your child already knows. Among those remaining, cross out duplicates. Show your child how much he already knows, and what's left will seem less daunting to him.
- Play math bingo. Draw a grid and write a number in each square. Draw flash cards one at a time and have your child cover up the squares that show the answers. Use small treats as markers. When a game is over, let your child eat his used markers, then start a new game.
- Play math concentration. Make several pairs of cards, one card showing a problem and the other card showing the answer. Spread out all the cards facedown and take turns turning over two at a time. If they make a pair, the player keeps them and takes another turn. If they don't make a pair, the next player gets a turn.

Calendar Math

Calendar

- Read the calendar with your child daily. Say the day of the week, the month, the date, and the year. Ask your child what yesterday's and tomorrow's dates are.
- Teach your child this rhyme to help him remember the number of days in each month:

    Thirty days has September,
    April, June, and November.
    All the rest have thirty-one,
    Save February, which alone
    Has twenty-eight, and one day more
    We add to it one year in four.

- Talk about calendar patterns. For example, why might there be five Sundays in a month but only four Mondays? If the first Tuesday of the month is the fifth, what will the second and third Tuesdays be?
- Make a blank calendar grid. Find out what day of the week the first of next month will be, then make a calendar for that month with your child. Write the days of the week across the top of the calendar. Write the date in the upper right corner of each square. Mark holidays, birthdays, and other special days with stickers or pictures.

Roman Numerals

Pencil
Paper

Explain to your child that the number symbols we use every day came from Arabia and are called Arabic numerals. A different system was used in ancient Rome. We call these symbols Roman numerals. The Roman numeral system uses six basic symbols: I (one), V (five), X (ten), L (fifty), C (one hundred), and M (one thousand). There are two rules for writing Roman numerals:

• Putting a numeral of lesser value before a numeral of greater value decreases the second numeral by the amount of the first. Thus IV equals four because V (five) is decreased by I (one).

• Putting a numeral of lesser value after a numeral of greater value increases the first numeral by the amount of the second. Thus VI equals six because V (five) is increased by I (one).

Write some Roman numerals on a sheet of paper and challenge your child to figure out what numbers they represent. Start with easy ones, such as I (one), II (two), III (three), IV (four), V (five), VI (six), VII (seven), VIII (eight), IX (nine), and X (ten). When your child masters these numbers, try more difficult ones, such as XL (forty), LX (sixty), XC (ninety), and so on. Take turns writing and interpreting Roman numerals.

Clock Arithmetic

The following activities will help your child learn to tell time and understand the passage of time.

Clocks (standard and digital)
Old clock or play clock

• Set a standard clock and a digital clock next to each other. Have your child look at the clocks whenever he goes outdoors, comes indoors, has a meal, and so on.

• Find an old clock or make a play clock by attaching construction paper hands to a paper plate with a brass fastener. Ask questions like *If it's six o'clock now, what time will it be in two hours?* Help your child move the hands to figure out the answers to your questions.

• See how many times your child can do something within a given time. For example, how many times can he jump up and down in a minute?

Skip-Counting Game

Learning to count by twos, fives, tens, fifties, and hundreds will make basic arithmetic easier for your child. Before you begin playing, learn the skip-counting jingle and its rhythmic accompaniment:

(slap knees)	(clap hands)	(snap left hand)	(snap right hand)
Counting,	counting,	1, 2,	3.
That's too	easy,	can't you	see?
Count in-	stead by	twos or	threes, or
By the	number	named by	me.

The players sit in a circle on the floor. To begin, they recite the jingle together while slapping, clapping, and snapping as shown above. All the players continue to slap, clap, and snap as the first player declares a number to count by (for example, ten). The player to his left then must say the next number in the series (in this case, twenty). Play continues around the circle. Each player must say the next number in the series during one *slap-clap-snap-snap* pattern. If a player is stumped or says the wrong number, he must drop out. To resume the game, the remaining players recite the jingle again and declare a new number. The last player remaining after all the others have dropped out is the winner.

SCIENCE

Isaac Asimov said, "Science can be introduced to children well or poorly. If poorly, children can...develop a lifelong antipathy; they will be in a far worse condition than if they had never been introduced to science at all." Asimov's words ring true with me. Thanks to one boring teacher, I grew up hating science, thinking it was dull and difficult.

As a home-schooling parent I almost made the same mistake. One year I decided we really should be "doing science," so I tried to teach it from a third-grade textbook. We all hated it, and soon we were coming up with daily excuses to avoid doing science. About halfway through the year I closed the book on our formal study of science.

Since then we've learned that science is anything but boring. It's in everything we do—from watching the phases of the moon to building sandcastles to blowing bubbles to collecting daddy-longlegs to baking cookies. Books like David Macaulay's *The New Way Things Work,* TV programs like *The Magic School Bus* and *Bill Nye the Science Guy* (available on DVD), and places like Vancouver's Science World make our world come alive.

The following activities will help your child learn about the world around him by doing. If you like to read to your child, you might also consider reading biographies of Albert Einstein, Leonardo da Vinci, Thomas Edison, or Galileo Galilei. There are also great picture books about scientists, such as *The Librarian Who Measured the Earth* by Kathryn Lasky and *Benjamin Franklin* by Ingri and Edgar d'Aulaire.

Float an Egg

This activity will help your child understand the concept of density and learn why objects sink or float.

2 clear drinking glasses   *Teaspoon*
Water   *Salt*
Marker   *2 eggs*

Fill one glass half-full of water. Mark the water level on the glass. Add salt a spoonful at a time and stir it into the water until it dissolves. Stop adding salt when it won't dissolve anymore. Notice what happens to the water level as you add salt. The level shouldn't rise; instead, the water gets denser as it becomes saturated with salt. When you dissolve salt in water, you cram more molecules into the water without making the water take up any more space. Fill the other glass half-full of plain water. Gently put an egg in each glass. The egg in the saltwater should float, and the egg in the freshwater should sink.
The saltwater is denser than the egg, so it holds up the egg, causing it to float. The freshwater is less dense than the egg, so it can't hold up the egg, and the egg sinks.

Make a Fossil

Most fossils form this way: A living thing decays and leaves a mold in its own shape behind in the earth. Then rock forms inside the mold, creating a copy of the living thing. This activity will help your child understand how fossils form.

4 cups plaster of Paris
2½ cups water
Disposable container
Old or disposable small baking pan
Petroleum jelly

Mix 2 cups of plaster of Paris with 1¼ cups of water in a disposable container. Spread the plaster in the bottom of an old or disposable small baking pan to a thickness of about 1 inch. Wait about 2 minutes until the plaster begins to set.

Coat your child's hand with petroleum jelly. Gently press his hand into the plaster just enough to dent the surface. Hold his hand in place for a few minutes, then remove it and let the plaster set until it's completely hard.

Coat the hand-shaped mold with petroleum jelly. Mix up another batch of plaster and pour it into the mold. Let the plaster harden, then gently separate the "fossil" from the mold. If they don't separate easily, hold the pan upright and tap it lightly with a hammer.

Homemade Hand Lotion

Does your child know that cosmetics like shampoo, soap, and hand lotion are created by scientists? This activity will help your child understand how it's done.

2 cups water
1 packet unflavored gelatin
4 tablespoons glycerin
Few drops of perfume or cologne
1 tablespoon rubbing alcohol

Heat 1 cup of water to nearly boiling. Stir in the gelatin, then stir in 1 cup of cold water. Let the mixture cool until it's just warm. Add the glycerin, perfume or cologne, and rubbing alcohol and mix well. Put the mixture in the refrigerator.

Stir the mixture every 15 minutes or so. In 1 hour, it should have the consistency of loose Jell-O. Take it out of the refrigerator and whip it with a fork or an eggbeater. Let it sit for about 30 minutes. If it's too thick, add water until it's thin enough to pour.

Homemade hand lotion makes a great gift. To package it, pour it into a clean baby food jar or other small jar. Tie a circle of fabric over the jar lid with a ribbon and label the jar however you like.

Amazing Inflating Balloon

Both chemistry and cooking are about combining ingredients to create something completely different. In cooking, certain ingredients, such as yeast and sugar, are vital to the finished product because of the chemical reaction they produce when they're combined. This activity demonstrates how yeast works.

3 tablespoons sugar
½ cup warm water
3 small packages active dry yeast
One empty 1-quart soda or juice bottle
Balloon
Rubber band

Have your child dissolve the sugar in the water. Stir in the yeast, then pour the mixture into the bottle. Stretch the open-ing of the balloon over the mouth of the bottle and secure it with the rubber band. Set the bottle in a warm place, such as on top of your refrigerator. In a while, the balloon will inflate. Why?

The yeast cells are eating the sugar, and as they do so, they produce a gas called carbon dioxide. Carbon dioxide is heavier than oxygen, so it pushes the oxygen in the bottle up and into the balloon. The same happens with yeast used in cooking. In that case, the release of carbon dioxide helps dough rise.

Invisible Ink

This activity uses iodine, which is poisonous, so please supervise it carefully.

½ teaspoon iodine
4–5 teaspoons water
Empty film canister or
   pill bottle
1 teaspoon cornstarch
¼ cup cold water

Small microwaveable
   container
Toothpick
Sheet of paper
Small sponge

Mix the iodine and 4–5 teaspoons of water in the empty canister or bottle to make a tan-colored solution. Label the canister or bottle with the word *poison* and keep it out of reach of small children.

Have your child mix the cornstarch and cold water in a microwaveable container until they're smooth. Microwave the mixture on high for 15 seconds. Stir it, then heat it on high for another 45 seconds. Dip a toothpick into the mixture and write with it on a sheet of paper.

To read the invisible message, dip a small sponge into the iodine solution and spread it lightly over the message. As the iodine mixes with the starch, the starch turns blue, and the message appears!

Copper Nail

Here's another activity that demonstrates how chemicals change when they're combined.

¼ cup vinegar   *10–20 copper pennies*
Glass jar   *Iron nail*
Pinch of salt   *Scouring powder*

Have your child pour the vinegar into the jar. Add a pinch of salt. Put the copper pennies in the vinegar and let them stand for a few minutes. Clean the iron nail with scouring powder and rinse it thoroughly. Drop the nail into the vinegar with the pennies and let them sit for about 15 minutes. What happens to the nail? What happens to the pennies?

After about 15 minutes, you'll notice that the iron nail is coated with copper and the pennies are bright and clean. The acid in the vinegar cleaned the pennies. It also combined with the copper to form a compound called copper acetate. The copper in the copper acetate is what covered the iron nail.

Rock Candy Crystals

2½ cups sugar
1 cup water
Medium saucepan
String

Button with large holes
Pencil
Drinking glass or glass jar

Help your child mix the sugar and water in the saucepan and cook the syrup over medium heat until it boils. Let it boil for 4 minutes without stirring it, then remove it from the heat and let it cool for a minute.

Thread the string through the button and tie it securely. Tie the other end of the string to the pencil. Leave several inches of string between the button and pencil.

Pour the syrup into the glass. Don't touch the glass after you've poured in the syrup; it will be very hot. Set the pencil across the top of the glass or jar. The button should hang suspended in the syrup. When the glass is cool enough to touch, move it to a place where it'll be easy to see but be undisturbed for a week or so.

Look at your syrup from time to time. First you'll see small crystals forming on the string. Eventually these will become larger chunks that can be broken off and eaten.

Rubber Egg

Chemical reactions occur inside our bodies all the time. If your child has trouble remembering to brush his teeth, this activity is a great way to show him how cavities form.

Egg
Small container
Vinegar
Chicken bone

Have your child place an egg in a small container and cover it with vinegar. Set the container aside for 24 hours. Pour out the vinegar and gently pick up the egg. Squeeze it. The acid in the vinegar will have dissolved the minerals in the eggshell so that it's now soft and rubbery.

Repeat the experiment with a chicken bone. In 3–4 days, the bone will be rubbery.

The bacteria in your mouth produce acid that dissolves the enamel on your teeth in the same way that the acid in the vinegar dissolved the minerals in the eggshell and chicken bone. Remind your children to brush their teeth often to remove bacteria and keep their teeth healthy and strong.

Electric Lemon

This activity demonstrates how batteries generate electricity.

Metal paper clip
Lemon
Length of copper wire

Have your child straighten the paper clip and insert one end into the lemon. Remove any insulation from both ends of the copper wire and insert one end into the lemon. Hold the exposed ends of the paper clip and the wire and touch both of them to your tongue at the same time. You'll feel a tingling sensation caused by electricity.

How does this work? You've created an electric battery. A battery needs two kinds of metal plus an acid. The paper clip and wire provide the metals, and the lemon provides citric acid. Water conducts electricity, so your wet tongue completes the electric circuit when you touch the wires to it.

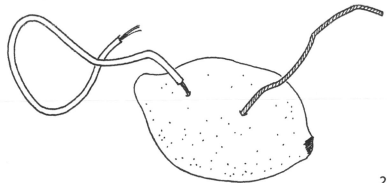

Fireplace Colors

This activity shows how different chemicals produce different-colored flames. Be sure to supervise it carefully.

2 gallons water
2 plastic pails
1 pound copper sulfate (available at a hardware store
  or garden center)
½ pound boric acid (available at a drugstore)
2 large mesh bags (laundry or onion bags)
Pine cones (enough to fill both mesh bags)
Rocks (optional)

Have your child measure 1 gallon of water into each pail. Mix the copper sulfate into one pail and the boric acid into the other. Fill each mesh bag with half the pine cones. Place one bag in the copper sulfate and the other in the boric acid. If the bags float, weigh them down with rocks. Let the pine cones soak for 3–4 days, then remove them and let them dry completely. To use the pine cones, toss them into a lit fireplace. The copper sulfate cones will burn green, and the boric acid cones will burn blue-green. To make cones that burn orange-red, use calcium chloride. For violet flames, use potassium chloride. Calcium chloride and potassium chloride may be available at your local hardware store, garden center, or drugstore. You can also check the Internet for chemical supply and scientific supply companies.

GEOGRAPHY

Geography is the study of Earth. It's divided into five major themes: location (where things and people are); place (what makes a location special, both physically and culturally); interaction (between people and the environment); movement (of people, products, and information); and regions (areas defined by distinctive characteristics).

Children are naturally curious, and you can do a lot to steer your child's curiosity toward geography. Prompt him to ask questions about his surroundings. Expose him to lots of maps and let him see you using maps regularly. To help him think geographically and build precise mental images, try to use basic geographical terms (*north, south, climate, highway, river,* and so on) whenever possible. Play games like *Where in the World Is Carmen Sandiego?* that teach your child how to ask questions about geography and use maps.

The following activities are only a few examples of the many ways your child can learn geography. They're informal and easy, but they'll help lay a solid foundation for your child's academic ventures into geography.

My Town

The following activities will help your child discover the personality of your city or town.

• Take a walk through your neighborhood and talk about what makes it unique. How is it similar to other places and how is it different? Talk about what the buildings are used for and notice features built to conform to the weather or topography. A visiting Swiss friend once pointed out to us that the homes in our neighborhood would never withstand the weight of the snow that falls in her mountain village.

• Study the weather. Weather can have a strong effect on the character of a place. Listen to a TV or radio forecast or read the weather map in the newspaper. Track the high and low temperatures of cities across the country and around the world. Watch cloud formations and forecast your neighborhood's weather.

• Ask your child, "Is what we eat affected by where we live?" Perhaps you live near the sea and eat a lot of seafood. If you live near an orchard, fresh fruit may be an important part of your diet. Farm families may eat lots of dairy, poultry, beef, and so on. If you like, go to various ethnic restaurants and talk about what ingredients are commonly used in certain areas.

People and Places

How do people adjust to their environment? What are the relationships between people and places? How do people change their environment to suit their needs? The following activities will help your child understand the interaction between people and their environment.

* Talk with your child about what would happen if you didn't change the natural environment of your yard by mowing grass, raking leaves, or watering.
* Go on a neighborhood litter patrol with your child. Wear gloves and/or use a pointed stick to pick up the litter. Talk about how we can help take care of our environment by controlling garbage and recycling.
* Notice how people sometimes adapt to their environment instead of changing their environment to suit them. For example, you might ask your child, "Why do people in hot countries wear long, loose clothes? Why do low-lying communities build dikes? Why are beach houses sometimes built on stilts?"

Maps

Maps help kids understand the concept of location. These activities will help your child practice making and reading maps.

- Help your child draw a simple map of his bedroom, house, yard, or neighborhood. Make a map leading your child to hidden treasures in your home or yard.
- To help your child understand direction (north, south, east, and west), use your home as a reference point, showing the sun rising in the east and setting in the west. Point out geographical features to the north and south. Ask your child questions like *What direction are you facing if the setting sun is on your right?*
- Find your city or town on a map. Point out familiar locations like friends' homes and your child's school. Discuss the purpose of a legend on a map.
- Hang a map of North America or the world on a wall. Use it to locate places you read or hear about.

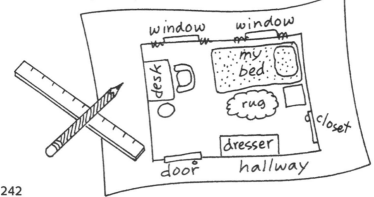

Here to There

Most people interact with places other than the places they're in almost every day—whether they're eating food or wearing clothes produced in another region or sharing information via telephone, newspaper, radio, TV, or Internet. The following activities are fun ways to learn about how people, products, and information move.

- Travel in as many different ways as you can: by foot, bicycle, car, bus, subway, train, airplane, ferry, and so on. Talk about the different routes each method of transportation takes. For example, ask your child how the walking route to his school differs from the driving route.
- Look around your house and find the origins of various objects. Look at clothing labels to learn where your clothes were made and think about where your food was produced. Ask your child questions like *Why are bananas grown in Central America?* and *Why does our milk come from a local dairy?*
- Talk about different ways people communicate with each other. Ask your child, "When would you use a phone? When would you write a letter? When would you send an e-mail?"

Divided Earth

Earth's regions can be defined by physical elements like land-forms, climate, and soil or by cultural differences like politics, economics, religion, and so on. The following activities will help your child understand regions.

- With your child, look at the physical regions in your home. Ask him, "Is there a sleeping region? An eating region? What other regions can you describe?"
- Take your child to plays, movies, and puppet shows about people from other countries. Read picture books, novels, and nonfiction about other countries. Listen to music from other countries. If possible, wear clothing and buy or make food typical of other countries. Learn simple words and phrases in another language.
- Have your child compare coins and stamps from various countries. Coins and stamps tell many things about a country, such as its political leaders, wildlife, history, sports, and so on.

FINE ARTS

The fine arts include visual arts, music, dance, and drama. Just as reading good books to children helps instill values, observing and participating in fine arts can help develop a child's artistic sensibilities and fill his mind with examples of beauty. And just as a child's early experiences with good books help him develop a lifelong habit of reading for pleasure, a child's early experiences with fine arts can give him a lifelong appreciation of the arts.

Fortunately, most elementary schools recognize the importance of fine arts and stress them even in the earliest grades. So do many parents. Those who are financially able may supplement their children's school experiences with music lessons, drama groups, or art classes. Parents can also provide many informal fine arts experiences, such as singing, playing, and listening to music as a family; attending music, drama, or dance performances; visiting art galleries and museums; looking at prints or books about famous works of art; acting out familiar stories; and so on.

The following activities are some fun and informal ways you and your child can experience the fine arts together.

Art Book

Your child can learn a lot about art just by looking at it, noticing details, and enjoying it. This activity will help your child do just that.

Scissors
Old magazines, newspapers, gallery catalogs, calendars, and
*   fine-art greeting cards and postcards*
Glue or tape
Large scrapbook

Have your child cut out pictures of art from magazines and so on and glue or tape the pictures into a scrapbook. Encourage him to jot notes telling what he knows about the artworks and artists and describing his thoughts about the artworks. Your child will enjoy looking at his art book and sharing it with others.

Instrument Dictionary

Making a musical instrument dictionary is a great way to introduce children to a variety of instruments.

Twenty-six sheets of paper
Two sheets of construction paper
Stapler
Old magazines, catalogs, books, calendars, and so on
Scissors
Markers
Glue

Stack the paper between the sheets of construction paper and staple the stack together along one edge. You now have a blank booklet with twenty-six leaves. On the front of each leaf have your child write one letter of the alphabet.

With your child, look through old magazines, catalogs, books, calendars, and so on for pictures of musical instruments that he can cut out or trace. You might also print pictures off the Internet. Read a little about each instrument you find.

Glue each picture onto the appropriate page in your booklet. For example, your *A* page may show an accordion, your *B* page may show a bassoon, and so on. Have your child write the instrument's name next to each picture and include any other information he finds interesting.

Artist of the Month

Declaring an artist or composer of the month is a fun way to learn about visual art and music.

Art prints
CDs or digital audio files
Simple biographies of visual artists and composers

Decide ahead of time which artists or composers you will feature. Look at your local library, on the Internet, or in an encyclopedia for some information on each. Find a few prints of each visual artist's work or a CD of each composer's work. You may want to base your choices on the seasons; for example, December is the perfect time to feature Pyotr Ilyich Tchaikovsky and *The Nutcracker.*

   In a prominent place, post the name and, if possible, a picture of the artist or composer for the current month. Display the artist's prints or spend some quiet time listening to the composer's music. If possible, attend an exhibit or concert that features the artist's or composer's work. Ask your child what he likes and/or dislikes about each work. Read a short biography of the artist or composer or simply share the interesting things you've learned about his or her life. Have a few books available for your child to read or leaf through. At the end of the month, change your display.

Act It Out

For most children, drama begins informally at a very young age. Playing with dolls is drama; playing store or hospital is drama; and playing cops and robbers is drama. Children also observe drama on TV, in movies, and onstage. This activity gives children an opportunity to participate in drama in a more structured and intentional way.

Choose a story your child is familiar with, such as *The Three Little Pigs, Little Red Riding Hood,* or a favorite picture book. The Bible is also a great source of stories; try the story of Moses parting the Red Sea or the story of the birth of Jesus.

To dramatize a story, your child can say the dialogue while performing the actions or simply perform the actions as you narrate the story. Costumes and props can be elaborate, simple, or nonexistent. Productions can be either impromptu or rehearsed and presented to friends and family members.

Write a Play

Pencil or pen
Paper

Encourage your child to write an original play. He may want to base his play on something that has happened to him, such as winning a special award or the birth of a new sibling. If he doesn't know where to begin, use a familiar nursery rhyme, song, or story as a starting point.

Explain to your child that a play includes more than just the words spoken by the actors. A play also includes set information, which tells about the scenery where the play takes place, and stage directions, which tell the actors what they should be doing as they say their lines. To distinguish stage directions from the actor's lines, have your child enclose stage directions in parentheses and underline them (like this).

Your child's play can be as simple or elaborate as he wishes to make it. The finished play can be read aloud or acted out complete with cast, costumes, and a set. This activity will probably require a lot of parental involvement, so be prepared to help your child as much as needed.

CHAPTER 7
My Family and Me

If you bungle raising your children, I don't think whatever else you do well matters very much.

—Jacqueline Kennedy Onassis

Family has been everything to your child until now. But as she enters middle childhood, her identity also becomes tied to her roles as a student and as a member of a peer group. These new roles can add enormous pressure to her life. As a student, she's expected to sit still, follow directions, and master academic skills. And socially, your child will seek acceptance among her peers—perhaps one of the most difficult aspects of her school years.

Your child's omniscient new teacher may usurp your role as the answerer of all questions, but you still have the critical job of maintaining your child's positive self-image. Spending time with your child by reading, talking, walking, and doing fun activities is the best way to accomplish this. No matter what happens while she's away from you, your smiles, hugs, and praise tell her she's special and loved.

The following activities promote family harmony and impart a sense of family history and tradition. They also help your child develop a positive self-image and affirm her identity as a loved and valued member of your family.

HARMONY BUILDERS

Ideally, a home is a place of harmony—but realistically, it's often a place of discord. Children are naturally self-centered, which probably accounts for a lot of conflict, and sometimes the personalities of family members clash. In addition, the dynamics within a family change when a new baby is born, when children enter and leave various childhood stages, and when parents go through various changes and experience stress in their own lives.

Some people believe whining, bickering, and fighting are normal. I believe that while perfect family harmony is rare, there are many things parents can do to prevent discord:

- Parents can approach life positively and fight the temptation to view everything negatively.
- Parents can demonstrate the respect with which family members should treat each other.
- Parents can set a standard for behavior and enforce it with firm, consistent discipline.
- Parents can expect their children to help out around the home.
- Parents can accept their children for who they are rather than who they want their children to be.

Living together harmoniously doesn't come naturally. It's an ongoing process that takes a lot of work, but the effort is worth it. The following ideas will help you encourage your child, build her self-esteem, and establish order and peace in your home.

Apples of Gold

The biblical wise man Solomon wrote, "A word aptly spoken is like apples of gold in settings of silver."

Scissors   *Glue*
Gold construction paper   *Poster board*
Markers

Cut apple shapes from the construction paper. Talk with your child about words that make you feel good. Write these words on the apples. Glue the apples onto the poster board. Hang your poster in a prominent place to remind your family to use encouraging words with each other.

What a Character!

Markers
Poster board or construction paper

Discuss the positive qualities of each member of your family. Write them all on a large sheet of poster board or use construction paper to make a miniature poster for each person. Display the poster(s) prominently to boost everyone's self-esteem and to remind family members to think about each other positively.

Praise Box

Utility knife
Shoebox with lid
Paint, markers, stickers,
   and so on

Pencil
String
Tape
Notepad

Use a utility knife to cut a slot in the lid of the shoebox. Let your child decorate the box with paint, markers, stickers, and so on. Attach a pencil to the box with string and a bit of tape. Place a notepad next to the box.

Use the box to praise and encourage everyone in your family. When you see your child playing nicely, write it down and slip the note into your praise box. When your child is especially kind, respectful, or obedient, do the same. Explain to your child that parents need encouragement as much as kids do, and that she's welcome to write positive comments about you to put into the praise box.

Open your praise box once a week or once every two weeks and take turns reading the notes in it. Afterward, celebrate your family by having a night of games or special snack together.

Love, Love, Love

The following ideas will help the members of your family communicate their love to each other.

- Ask your child why she loves a particular parent, sibling, grandparent, or friend. Alternatively, you might ask your child about the funniest thing that person ever did. You're sure to get some priceless answers! Write down your child's answers and have her decorate the note with crayons or markers. Sneak the love note into the appropriate person's lunch the next day.
- Ask your child, "Who loves you?" and write down her answer. Keep asking her, "Who else loves you?" and write down each name she says. Read her the list when she's finished. Title the list "Look Who Loves _____" and let her decorate it. Display the list on your refrigerator or in your child's bedroom to remind her how much she's loved.
- If you have access to a tape recorder, make an audiotape for your child to play before bed. Sing her favorite songs; tell her a story; talk about the things you enjoy doing together; tell her you love her and why you're thankful for her. Your child will enjoy listening to it over and over again.

Chore Chart

A busy home functions best if household chores are shared, and doing chores helps children learn responsibility, teamwork, and practical skills.

Sheet of poster board or paper
Markers

Divide a sheet of poster board or paper into eight rows. Divide the rows into columns, allowing one column for each child in your family plus one extra. Starting with the second row in the far left column, label each row for one day of the week. Starting with the second column in the top row, label each column with one child's name.

Now assign chores. Use words for readers and pictures or symbols for nonreaders. Be specific about which chores to do on what days. For example, it's not enough just to say "vacuum." Make it clear that the living room is vacuumed on Monday, the playroom on Tuesday, and so on. Also, provide a list of job descriptions that tell exactly what each chore entails. (For example, washing dishes also includes wiping up the sink and putting the dishes away.)

We assign chores yearly because this helps our children gain proficiency with their chores; because then chores can be better assigned according to abilities; and because our children need less reminding when certain chores are always their responsibilities.

Rule of the Day

Peaceful homes are usually those in which children obey the rules of the home and respect their parents and each other. But most children don't do this naturally. Teaching a child obedience and respect is an ongoing process—and one she's more receptive to when her family knows how to laugh and have fun together. Telling jokes and doing fun family activities are good ways to share a few laughs and enjoy each other. So is having a "rule of the day."

Establish a silly rule that your family must follow for a day. For example, can your family go a whole day without saying the word *mom?* Or how about making a rule that all meals must be eaten standing up? Try singing everything instead of speaking…or addressing family members by their full names…or wearing your clothes backward…or singing "Twinkle, Twinkle, Little Star" before you sit anywhere…and watch the giggles flow!

You needn't do this every day. Perhaps you'll do it only on weekends, holidays, or when your family is stressed out. Have a special treat or family movie night at the end of every "rule" day.

Family Rules

Posting a list of acceptable and unacceptable behavior goes a long way toward establishing a peaceful home. It helps parents be consistent in discipline and helps children know exactly what is expected of them.

Markers
Poster board

Gather everyone in your family and brainstorm a list of family rules. For example, your rules might include *We speak quietly with each other, We put others first, We always tell the truth,* and so on. Write the rules with a marker on poster board and let your child illustrate the poster.

Post your family rules in a prominent place and add to them as necessary. When your child's behavior needs correcting, refer to the rules to reinforce that her behavior doesn't meet your family's standards and to help her understand that she's responsible for her misbehavior—it really is against the rules; it's not just that Mom or Dad is having a bad day. If you like, choose appropriate consequences for breaking each rule and write those down, too. This technique helps you apply discipline consistently and helps your child know what to expect when she does wrong.

MEMORY LANE

Hearing stories of their births and babyhoods helps children feel special and loved, and it naturally builds their self-esteem. And as much as they enjoy hearing about themselves, children also love looking at photos and keepsakes from their parents' childhoods and hearing stories about the "olden days." Use the following activities to take a walk down memory lane with your child.

When You Were Born

Baby scrapbook and/or keepsakes

On a quiet afternoon or evening, cuddle up with your child to look at her baby scrapbook together. If you haven't made a scrapbook, look through keepsakes like her hospital identification bracelet, her baby booties, and maybe even a prenatal ultrasound image. Talk about the day your child was born, the day she came home from the hospital, how and why you chose her name, and so on. You'll probably enjoy telling these tales as much as your child will enjoy hearing them.

Family Photos

Family photo albums

Set aside a few hours one day to look through family photo albums with your child. You might look at photos of your wedding, of family vacations, of your child's toddler years, or of friends and relatives your child hasn't met. Looking at photos together and telling your child the "thousand words" behind each photo will help you give your child a sense of tradition and belonging.

The Olden Days

Most kids can't imagine a world without them in it, and many think their parents were born old! Prove that you used to be a kid by sharing memories from your childhood.

Photos, scrapbooks, and/or keepsakes from your childhood

Set aside an afternoon or evening to look through your childhood photos, scrapbooks, and/or keepsakes with your child. Talk about what you were like as a child and describe your parents and siblings, the things your family did together, your friends, your school memories, and so on. My kids love to do this activity, and I love turning the clock back for a few hours. Remembering my childhood also helps me look at life from a child's perspective.

Family Movie Night

Family videos   *Special snack*

If your family owns a video camera, you've probably got hours and hours of footage that you haven't watched in a while. Snuggle under a blanket or lie on the floor and share a special snack as you turn back the clock and relive your early days as a family.

Personal Time Line

Paper   *Scissors, tape, glue, and*
Markers   *photos (optional)*

A time line can be as short as one page or as long as a wall.

To make a short time line, draw a vertical line down the middle of a sheet of paper. Write your child's birth date on the left side of the line at the top of the page. On the right side of the line, write the corresponding event. ("I was born!") Add other important dates and events, such as when your child started to walk and talk, when siblings were born, when your child started preschool, when you took family trips, and so on, in chronological order.

To make a long time line, cut a length of paper from a large roll or tape several sheets of paper together. Draw a horizontal line across the middle of the banner. Write the dates and events of your child's life from left to right. Glue on photos or let your child illustrate each event. Hang the time line in your child's room and add to it occasionally.

Family Tree

Making a visual family tree that shows your extended family is a project your child will really enjoy.

Photos

Pencil

Scrap paper

Poster board

Markers

Glue

Collect photos of the people you want to include in your family tree. Before you draw your tree on poster board, sketch it on scrap paper. Show your child and her siblings at the bottom of the tree and work your way up the branches to show her extended family.

Using your sketch as a guide, pencil your family tree on poster board, then draw over your pencil lines with markers. Glue each photo in its proper spot onto the tree and label it with the name and birth date of the person pictured. You might also note marriage and death dates if you like.

Post your family tree in a prominent place where the whole family can admire it.

Family Time Line

Scissors   *Glue*
Paper   *Photos*
Tape   *Three-ring binder*
Markers

A family time line covers many years and many people, so consider making yours on a long banner or in book format.

To make a banner time line, cut a length of paper from a large roll or tape several sheets of paper together. Draw a horizontal line across the middle of the banner. At the left edge, record your first event. Write the date on one side of the line and describe the event on the other side. Add other events, such as births, deaths, marriages, and other important family milestones, in chronological order. Glue on photos or let your child illustrate each event.

To make a book time line, use plain white paper in a three-ring binder. Draw a horizontal line across the middle of each page. Decide on the period of time each page will cover and label the pages accordingly. Record events and illustrate them in the same way as the banner time line described above.

Don't forget to update your time line as new events occur!

TOMORROW'S MEMORIES

Imagine your child as a parent, twenty or thirty years from now. On her lap she holds your young grandchild. Together they're looking at mementos from your child's past—perhaps a scrapbook, report cards, class photos, and so on. The following activities will help your child create many treasures she can enjoy herself and share with her own family in the years to come.

Memory Box

Help your child make a memory box where she can store her special mementos and childhood treasures.

Cardboard box with lid
Magazines, photos, paint, markers, and/or stickers
Clear contact paper (optional)

Have your child decorate a cardboard box and its lid. She might want to glue magazine pictures or photos of herself onto the outside of the box, paint pictures on the box, or simply decorate it with markers and/or stickers. If you like, cover the box with clear contact paper.

Encourage your child to store photos, report cards, award certificates, and other mementos in her memory box. Looking through her box will be a great activity for your child when she's sick, on rainy days, or when there's just "nothing to do."

Family Book of Records

This idea is adapted from *365 TV-Free Activities You Can Do with Your Child* by Steve and Ruth Bennett.

Page dividers   *Three-ring binder*
Loose-leaf paper   *Markers or crayons*

Label the dividers with categories like *Academic Achievements, Athletics, Family Games, Food, Random Acts of Kindness,* and so on. Place the dividers and a supply of paper into the binder.

Now you're ready to record your family's day-to-day records. For example, what's the longest Monopoly game you've ever played? Who read the most books last month? Who has eaten the most lima beans in one sitting? Who did something unusually kind for someone else? For younger family members, record how many blocks they can stack, how many times they can jump on one foot, and so on. For each record, be sure to describe the feat, the record, the record holder, and the date.

If you have more than one child and don't want your kids competing against each other, keep a separate book of records for each child and encourage your kids to beat their own records, not those of others. And to ensure that everyone has her moment of glory, let each record stand for at least twenty-four hours before it can be challenged.

A Day in the Life of...

When I was growing up, the high price of photography meant photo taking was reserved for special occasions. Now, however, cameras are readily available and fairly inexpensive. Encourage your child to be a photographer now and then, recording people, places, things, and events that are meaningful to her.

Digital camera or camera with film

Let your child use your camera or buy your child an inexpensive camera of her own. (Even disposable cameras take fairly good pictures.) Encourage her to take photos of subjects that interest her, whether they're people, pets, or your weed-filled garden. Remind her to pay attention to the background of the photo, to keep her fingers away from the lens, and to hold the camera steady when squeezing the shutter release. Encourage her to view subjects from different angles and distances.

Your child can use her photos to illustrate a story or mount them in a small scrapbook as a photo diary. She can make photo books with various themes—perhaps nature, animals, or people in your neighborhood. She can combine photography with other hobbies by taking photos of things like her rock collection or her efforts at gardening or cooking. She can use photos to create place mats, greeting cards, or bookmarks.

Memory Book

Make memory books with your child based on various subjects or events in her life—soccer, birthday parties, your vacation at the ocean, her visit to her grandparents' house, and so on. (Memory books also make great gifts.)

Keepsakes
Scissors
Several sheets of
  construction paper

Hole punch
Ribbon
Glue
Markers or gel pens

Collect all the keepsakes you want to include in the book: photos, scraps of gift-wrap, ticket stubs, brochures, programs, and so on. Decide what your memory book will look like. Perhaps you want to make a heart-shaped one or a soccer ball–shaped one or a square one. Cut paper to the size and shape you want, punch holes in it, and tie the pages together with ribbon. Glue the keepsakes onto each page and use markers or gel pens to add names, dates, and comments. For bulky items, attach a small envelope or a construction paper pocket.

Family Newspaper

Paper
Pens and markers
Scissors

Glue
Computer and printer
(optional)

Create a family newspaper to report on happenings in your home, record opinions on current events, and showcase hobbies, interests, and achievements. Encourage each family member to contribute to the newspaper. Younger children can dictate stories and draw pictures, while older children can write or type their own pieces. Here are some topics children may enjoy:

family vacation
arrival of a new pet
new neighbors
school happenings
sports
hobbies
recipes
jokes
creative writing

birthday celebrations
holidays
interview with parents or
    grandparents
survey on favorite foods, toys,
    books, movies
opinions on cooking, family rules,
    chores

Assemble your newspaper on a computer or by cutting and gluing articles to sheets of paper. Circulate your newspaper by posting it on your refrigerator or by sending copies to relatives and family friends. Be sure to make enough copies so that each child can save one for posterity.

Time Capsule

Help your child create a time capsule to be opened next year—or ten years from now.

Pen
Paper
Small shoebox
Current photo of your child
Current photo of your family
Other meaningful keepsakes
Tape or ribbon

Help your child prepare information to put into her time capsule by asking her questions (and writing down her responses if necessary). You might ask about favorite foods, songs, activities, friends, and so on. Ask your child what she looks forward to in the coming years and what she expects life to be like next year or when she's a teenager or an adult. When everything is written down, place the paper in a small shoebox along with a current photo of your child, a current photo of your family, and other meaningful keepsakes. Place the lid on the shoebox and write your child's name on it, the date on which the time capsule is being closed, and the date on which it's to be opened. Secure the time capsule with tape or ribbon and keep it in a safe place until it's time to open it.

Video Time Capsule

Video camera

Ask your child questions on camera, such as who her friends are, what she likes to do and eat, and so on. She may also enjoy just chatting about herself and her day-to-day life. Record your child's world: her friends, home, school, church, sports activities, and so on. Label the finished recording with your child's name, the current date, and the date it's to be viewed. Keep it in a safe place until it's time to watch it. If you have more than one child, make a different recording for each child. If you like, add a new segment every year so that in the future, you'll be able to watch your child grow up on her video time capsule.

Journal

Diary or notebook
Pen

Suggest to your child that she begin the habit of writing in a journal. She needn't do it every day; once or twice a week is fine, too. Encourage her to describe her thoughts and feelings as well as events. She'll find that a journal is a great way to remember her past and see how far she's come.

Book of Me

Photos
Old magazines
Scissors
Glue
Construction paper
Markers, stickers, rubber stamps, and so on
Hole punch
Ribbon

Help your child make a book about herself and her life.
Choose photos to include and look through old magazines for
pictures and words that help portray who she is. Glue the
photos and cutouts onto construction paper. Add text that
tells about your child. Your child can decorate the pages with
drawings, stickers, rubber stamps, and so on. Make a title
page that includes the name of your child and the date.
When the book is complete, assemble the pages, punch holes
in them, and tie them together with ribbon.

If you like, make a bound book for your child by following the directions on pages 411–412.

Me Collage

Photos
Old magazines
Scissors
Glue

Heavy matte board
Markers, stickers, rubber
  stamps, and so on
Clear acrylic spray (optional)

Help your child make a collage about herself and her life. Choose photos to include and look through old magazines for pictures and words that help portray who she is. Glue the photos and cutouts onto a sheet of heavy matte board. Your child can add drawings, stickers, rubber stamps, and so on to the collage. When the collage is complete, preserve it with clear acrylic spray if you like. Ask your child about the pictures and words she's used.

Book of Lists

Books of lists are popular with children. My kids enjoy *The Best Ever Kids' Book of Lists* by Eugenie Allen, which lists things like the natural wonders of the world, the scariest people ever, and the grossest vegetables. Your child may enjoy making her own book of lists.

Plain paper
Pen or markers
Old magazines (optional)
Hole punch
Ribbon

Help your child make a book of lists about herself, her life, or anything else that interests her. She might want to list food she likes and dislikes, friends, favorite books, music, movies, TV shows, sports she plays or would like to play, pets she owns or would like to own, and so on. Your child can illustrate her book or, if she likes, include pictures from old magazines.

When the book is complete, assemble the pages, punch holes in them, and tie them together with ribbon. If you like, make a bound book for your child by following the directions on pages 411–412.

CHAPTER 8
Arts and Crafts

Every child is an artist. The problem is how to remain an artist once he grows up.

—*Pablo Picasso*

Arts and crafts develop your child's coordination, concentration, and creative-thinking, artistic, organizational, and manipulative skills. Most kids enjoy arts and crafts, and fortunately they're a big part of the early school years. If you want to supplement your child's arts-and-crafts education, this chapter provides experiences in drawing, painting, printmaking, sculpting, modeling, and more.

An old phone book is useful for coloring, painting, and gluing. Just open the book and place your child's paper on the first page. For the next project, turn the page and—voilà!— another clean surface. You'll never have to hunt for scrap paper to protect your table and you'll spend a lot less time cleaning it, too. Save your child's outstanding creations in a three-ring binder with plastic page protectors. Label each artwork with the date or your child's age. Photograph three-dimensional and extralarge creations.

Encourage your child to experiment and express himself. Make sure he understands that there's no right or wrong way to create arts and crafts.

DRAWING

Drawing is probably the first art form your child experienced. During his toddler and preschool years, it was both a creative exercise and one that helped develop his small muscles and hand-eye coordination. As he enters middle childhood, he'll develop the ability to create more realistic-looking drawings, although he may get frustrated when his efforts don't yield his desired results. He may enjoy drawing lessons—presented in either an art class or a book. A series we've enjoyed is the Draw Write Now series by Marie Hablitzel and Kim Stitzer.

The following ideas will help you encourage your child's drawing efforts:

- Give your child a variety of drawing tools: crayons, pens, pencils, colored pencils, chalk, markers, and charcoal.
- Give your child a variety of papers: plain paper, construction paper, newsprint, tracing paper, shiny paper, fine sandpaper, cardboard, and matte board.
- Cut paper into shapes, such as circles, triangles, and stars.
- Give your child three-dimensional surfaces, such as boxes and rocks, to draw on.
- Give your child a small notebook or sketchbook.
- Let your child draw while you read a book to him.
- Encourage your child to draw pictures in various shades of the same color.
- Have your child draw with wet chalk on dry paper or with dry chalk on wet paper.

Flipbook

An animated cartoon is made up of a series of drawings that are shown quickly, one after the other, so that the figures appear to move. Your child can bring his own drawings to life by making a flipbook.

Small notebook or pad of paper
Colored pencils or markers

Have your child choose a simple action to show with his flipbook—perhaps a face changing from sad to happy, a person walking, or an apple falling from a tree. On the last page of the flipbook, have him draw the first picture in the action sequence (for example, the sad face). On the next-to-last page, he should draw the same picture but with a slight change (for example, the frown lifting a bit). He should draw each subsequent picture so it's slightly different from the one before it until the action sequence is complete. Show your child how to flip the pages from back to front to see his homemade animated cartoon.

Line Design

Scissors
Plain paper
Construction paper or
*   matte board*

Crayons, colored pencils,
*   or markers*
Glue

Cut a sheet of plain paper two inches shorter and two inches narrower than your construction paper or matte board. Have your child draw a long, twisting line all over the plain paper. The line should cross itself many times. Your child can color in the spaces with solid colors and/or patterns, then glue the finished drawing on the construction paper or matte board and display it on a wall.

Drawing Fun

Plain paper
Crayons, colored pencils, or markers
Mirror

- Challenge your child to draw a simple picture or write his name with his non-dominant hand.
- Challenge your child to write a message or his name backward and hold it up to a mirror to see how he did.
- Have your child close his eyes and try to draw a simple picture or write his name or a message.

Near and Far

Use several layers of paper to make a landscape appear more three-dimensional and realistic.

Scissors
One sheet of plain paper
Two sheets of tracing paper
Markers or crayons
Tape or glue

If necessary, cut the plain paper and/or tracing paper to the same size. Have your child draw the background of a landscape on the plain paper. The objects in the background should look small and far away.

Lay a sheet of tracing paper over the plain paper and attach it at the top with a bit of tape or glue. Have your child add more details to the landscape by drawing on the sheet of tracing paper. These objects should be bigger than those in the background so they appear nearer.

Now attach another sheet of tracing paper on top of the first. On the top sheet of tracing paper, have your child draw the foreground of the landscape. The objects in the foreground should be the largest so that they appear the closest.

Dot Drawing

This drawing technique, called pointillism, creates an optical illusion. A picture made with many little dots looks like one solid image when viewed from a distance.

Have your child draw a picture with dotted lines very lightly in pencil. He can use any of the following methods to fill in the picture:

- Fill in the picture with colored dots using colored pencils or fine-tip markers.
- Dip the pointed end of a sharpened pencil in paint, then press it lightly on the paper to make dots. Use a different pencil for each color of paint. To make larger dots, use the eraser end of the pencil.
- Fill in the picture with colored dot stickers.

When your child's picture is complete, stand back and look at it. The dots will blend together to form blocks of solid color. If you look at the picture with your eyes out of focus, the colors will seem to move.

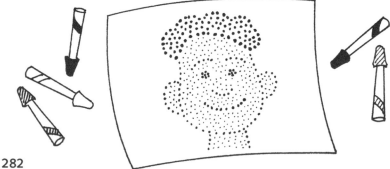

Popsicle Stick Puzzle

Several Popsicle sticks
Tape
Markers or acrylic paints

Lay several Popsicle sticks side by side on a flat surface to form a square. Lay two pieces of tape across all the sticks to join them. Turn them over so the tape is on the underside. Draw or paint a picture on the Popsicle stick square. When the picture is complete, remove the tape. Have your child mix up the pieces and put them in the right order again. If you like, have two or more kids make puzzles then trade and try to put each other's puzzles together.

Crayon Rubbings

Textured objects
Paper
Crayons, paper removed

Collect textured objects like leaves, string, doilies, paper clips, keys, fabric, tiles, coins, cardboard shapes, and bricks. Place a sheet of paper over an object, then have your child rub the side of a crayon on the paper. Shift the paper and change colors for an interesting effect.

Fun with Chalk

When I was a girl, chalk was just for chalkboards and side-walks. Today chalk is affordable and widely available in a variety of colors and sizes. Encourage your child to use chalk in the creative ways described below.

Colored chalk   Water, liquid starch, or
Paper   buttermilk
Hair spray   Sugar
Sponge   Cotton ball
Paintbrush

- Have your child draw with chalk on a sheet of paper. Spray the drawing with hair spray to set the chalk.
- Use a sponge or paintbrush to paint a sheet of paper with water, liquid starch, or buttermilk. Let your child draw on the wet paper with colored chalk.
- Have your child make a chalk rubbing by placing a sheet of paper on a textured surface and rubbing chalk over the paper.
- Let your child draw on a window with wet chalk.
- Soak chalk in a mixture of one cup of water and one-third cup of sugar for ten minutes. Let your child draw on paper with the wet chalk, then smudge the drawing with a cotton ball.
- Have your child draw on a damp sponge with chalk. Press the sponge on paper to print the design.

PAINTING AND PRINTMAKING

Kids of all ages love to paint. Toddlers and preschoolers are best suited to large sheets of paper and pots of liquid tempera, but older children will enjoy more refined materials and techniques. Provide acrylic paints as well as tempera paints. Provide high-quality brushes in a variety of sizes. Encourage your child to paint on paper, fabric, matte board, and ceramic tile as well as on three-dimensional objects like rocks, terra cotta pots, wood blocks, cardboard boxes, and Popsicle sticks.

The following activities will create a variety of painted objects your child will be proud to display. Many also make great gifts for friends and family.

Painting

The following painting activities are suitable for children of all ages.

String
Clothespin
Tempera paint
Paper
Marbles
Drinking straw
Old toothbrush
Balloons

- Have your child clip a length of string to a clothespin then dip the string in the paint and drag it around the paper.
- Let your child drop marbles into various colors of paint and roll them across a sheet of paper.
- Drop thinned paint onto a sheet of paper. Have your child use a drinking straw to blow the paint around.
- Let your child dip an old toothbrush into paint and spatter it over the paper.
- Blow up balloons of various sizes and tie the ends. Have your child hold onto the tied end of each balloon, dip the balloon in paint, and press it onto the paper.

Wall Hanging

Scissors
Solid-colored fabric
Iron
Two 2-foot-long wooden
   dowels

Darning needle
Yarn or heavy thread
Tempera or acrylic paint
Paintbrushes
2-foot length of string

Cut the fabric into a rectangle 1½ by 2 feet. Iron the fabric, then lay it right side down and place a dowel parallel to and 1½ inches from a short edge. Fold the edge of the fabric over the dowel. Use a darning needle and yarn or heavy thread to sew down the edge and form a casing for the dowel. Make a similar casing on the other short edge of the fabric. Set aside the dowels.

    Have your child paint a design or picture on the fabric, making sure a short edge is at the top. When the paint is dry, insert the dowels into the casings. Tie one end of the string to each end of the top dowel so your child can hang his artwork.

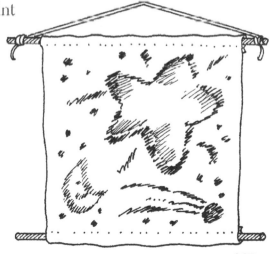

Popsicle Stick Sign

Craft glue or glue gun
3-by-8-inch piece of cardboard
24 Popsicle sticks
Acrylic paints
Paintbrush
Clear acrylic spray
Tape and string or wire (optional)
Magnetic strip (optional)

Help your child spread glue over the cardboard and arrange the Popsicle sticks side by side across the length of the cardboard. Press the sticks down firmly, then let the glue dry.

Have your child paint the Popsicle sticks to create whatever kind of sign he wants. He may want a sign that he can hang on his bedroom door (for example, "Joshua's Room") or he may want to display a motto or phrase he likes (for example, "I love hockey!"). Let the paint dry, then spray the sign with clear acrylic spray.

If you like, tape string or wire to the back of the sign so that it can be hung on a door or wall. If it will be hung on a metal surface like a refrigerator, glue a magnetic strip onto the back of the sign.

Painted Tile

Odds and ends of plain ceramic tile are great fun to paint.
You can hang painted tiles on a wall or use them for coasters
or trivets.

Acrylic paints
Paintbrushes, sponges, and/or small stickers
Plain ceramic tile
Clear acrylic spray
Glue gun (optional)
Marbles or wooden beads (optional)

Let your child paint on a plain piece of tile. He can paint a
design, scene, or message; use sponges to make a colorful
design; or stick stickers on the tile, paint over them, and
remove the stickers when the paint is dry.

When your child's masterpiece is finished, spray the tile
with clear acrylic spray. If your child has made a trivet, you
might also use a glue gun to glue marbles or wooden beads
to the underside of the tile (one in each corner).

Painted Pots

These colorful pots can be used for more than just plants!
Fill them with candies and give them as gifts or use them to
hold earrings, spare change, or candles.

Terra cotta pot   *Sponges*
Acrylic paints   *Small stickers*
Paintbrushes   *Clear acrylic spray*

Have your child paint a terra cotta pot using one of the following techniques:

- Paint the outside of the pot one color; paint the rim and
  inside a different color.
- Paint the pot one color inside and out. When the paint is
  dry, use sponges to dab on two or three other colors.
- Paint the pot one color inside and out. When the paint is
  dry, stick small stickers on the outside of
  the pot. Paint the outside of the pot again
  with a different color. Remove the
  stickers when the second coat of
  paint is dry.

When the paint is completely dry,
spray your pot with clear acrylic spray.

Rock Creatures

Smooth rocks
Pencil (optional)
Paintbrushes and acrylic paints and/or permanent markers
Clear acrylic spray

Collect a variety of smooth rocks.

Have your child pencil a design on each rock before painting it, if he likes. He can also paint the rock freehand. It's best to paint the entire rock in a solid color first, then add details in contrasting colors using paint and/or markers.

Sometimes the shapes of rocks suggest how they might be painted. Small, round, or flat rocks make great bugs, and larger rocks make good birds, mice, or imaginary creatures. Some rocks are even shaped like hearts, fish, or cars. Encourage your child to use his imagination as he looks at the rocks and decides how to paint them.

Spray the painted rocks with clear acrylic spray to give them a shiny finish. Arrange them on a shelf, perch them in a potted plant, or use them for paperweights on a desk or table.

Sand Painting

Sand
Powdered tempera paint
   in several colors
Large, shallow containers

Cardboard or matte board
Paintbrushes
Glue
Charcoal or marker

Color the sand by mixing it with powdered tempera paint. Leave some sand uncolored. Place each color of sand in a separate container.

Have your child paint the entire surface of one side of the cardboard or matte board with glue, then completely cover the glue with uncolored sand. Help him tilt the board and tap it lightly over the container to shake off any excess sand. Let the glue dry.

Have your child sketch a simple design on the sand-covered board using a piece of charcoal or a marker, then use a fine brush to paint a small part of the design with glue. Help him hold the board over a sand container, sprinkle the desired color of sand onto the glue, and shake off any excess sand. Continue in this way until your child has painted his entire design with colored sand.

Printmaking

Paring knife and potato
Liquid tempera paint
Paper
Scissors, thin foam, glue,
  cardboard tube, and
  shallow pan

Sponges
String or yarn and block of
  wood
Griddle, aluminum foil,
  and crayons

- Use a paring knife to cut a potato in half and carve a relief design. Let your child dip the potato in paint and then press it on paper.
- Help your child cut shapes from thin foam and glue them onto a cardboard tube. Pour paint into a shallow pan and have your child dip his "roller" into the paint and roll it onto paper.
- Cut shapes from sponges. Have your child dip the shapes in paint and press them on paper.
- Wrap string or yarn around a block of wood. Have your child press the block in paint, then on paper.
- Cover a griddle with foil. Warm the griddle slightly, then have your child draw on the foil with a crayon. Show him how to carefully press paper on the design and lift it off to make a print. Wipe the foil with a damp cloth and start over to make a new print.

MODELING AND SCULPTING

Modeling and sculpting are activities that create three-dimensional structures out of a variety of materials. Although such activities (using papier-mâché, for example) can be messy and complicated, they can also be quite simple (for example, sculpting with play dough or modeling clay). The following activities use a variety of modeling compounds and techniques to create interesting and beautiful pieces of art.

Marshmallow Sculpture

This is an easy, clean activity that even adults will enjoy. It'll keep your child occupied for a long time.

Toothpicks
Miniature marshmallows

Make three-dimensional sculptures by joining toothpicks and miniature marshmallows. Your sculptures can be simple or complicated. Challenge your child to see who can build the most elaborate house, the most interesting car, or the funniest animal.

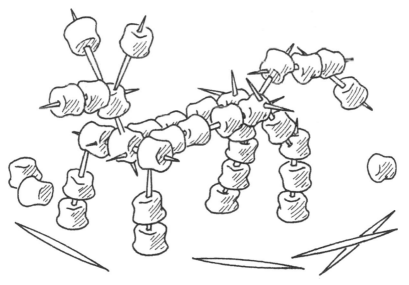

Newspaper Bowl

Plastic or glass bowl
Eight single sheets of newspaper
Large container full of warm water
Scissors
Liquid tempera, acrylic, or spray paint
Shellac or clear acrylic spray

Turn the bowl upside down on a flat surface. Place a sheet of newspaper in a large container of warm water. When the newspaper is soaked, remove it from the water and lay it over the bowl. Shape it firmly to the bowl and press it firmly along the rim of the bowl.

Repeat the procedure described above with the remaining sheets of newspaper, being sure to alternate the direction of the paper for each layer. Let the newspaper dry.

When the newspaper is dry, it will lift off the bowl easily and retain its shape. Lift the newspaper bowl and trim its edges with scissors. Let your child paint the paper bowl. Finish the bowl with a coat of shellac or clear acrylic spray.

Papier-Mâché Piggy Bank

¼ cup flour
6 cups water
Shallow pan
Several sheets of newspaper
Balloon
Scissors
Empty paper egg carton

Glue
Pipe cleaner
Paintbrush
Pink paint
Black paint or marker
Utility knife

Let your child mix the flour with 1 cup of water. Add the mixture to 5 cups of boiling water. Gently boil and stir the paste for 3 minutes. Let it cool, then pour it into a shallow pan.

Tear the newspaper into squares or strips. Then inflate and tie the balloon. Have your child dip the squares or strips of paper into the paste, then place them on the balloon, making sure their edges overlap. Cover the balloon with many layers of pasty paper and let it dry for a day or two.

Cut 6 sections from the egg carton. Glue 1 section onto the tied end of the balloon for the pig's nose. Glue 4 sections onto the underside of the pig for its feet. Cut the remaining section in half and glue 1 piece onto each side of the pig's head for its ears. Use a curled pipe cleaner for the pig's tail. Cover the nose, feet, ears, and tail with papier-mâché and let them dry. Then paint the pig pink and add details with black paint or marker. Use a utility knife to cut a money slot in the top of the pig.

Refrigerator Magnets

1 cup flour
½ cup salt
Water
Food coloring (optional)
Baking sheet

Liquid tempera or acrylic
*   paint and paintbrush*
*   (optional)*
Clear acrylic spray
Magnetic strip
Glue gun

Preheat your oven to 200°F. Mix the flour and salt with enough water to make a dough that feels like modeling clay. If you like, tint the dough with food coloring. Let your child use his imagination to shape the dough into small figures. If he wants to make letters, have him roll the dough into ropes and then shape the ropes into letters. Bake the figures on a baking sheet until they're very hard. (This may take an hour or two.) If you like, your child can paint the figures. Finish the figures with clear acrylic spray, then use a glue gun to attach a magnetic strip to the back of each figure.

Plaster Imprints

Modeling clay (See page 404.)
Shallow box or old baking pan
Small objects like keys, coins, string, and leaves
2 cups water
Bucket
3 cups plaster of Paris
Paint stick or wooden spoon
Paintbrush and acrylic paints (optional)
Clear acrylic spray (optional)

Press the clay into the bottom of the box or pan to make a smooth, flat surface. Press small objects into the clay.

Pour the water into the bucket. Sprinkle the plaster of Paris over the water and stir the mixture until it's about as thick as pea soup. Pour a thin layer of plaster over the objects in the clay and wait 10–20 minutes for the plaster to harden.

Now carefully remove the plaster. The objects will have made an imprint in the hardened plaster. This is called a negative imprint because the image is backward. If you like, have your child paint the plaster with acrylic paint. Then spray the plaster with clear acrylic spray.

Clay Pot (No-Kiln Method)

Clay that can be oven-dried, such as Fimo or Sculpey,
*   or air-dried*
Spoon (optional)
Paintbrush and tempera or acrylic paint (optional)
Clear acrylic spray

Help your child use one of these methods to make a pot:

• Roll the clay into a ball and make a hole in the center with your thumb. Push outward from the hole with your thumb and place your fingers on the outside of the ball as you press and shape the pot, turning the clay as you work. Try to keep the clay the same thickness all the way around.

• Make long ropes of clay about as thick as a large crayon. Coil the ropes around and around, piling the coils on top of each other to make a pot shape. You can leave the pot as is or use a spoon to smooth the coils into a flat surface.

Follow the clay manufacturer's directions to dry your pot. If you like, have your child decorate the dried pot with tempera or acrylic paint. Finish the pot with clear acrylic spray.

Clay Pot (Kiln Method)

Use this method if you plan to build an outdoor kiln. (See page 302.)

Clay
Water
Airtight plastic bag (optional)
Slip, a water-clay mixture available at art supply stores, and
spoon or smooth stone (optional)

Follow the directions for making a clay pot on the previous page using regular clay instead of clay that can be air- or oven-dried. If the clay starts to dry out as your child works with it, add a little water.

Don't let your child's pot dry out before you fire it. If you can't fire it right away, keep it at the "leather-hard" stage (hard enough to hold its shape but soft enough to cut easily) by storing it in an airtight plastic bag. If you like, polish a leather-hard pot before firing it by applying a coat of slip and rubbing the pot with the back of a spoon or a smooth stone.

Fire your pottery by following the directions on the next page.

Outdoor Kiln

72 bricks
Wet clay
Dry sawdust
Unpainted leather-hard
  pots (See page 301.)

Newspapers
Matches
19-by-19-inch sheet of heavy
  metal

This kiln is big enough to fire thirty 4-inch pots. Check your local fire regulations before building it.

Arrange 8 bricks in a square. Arrange another 8 on top of the first 8 to cover the cracks in the first layer. Repeat this process until all the bricks are used. Seal all the cracks between the bricks with wet clay. Put 3 inches of sawdust in the bottom of the kiln. Put a layer of pots 1 inch apart upside down on the sawdust. Add sawdust until there's 1 inch of sawdust on top of the pots. Continue adding pots and sawdust this way. Top the last layer of pots with 3 inches of sawdust. Put crumpled newspapers on the top layer of sawdust. Light the newspapers and put the metal on top of the kiln. (You may need to weight it.) Let the kiln burn until the smoking stops.

If the firing has gone correctly, when you open the kiln, you'll find all the sawdust burned up and the pots together at the bottom. Pottery fired this way isn't as hard as pottery fired in a regular kiln, but it is quite hard. Your pots will have turned black and, if you polished them with slip before firing, they will have retained a fine polish.

GIFTS TO MAKE

I'm always looking for good ideas for gifts my kids can make
for their friends, music teachers, coaches, and others at
Christmas, year-end, and so on. Here are some of the items
we've made over the years that have been fun both to make
and to give.

Keepsake Box

Use this box to store photos, jewelry, or other treasures.

Tissue paper, patterned or in complementary colors
Sponge brush
Decoupage glue
Small box with removable lid
Three disposable cups
Craft glue or glue gun (optional)
Dried or silk flowers (optional)
Ribbon (optional)
Metallic-ink pen or permanent marker (optional)

Have your child tear the tissue paper into small pieces.

Use the sponge brush to paint a thin layer of decoupage glue on the outside of the box lid. Have your child quickly cover the glue with overlapping tissue pieces. (If your child works slowly, use only a little glue at a time.) When the lid is covered to your child's satisfaction, balance it on a disposable cup to dry for about an hour.

Repeat the process above for the sides of the box. Balance it on two disposable cups to dry for an hour, then flip it over and do the same for the bottom of the box.

If you like, decorate the lid by gluing on dried or silk flowers tied with ribbon. You can also use a metallic-ink pen or permanent marker to write a label on the box, such as *Emily's Treasures* or *Grandma's Photos.*

Picture Frame

Heavy cardboard   *Heavy book*
Utility knife   *Glitter glue, paint, beads,*
Pencil and ruler   *buttons, dried flowers,*
Craft glue or glue gun   *and so on*

Place the cardboard on a protected surface and cut out a 6-by-8-inch rectangle, a 5-by-7-inch rectangle, and a 7-by-1½-inch strip. In the center of the large rectangle, pencil a small rectangle whose sides are 1¼ inches from the edges of the large rectangle. Cut along the lines and discard the cutout. Apply craft glue along the very edge of the top third of the small rectangle. (Don't glue all around it, or you'll have no opening to slip a photo into the frame.) Center the small rectangle glue side down on the large rectangle and press on it. Now bend the end of the cardboard strip and glue the bent end to the center of the small rectangle to make a stand. Put the frame under a heavy book until the glue dries. When the glue is dry, have your child decorate it with glitter glue, paint, beads, buttons, dried flowers, and so on. The frame will hold a 4-by-6-inch photo.

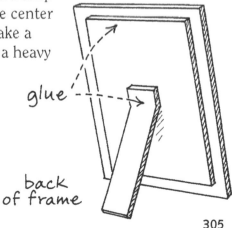

glue

back
of frame

Friendship Bracelet

Your child can make one of these nifty, easy bracelets for each of his friends.

Assorted beads   *Elastic cord or fishing line*
Towel   *Clear nail polish*
Scissors   *Clasp (with fishing line)*

Lay the beads on a towel to keep them from rolling around and have your child arrange them in any pattern he likes. Cut a length of elastic cord or fishing line six inches longer than the circumference of your child's wrist. Then string the beads in one of the following ways:

- If you're using cord, tie an anchor bead to the end of the cord. Have your child string the beads in the order he's chosen. (If he's using letter beads, make sure they're facing the right way.) Tie the ends together so the bracelet fits your child's wrist snugly but stretches enough to slip over his hand. Brush nail polish on the knot to make it more secure.
- If you're using fishing line, tie a clasp to one end of the line. Have your child string the beads in the order he's chosen. (If he's using letter beads, make sure they're facing the right way.) Tie the other end of the line to the clasp, making sure the bracelet will fit your child's wrist when the clasp is fastened. Brush nail polish onto the knots to make them more secure.

Clothespin Trivet

21 spring-style clothespins *Paint and paintbrush*
Craft glue *Clear acrylic spray*

Pull the clothespins apart and discard the springs. Glue the smooth sides of the pieces in each pair together. Let the glue dry. Arrange the pairs in a flower blossom shape with the pointed ends touching in the center. Glue the parts that are touching and press them together. Let the glue dry. Have your child paint the trivet. Finish it with clear acrylic spray.

Notepad Holder

Scissors *Craft glue*
Heavy cardboard *Rickrack*
Fabric *Two magnetic strips*
Notepad *Decorations*

Cut the cardboard and the fabric two inches longer and two inches wider than the notepad. Glue the fabric onto the cardboard. Glue rickrack around the edge of the cardboard. Glue two magnetic strips onto the back of the cardboard. Glue the notepad onto the center of the fabric. Have your child decorate the fabric with glitter glue, fabric paint, or tiny dried flowers. Let the glue and/or paint dry.

Treasure Box

Popsicle sticks
Craft glue or glue gun
Paint and paintbrush

Clear acrylic spray
Marbles

- **Base:** Lay several Popsicle sticks side by side to make a square. Spread glue on four more sticks and lay them across the square at even intervals to hold the square together. Let the glue dry. Turn the base over.
- **Sides:** Glue a stick onto the base along each "bumpy" edge. Put a dab of glue at each end of these two sticks. Lay two more sticks on the first two and along the other edges of the base. Continue gluing sticks in this log-cabin style until the box is as tall as you want it.
- **Lid:** Follow the directions for the base.

Have your child paint the box. Finish it with clear acrylic spray. Glue a marble onto each corner of the base (for legs) and one onto the center of the lid (for a handle).

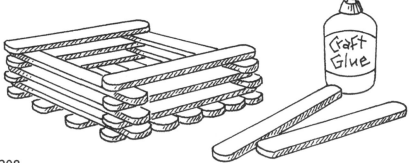

Potpourri Ball

Paintbrush   *Potpourri*
Craft glue   *Ribbon*
Tennis ball

Have your child brush a thick coat of glue all over the ball.
Roll the ball in potpourri until it's covered. Let the glue dry
completely. Tie a length of ribbon around the ball and secure
it with glue. Place the ball in a drawer or hang it in a closet.

Message Clip

Precut wood shape   *Clear acrylic spray*
Paintbrush   *Spring-style clothespin*
Acrylic paints   *Magnetic strip*
Permanent black marker   *Glue gun*

Buy an appropriate precut wood shape (for example, an apple
shape for a teacher) from a craft store. Have your child paint
the shape with acrylic paints and let it dry completely. Add
words with a permanent black marker. Finish the shape with
clear acrylic spray. Attach a clothespin to the front of the
shape and a magnetic strip to the back with a glue gun. The
message clip will adhere to any metal surface and can hold
messages, recipes, to-do lists, photos, and more.

Napkin Holder

23 spring-style clothespins   *Paint and paintbrush*
Craft glue   *Clear acrylic spray*

Have your child pull the clothespins apart and discard the springs. Glue the smooth sides of the pieces in each pair together. Let the glue dry. Lay three pairs on a flat surface so that their sides are touching and glue them together. Let the glue dry. This will be the base of the napkin holder. Sort the remaining pairs into two sets of ten. Arrange each set in a semicircle with the pointed ends touching in the center. Glue the parts that are touching and press them together. Let the glue dry. The two semicircles will be the sides of the napkin holder. Apply glue to the two long outer edges of the base. Press the bottom of one semicircle to each side. Let the glue dry. Let your child paint the napkin holder. Finish it with clear acrylic spray.

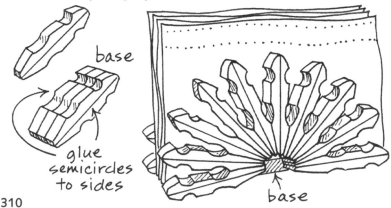

base

glue
semicircles
to sides

base

PAPER CRAFTS

An amazing variety of crafts can be made from a simple supply of paper, scissors, and glue. The following activities use very basic materials but will challenge your child artistically.

Paper Mosaic

If your child has never made a mosaic, make a small sample to show him before he begins.

Scissors
Construction paper in many colors
Glue stick
Shellac

Help your child cut light- and bright-colored construction paper into ½-inch-wide strips, then cut the strips into ½-inch squares. Have your child sort the squares by color. Then give him a sheet of dark-colored construction paper and a glue stick.

Let your child glue squares onto the dark paper in any design he likes. Your child may want to start with a large central image, such as a tree, flower, whale, or car, then fill in the background with a contrasting color. Explain to your child that the tiles should not touch each other but should only have a tiny bit of space between them.

When the mosaic is finished, apply a coat of shellac. Mount the mosaic on one or two larger sheets of colored construction paper to give it a border.

Envelopes

Envelopes made from gift-wrap or wallpaper add a special touch to holiday cards, invitations, and thank-you notes.

Envelope
Gift-wrap or wallpaper
Pen or pencil
Scissors
Glue, tape or stickers

Let your child choose an envelope the same size as the envelope he'd like to make. Help him carefully pull apart and open the envelope flaps to create a flat pattern for tracing. Lay the pattern on the wrong side of a piece of gift-wrap or wallpaper and have your child trace it.

Carefully cut out the traced shape. Fold in the side flaps and glue the bottom flap onto the side flaps. (Look at the original envelope if you're not sure where to fold.)

Let your child place a card or letter inside the envelope and seal it with glue, tape, or stickers.

Books, Books, Books

Scissors
Book club fliers
Construction paper or lightweight cardboard
Glue
Clear contact paper
Hole punch
Satin ribbon

Have your child cut pictures of his favorite books from book club fliers. If his class doesn't participate in a book club, ask friends and relatives to save their fliers. Your child can use the pictures for the following crafts:

- To make a bookmark, cut a strip of construction paper or lightweight cardboard about two inches wide and six to eight inches long and glue pictures of books onto it. Cover the bookmark with clear contact paper. Punch a hole in the top, thread a ribbon through the hole, and tie the ends of the ribbon together.
- To make a collage, glue pictures of books onto a sheet of construction paper. Cover the pictures with clear contact paper and use the collage as a place mat or wall hanging.
- If your child is keeping a reading journal (page 213), pictures of books make great decorations for the journal cover and pages.

Greeting Card Box

Scissors
Rectangular greeting card
Pencil and ruler
Glue and paper clips

Have your child cut the card along the fold.

- **Lid:** Turn over the front of the card and draw a line 1 inch from each long edge and 1½ inches from each short edge. Fold along each line, then open the folds to make a little rectangle in each corner of the card. For each little rectangle, cut along the line that starts at a short side so the rectangles become flaps. Fold the long sides up and fold the flaps inward. Brush glue on the outsides of the flaps. Fold up the short sides of the card and press them onto the flaps. Fold the top edges of the short sides over the flaps and glue them down. Secure the glued spots with paper clips until the glue dries.
- **Box:** Repeat the process above using the other half of the card. Make the bottom slightly smaller so the lid will fit over it by increasing each measurement ⅛ inch.

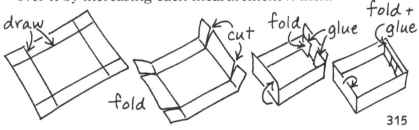

Budding Author

Making a book with your child is a fun way to encourage a child who likes to write or illustrate stories. A book can be:

- paper stapled together with a construction paper cover
- a small notebook with blank pages
- an inexpensive scrapbook
- a three-ring binder with plastic page protectors
- a hand-bound volume (See page 411.)

Let your child write a story along the bottom of each page and illustrate it with drawings, photos, or cut-out pictures.

Silhouette

Tape   *Chalk*
Black construction paper   *Scissors*
Lamp   *White paper or matte board*

Tape a sheet of black construction paper to a wall. Shine a lamp on your child so the shadow of his profile falls on the paper. Play with distances and angles until the shadow's proportions are accurate. Trace the shadow with chalk. Have your child cut along the chalk line. Glue your child's silhouette onto a sheet of white paper or matte board. Mark his name and age on the back of the silhouette, then tape it to the wall or put it in his scrapbook.

Woven Place Mat

Construction paper in two
   or three colors
Pencil

Ruler
Scissors
Stapler or glue

Fold a sheet of construction paper in half so the long edges
meet. Hold the paper so the fold faces you. Starting 1 inch
from the left edge, mark every ½ inch along the fold. Stop
marking 1 inch from the right edge. At each mark, cut a
straight slit from the fold to 1 inch from the top edge. Then
unfold the sheet of paper. This is the mat that will be woven.

    Cut ½-inch-wide strips of construction paper in one or two
other colors. The strips should be as long as the long sides of
the mat. Beginning at one of the short sides of the mat, help
your child weave a strip down through the first slit, up
through the second, down through the third, and so on
through all
the slits. Weave another strip up through the first slit, down
through the second, up through the third, and so on.
Continue weaving strips in this way until there's no room for
any more strips. Adjust each strip after weaving it so it's snug
against its neighbor and/or the edge of the mat. Secure the
strips along the short edges of the mat with staples or glue.

Paper Border

Generations of children have enjoyed making paper-doll chains. Your child can use this technique to make a border for his bed-room, the mantel, or a plain wall in your home.

Large sheet of paper   *Pencil*
Scissors   *Crayons, markers, or paint*

Cut a strip of paper about 36 inches long and 6 inches wide. Fold the strip of paper accordion style, making each panel about 3 inches wide. Have your child draw a simple figure on the top panel. Make sure part of the figure touches the fold on each side. Carefully cut out the figure, making sure not to cut along the folds. Let your child unfold the chain of figures and decorate it with crayons, markers, or paint.

draw figure

but don't cut along folds!

cut along lines of figure through every panel

Wallpaper Art

Wallpaper scraps come in handy for these quick, easy projects. If you don't have wallpaper, gift-wrap is a great alternative.

Scissors
Wallpaper or gift-wrap scraps
Glue
Construction paper
Clear contact paper
Plain paper and envelopes
Cardboard, matte board, or paper plate

Cut shapes from wallpaper or gift-wrap scraps. Let your child use them as follows:

- Glue cutouts onto a sheet of construction paper. Cover the paper with clear contact paper and use it as a place mat.
- Glue small cutouts onto plain paper and envelopes to create stationery.
- Use cutouts to decorate homemade greeting cards.
- Glue cutouts onto cardboard, matte board, or a paper plate to create a picture. Tape a matching set of paper plate pictures to the wall.

OTHER CRAFTS

The craft projects that follow use a variety of materials and will challenge your child's imagination and artistic ability. They're fun to make and great for rainy afternoons or when your child is feeling a little under the weather. Your child can make crafts as gifts for friends and family or use them to brighten up your home. If he plans to give a craft away, remember to photograph it first and store the photo in your child's portfolio or scrapbook.

Diorama

Making dioramas is educational, but it's also just plain fun!

Paintbrush and paints or glue and construction paper
Shoebox or small box
Scissors
Small toy figures, magazine pictures, dried or silk flowers,
   fabric scraps, thread, tape, and so on
Plastic wrap

Let your child choose a theme for the diorama, such as a jungle or a pioneer village. Have him paint the inside bottom of the box an appropriate background color or glue a sheet of construction paper onto it. Set the box on its side so the inside bottom of the box becomes the back of the diorama.

The objects your child uses in his diorama will depend on his theme. He might use small toy figures of people or animals, pictures cut from magazines, dried or silk flowers, fabric scraps, and so on. If he wants items like birds or fish to appear suspended in the diorama, he can tape one end of a short length of thread to each item and the other end to the ceiling of the diorama.

When your child's diorama is complete, stretch plastic wrap tightly across the front of the diorama and secure it with tape.

Tile Mosaic

¼-by-¾-inch molding (optional)
8-by-8-inch piece of ¼-inch plywood
Craft glue
½- or ¾-inch ceramic tiles in several colors
Tape
Grout
Water
Cardboard with straight edge
Sponge

If your child wants a framed mosaic, cut molding to fit the edges of the plywood and glue the molding to the plywood.

Have your child arrange the tiles about ⅛ inch apart on the plywood in a colorful pattern. Show him how to glue the tiles onto the plywood by starting at one corner of the plywood and gluing them one row at a time. Coat the underside of each tile with glue and place it back in position. Let the mosaic dry for 24 hours. Reglue any loose tiles and again let the glue dry. Seal the edges of the mosaic with tape if it isn't framed.

Mix the grout with water until it's thick and creamy. Spread grout over the mosaic with the cardboard, pressing the grout into the spaces between the tiles. Wipe the tiles gently with a damp sponge to remove excess grout. When the grout is dry, remove any tape and clean the mosaic thoroughly. A framed mosaic looks great hanging on the wall, and an unframed mosaic makes an attractive trivet.

Seed Necklace

A child who doesn't like to wear necklaces will still enjoy making one for a friend or family member.

Beans and seeds   *Heavy thread*
Strong needle   *Scissors*

Collect an assortment of beans and seeds, such as apple, cantaloupe, acorn squash, pumpkin, watermelon, brown allspice, and sunflower seeds. Coffee beans also work well. Soak hard beans or seeds in warm water for several hours.

Lay the beans and seeds on a towel to keep them from rolling around and have your child arrange them in any pattern he likes. Thread a strong needle with heavy thread. Tie a knot in the end of the thread and help your child string beans and seeds onto it. When the necklace is long enough, knot the thread and trim the ends.

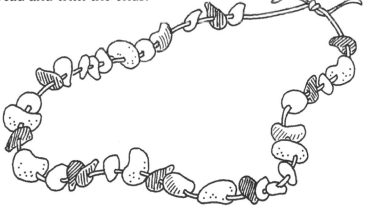

Flower Press

Pressed flowers can be used to decorate a variety of paper items.

Small flowers
Newsprint or other absorbent paper
Heavy book
Glue
Plain note cards, note paper, or construction paper
Clear contact paper

Have your child pick an assortment of small flowers, such as pansies, violets, buttercups, and daisies. Make sure he picks them when they're free of rain or dew. Place them between sheets of absorbent paper, making sure the flowers don't touch each other. Cover the paper with a heavy book. Leave the flowers for a week or so until they're completely dried.

To make stationery, have your child glue the pressed flowers onto plain note cards or note paper. He can also glue the flowers onto construction paper to make bookmarks or gift tags. To make a collage, have your child glue the flowers onto a sheet of construction paper. Turn the collage into a place mat by covering it with clear contact paper.

Rain Gauge

Popsicle stick
Ruler
Waterproof marker
Clean, empty soup can
Colorful contact paper or paintbrush, acrylic paints, and
  clear acrylic spray (optional)
Glue
Plastic bucket and sand (optional)

Lay a Popsicle stick next to a ruler, aligning the ends. Use a waterproof marker to copy the ruler markings onto the Popsicle stick. Mark every inch, half-inch, quarter-inch, and eighth-inch on the Popsicle stick.

If you like, have your child decorate a clean, empty soup can with colorful contact paper or acrylic paint. If your child paints the can, finish it with clear acrylic spray.

Stand the Popsicle stick inside the can and glue it onto the side of the can. Set the can outside in a place where it won't tip over. If you like, place the can in a plastic bucket and pack sand around it.

After a rainfall, read your Popsicle stick ruler to see how much rain has fallen. If you like, log your readings on a calendar or in a weather notebook. Pour the rain out of the can after each reading.

Stuffed Animal Holder

18-by-36-inch piece of felt
Plastic clothes hanger
Craft glue or glue gun
Heavy books
Fabric scraps in various colors
Glitter glue, buttons, lace, and
*   so on*

Lay the felt on a flat surface and set the hanger at one of the short edges so the hook is off the felt but the rest of the hanger is on it. Have your child spread glue on both corners of the felt near the hanger, stopping at the hanger. Fold the corners over the hanger and press hard. Set a heavy book on the hanger and let the glue dry completely.

Cut out 8 fabric pockets, each about 5–6 inches square. Turn the felt over and arrange the pockets on top of the felt. Spread glue along the sides and bottom of each pocket and press the pockets onto the felt. Set a heavy book on each pocket and let the glue dry. Let your child decorate the pockets with glitter glue, buttons, lace, and so on. Your child can slip a small stuffed animal into each pocket and hang the holder in his closet or on his bedroom door or wall.

Hair Scrunchie

4-by-22-inch piece of fabric
Straight pins
Needle and thread
Safety pin
Scissors
9-inch length of ¼-inch elastic
Tape

Have your child fold the fabric in half lengthwise with the wrong side out and pin the long edges together. Sew a seam along the pinned edge to make a fabric tube.

Attach a safety pin to one end of the tube. Tuck it inside the tube and push it all the way through the tube so that the tube turns inside out. (The fabric will now be right side out.) Remove the safety pin.

Attach the safety pin to one end of the elastic. Tape the other end of the elastic to your work surface. Use the safety pin to thread the elastic through the fabric tube. Remove the tape, overlap the ends of the elastic, and sew them together.

Tuck one end of the fabric tube into the other, making sure the seam matches up. Fold the edge of the outer end under. Stitch the folded end to the tucked-in end all the way around.

God's Eye

This craft is found among many cultures of the world. Its Spanish name is *ojo de Dios,* which means "eye of God."

Two sticks (any kind)
Yarn in several colors or variegated yarn
Scissors

Have your child cross two sticks so they're perpendicular to each other. As your child holds the sticks, bind them together by crisscrossing yarn around the center of the cross.

Tie one end of a length of yarn to one arm of the cross. Show your child how to wrap the yarn over and around an adjacent arm. (Be sure to wrap the yarn around the arm, not just over or under it.) Wrap the yarn around the next arm in the same way. Keep wrapping yarn in this way, creating a diamond shape, until you want to change colors. Tie off the end of the yarn and repeat the process above with a new length of yarn in a different color. Do this as many times as you like.

If your child has difficulty changing yarn, use variegated yarn. You can make your own variegated yarn by cutting yarn of various colors into two-yard lengths. Tie the lengths together end to end.

Fork Flower

This simple, easy craft is a great way for your child to keep busy while he's waiting for his meal in a restaurant or at home.

Yarn
Fork with four tines
Scissors
Green pipe cleaner or floral wire (optional)

Tie the end of a length of yarn (at least 12 inches long) to one of the end tines of the fork. Show your child how to weave the yarn over the adjacent tine, under the next one, and so on. Wrap the yarn around the other end tine and weave another row in the other direction. Continue weaving until the fork is full of yarn.

Help your child thread a separate length of yarn (about 6 inches long) between the two middle tines at the bottom of the weaving. Pull the yarn tightly around the center of the weaving and tie a knot. Pull the weaving off the fork to reveal a puffy little yarn flower. You can trim any long yarn ends whenever it's convenient to do so.

If you like, have your child make several flowers. Attach each to a stem of green pipe cleaner or floral wire. Let your child arrange his bouquet of fork flowers in a vase.

Tie-Dyed T-Shirt

White or light-colored all-cotton T-shirt
Rubber bands
Old pail
Old towel
8 cups cold water

4 cups hot water
Old bowl
Cold-water dye
Cold dye fix
Old wooden spoon
6 tablespoons table salt

Wash the shirt but don't dry it. Squeeze out the excess water. Let your child gather large and small bunches of fabric all over the shirt and fasten them with rubber bands.

Place the pail in a sink or bathtub or on a surface covered with an old towel. Pour the cold water into the pail. Pour 2 cups of hot water into the bowl. Stir the dye into the hot water. Pour the dye mixture into the pail of cold water. Rinse the bowl.

Pour another 2 cups of hot water into the bowl. Stir in the cold dye fix and the salt until the salt dissolves. Stir this mixture into the contents of the pail.

Have your child place the shirt in the pail and stir it slowly and gently for about 10 minutes. Let it sit in the pail for another 50 minutes, stirring occasionally.

Remove the T-shirt from the dye and rinse it under cold running water until the water runs almost clear. Squeeze the shirt and roll it in a clean old towel to remove excess water. Remove the rubber bands. Wash and dry the T-shirt by itself before your child wears it.

Grass Buddy

My son made this craft early one spring and had fun cutting his grass buddy's hair for months afterward.

Grass seeds   *Styrofoam cup*
Old sock   *Spray bottle full of water*
Potting soil   *Safety scissors*
Waterproof markers

Have your child sprinkle grass seeds into the toe of an old sock, then add about two cups of potting soil. Knot the sock right above the soil to make a head shape. Turn the head knot side down and have your child draw facial features on it. If he likes, he can draw details like clothing and jewelry on the Styrofoam cup. Balance the head on the rim of the cup. The knot and the rest of the sock go inside the cup.

Have your child spray his grass buddy's head with water and set it in a warm place. If he keeps the soil moist, in a couple of weeks the grass buddy will sprout delicate blades of grassy hair. Your child can use a pair of safety scissors to give his grass buddy a haircut as needed.

CHAPTER 9
Holiday Fun

There is always one moment in childhood when the door opens and lets the future in.

—Graham Greene

Holidays are the exclamation points of life. As Marguerite Kelly and Elia Parsons write in *The Mother's Almanac,* "The first holiday may have been invented to celebrate fertility or planting or harvest, but we're sure a mother was behind it. Even then she must have known that nothing could cure her day-to-day drudgery as well as a holiday or brighten the eye of a small child so quickly."

Holidays provide an important break from routine. Even when we feel too busy or tired or broke to plan a celebration, anticipating a special day can lift our spirits and impart a sense of tradition. Holidays give us a chance to spend time together, enjoy good food, exchange gifts or other tokens of our love, play games, and have fun.

This chapter suggests many ways of celebrating holidays with children. In it you'll find crafts, gifts, cooking, baking, games, books to read, and more.

However you choose to celebrate holidays, remember that anticipation is half the fun. Be sure to let your child help you plan each celebration.

VALENTINE'S DAY (FEBRUARY 14)

Valentine's Day is for celebrating love. Although no one is quite sure how Valentine's Day and its traditions started, most of us enjoy sharing cards, sweets, hugs, and kisses with those we love.

Children who are in school will likely begin Valentine's Day preparations several weeks in advance. At home, you can do the same by making heart-shaped cookies and cards and Valentine's Day crafts and gifts. Read a book or two about Valentine's Day in the days leading up to February 14. On Valentine's Day, dress the whole family in red and put your heart-shaped cookie cutter to work for toast, sandwiches, cheese, and finger Jell-O. A family dinner or small party with a few friends is a simple and fun way to celebrate this special day.

Recommended Reading

Hearts, Cupids, and Red Roses: The Story of the Valentine Symbols by Edna Barth

It's Valentine's Day by Jack Prelutsky

Saint Valentine by Robert Sabuda

Secret Messages

Instead of handing out traditional valentines, your child can send messages in the following fun ways.

- Write on plain white paper with a toothpick dipped in lemon juice. Iron the paper to reveal the message.
- Lay several Popsicle sticks side by side to form a square. Lay strips of tape across all the sticks to join them. Turn the square over. Write a message on the front of it. Remove the tape and put the sticks in an envelope. Put the puzzle back together to read the message.
- Write on a small valentine card. Roll up the card and insert it into a balloon with some confetti. Blow up the balloon and pop it to reveal the valentine inside.
- Blow up a red, pink, or white balloon and pinch the opening shut. Write on the inflated balloon, then deflate it. Blow up the balloon to read the message.

Clay Hearts

1 cup flour
½ cup salt
⅓ cup water
Red food coloring (optional)
Rolling pin
Heart-shaped cookie cutter
Drinking straw
Baking sheet

Paintbrush
Tempera or acrylic paints
Clear acrylic spray
Glue gun (optional)
Magnetic strips (optional)
Jewelry pins (optional)
Satin cord (optional)

Have your child mix the flour and salt, then add the water and stir the mixture well to make clay. If you like, tint the clay with red food coloring.

   Roll out the clay and let your child cut heart shapes from it with the cookie cutter. If a heart will be strung on a necklace, poke a hole near the top of it with a straw. Bake the hearts on a baking sheet at 200°F until they're hard. (This may take an hour or more.) Let your child paint the hearts. Finish them with clear acrylic spray.

- Glue magnetic strips onto the backs of the hearts to make refrigerator magnets.
- Glue jewelry pins onto the backs of the hearts to make brooches.
- String a heart on a 2-foot length of satin cord to make a necklace.
- Glue the hearts onto a plain picture frame. (See page 305.)

Valentine Soaps

Heart-shaped soap is easy to make and is a nice gift for teachers, friends, and family members.

Heart-shaped cookie cutters, baking sheet, and tape (or foil
*   liners and miniature muffin pan)*
1½ cups pure soap flakes or grated bar soap
½ cup water
Red food coloring
Funnel
Cellophane and red or pink ribbon

Place several heart-shaped cookie cutters on the baking sheet and crisscross 2 strips of tape over each cookie cutter to attach it firmly to the baking sheet. Or if you like, use foil liners in a miniature muffin pan to make little round soaps rather than heart-shaped ones.

Have your child mix the soap and water. Add enough red food coloring to get the color you want. Pour the soap into the molds using a funnel. Let the soaps harden before you remove them from the molds.

Wrap the soaps in cellophane and tie them with red or pink ribbons.

Crispy Kisses

Scissors
Paper
Red marker
¼ cup butter
4 cups miniature or 40
   large marshmallows

5 cups crispy rice cereal
Funnel
Cooking spray
12-inch square of
   aluminum foil

Cut paper into 8½-by-1-inch strips. Have your child write a Valentine's Day message on each strip. Melt the butter in a large saucepan. Add the marshmallows and stir the mixture constantly over low heat until it's syrupy. Turn off the heat. Stir in the cereal until it's well coated. Spray the inside of a funnel with cooking spray. Press the cereal mixture into the funnel. Gently remove the cereal kiss and place it flat side down on the foil. Pull the corners of the foil up around the kiss. Insert a paper strip so that half the strip sticks out the top of the kiss. Twist the foil ends at the top. This recipe makes 6 large kisses.

Peppermint Patties

4 cups powdered sugar
3 tablespoons soft butter
2–3 teaspoons peppermint
  extract

½ teaspoon vanilla
¼ cup evaporated milk
2 cups chocolate chips
2 tablespoons shortening

Have your child combine the powdered sugar, butter, peppermint extract, and vanilla. Add the milk and mix the dough well. Roll it into 1-inch balls and place them on a wax-paper-lined baking sheet. Chill them for 20 minutes. Flatten the balls to ¼ inch patties. Chill them for another 30 minutes. Stir and melt the chocolate chips and shortening in a double boiler. Use tongs to dip each patty in the chocolate. Place the dipped patties on wax paper and let them harden.

Valentine's Day Cake

One package white cake mix
Red food coloring
Whipped cream or frosting

Red candy sprinkles or heart-
  shaped candies

Help your child prepare the cake mix and pour it into the pan(s). Squeeze a few drops of red food coloring into the batter and swirl it through the batter with a knife. Bake the cake and let it cool completely. Frost it with whipped cream or frosting and top it with red candy sprinkles or heart-shaped candies.

Penny Pitch

Marker
Poster board or sheet of paper at least two feet square
Small treats and prizes
Ten pennies per player
One small container per player
One small bag per player
Paper hearts

Draw a grid of three- or four-inch squares on the poster board or paper. In each square, place a small treat or prize like a piece of candy or a pencil, eraser, sticker, or any small trinket or toy.

Give each player ten pennies in a small container. The players take turns standing at a distance and pitching pennies at the grid. If a player lands a penny in a square, she claims the treat or prize in that square and collects it in her goodie bag.

If any treats or prizes are too large to fit in the squares, place paper hearts in the squares instead. Keep the large treats and prizes in a box. Let players whose pennies land in the squares with paper hearts choose their own treats and prizes from the box.

SAINT PATRICK'S DAY (MARCH 17)

Saint Patrick's Day celebrates the patron saint of Ireland. Bishop Patrick introduced Christianity to Ireland during the fifth century, and in Ireland he is still honored with a national holiday and a week of religious festivities.

Regardless of your nationality or faith, celebrating Saint Patrick's Day can help break the monotony of the end of winter. Dress in green and invite a few friends over for a small party. Make a craft together and play a few simple games. Decorate and enjoy green food like cupcakes or sugar cookies with green frosting. Tint white grape juice with a drop or two of green food coloring or serve limeade or green Kool-Aid. If you like, listen to a CD of Irish folk music or watch a DVD like *Riverdance* or *Lord of the Dance* together.

Recommended Reading
Patrick: Patron Saint of Ireland by Tomie DePaola
The St. Patrick's Day Shamrock Mystery by Marion M. Markham
Shamrocks, Harps, and Shillelaghs: The Story of the St. Patrick's Day Symbols by Edna Barth

Shamrock Pancakes

These green shamrock-shaped pancakes are perfect for a
Saint Patrick's Day breakfast or lunch.

*3 tablespoons plus more
  vegetable oil
1¼ cups all-purpose flour
2 tablespoons sugar
2 teaspoons baking powder*

*¾ teaspoon salt
1 cup milk
1 egg, slightly beaten
Green food coloring
Syrup or jam*

Preheat an electric griddle or skillet and grease it lightly
with oil.

In a large bowl, have your child mix the flour, sugar, baking powder, and salt with a fork, then add the milk, egg, a
few drops of food coloring, and 3 tablespoons of oil. Have her
stir the batter just until the dry ingredients are moistened.

Pour the batter into the pan to make shamrock-shaped
pancakes. (For each pancake, pour 3 small circles close
enough to touch each other, but not so close that they run
together into one indistinguishable shape.) Turn each pancake when its top begins to bubble and cook the other side
until it's golden brown. Serve the pancakes with syrup or
jam.

Potato Head

Large baking potato
Scrub brush
Play dough or clay, felt scraps, buttons, raisins, miniature
*   marshmallows, toothpicks, yarn or old plastic scouring*
*   pad, fabric or ribbon scraps*

Clean the potato well with a scrub brush. Give your child an
assortment of items with which to decorate her potato. She
can make facial features from play dough or clay, felt scraps,
buttons, raisins, or miniature marshmallows and attach
them with short toothpick pieces. She
can use yarn or an old plastic scouring pad for hair and use fabric or ribbon scraps for a collar or hair deco-
ration.

   If you like, have each family
member create her own potato
head. Photograph the potato head
family before they become dinner.

Twice-Baked Potatoes

What Saint Patrick's Day dinner would be complete without potatoes? These are delicious and simple to make.

4 potatoes
½ cup butter
½ cup sour cream
2 teaspoons salt
Pepper to taste
1 cup grated Cheddar

Preheat your oven to 425°F. Scrub the potatoes thoroughly and pierce each one in several spots with a fork. Bake the potatoes for about 1 hour or until they're tender when pierced with a fork. Remove them from the oven and let them cool. Reduce the oven temperature to 350°F.

When the potatoes are cool enough to handle, slice each in half lengthwise. Scoop out the center of the potato with a small spoon, leaving the skin intact. Put the scooped-out potato in a mixing bowl.

Let your child add the butter, sour cream, salt, and pepper to the scooped-out potato, and help her use an electric mixer to mix it until it's smooth. Have her spoon the potato mixture back into the skins, then place the filled skins on a baking sheet and sprinkle grated cheese on top of them. Bake them for 10 minutes or until the cheese melts.

Shamrock Hop

This is a fun, active game for four or more players. Play it on a carpeted floor to prevent slips and falls.

Scissors
One sheet of green construction paper per player
Tape or string

Cut one large shamrock shape from each sheet of paper.

Mark a start and finish line with tape or string. Have players form pairs. One player in each pair stands at the starting line. Place one shamrock shape in front of each player at the starting line. Give another shamrock to the player in each pair who's not at the starting line.

At your signal, each player at the starting line hops with her feet together onto the shamrock in front of her. The player's partner then places the other shamrock in front of the hopping player. The hopping player then hops onto the second shamrock while her partner moves the other shamrock in front of her. Players continue moving shamrocks and hopping onto them in this way until one pair moves both of its shamrocks across the finish line.

Green Guessing Game

Tape
Shoebox with lid
Utility knife
Jar with lid

Green candy
Slips of paper
Pencil

Tape the lid to the box and cut a slit in the lid. Fill a jar with green candy, counting the pieces you put in the jar.

Place the jar, the box, the slips of paper, and the pencil on a counter. Have each family member guess the number of candies in the jar, write her name and guess on a slip of paper, and place it in the box.

On Saint Patrick's Day, let your child count the candies in the jar. Then let her open the box and read the guesses. The person who made the closest guess wins the candy.

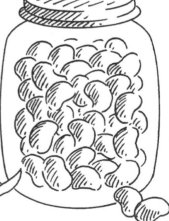

Hot Potato

This game is best played with five or more players.

Potato

Have the players sit cross-legged in a circle. One player sits in the middle of the circle; this player is the leprechaun. The leprechaun starts the game by throwing a potato to one of the players in the circle. The leprechaun then closes her eyes and keeps them closed while the potato is passed among the players in the circle.

After the potato has been passed for a while, the leprechaun shouts, "Shamrock!" and opens her eyes. The player holding the potato at that moment leaves the circle and is out of the game. Play continues until only one player is left in the circle. That player is the winner and gets to be the leprechaun for the next game.

Keep playing until each player has had a turn as the leprechaun.

EASTER (DATE VARIES)

Easter is a Christian holiday that celebrates the resurrection of Jesus Christ. It is also a time to celebrate the coming of spring and all its delightful signs of new life.

Easter is a good time for family dinners and small get-togethers with friends. Decorate eggs or make candy together. Construct a simple craft and play a few games. Hold an egg or candy hunt outdoors or in, depending on the weather. Have an informal parade in your neighborhood with decorated bicycles, wagons, and tricycles. If you start your Easter activities early, this holiday can help bring some sunshine to the last few days of winter.

Recommended Reading
Easter by Gail Gibbons
The Easter Egg Farm by Mary Jane Auch
The Story of Easter by Aileen Fisher

Jiggle Eggs

Eggs	*One 12-ounce can bright-*
Skewer or large needle	*colored frozen juice concen-*
Empty egg carton	*trate, thawed*
3 packets unflavored gelatin	*1½ cups water*
	Small funnel

Show your child how to poke a ½-inch hole in the end of
each egg, then twist the skewer or needle around inside the
egg to break the yolk. Have your child drain the egg into a
bowl and rinse the empty shell carefully with cool water. Set
the shell hole side down in an egg carton to dry and save the
contents of the egg for cooking or baking.

Mix the gelatin with the juice concentrate. In a medium
saucepan, bring the water to a boil. Add the juice-gelatin
mixture and stir the mixture until the gelatin dissolves.
Remove the mixture from the heat and let it cool to lukewarm.

Have your child hold an eggshell hole side up over a
bowl. Insert the funnel into the hole. Carefully fill the egg
with the juice-gelatin mixture. Set the egg back in the carton, hole side up. After you've filled all the eggs, refrigerate
them for at least 2 hours.

Serve the eggs in a basket. Guests will enjoy cracking
open the eggs and discovering the surprise inside.

Easter Candy

⅓ cup soft butter
⅓ cup light corn syrup
½ teaspoon salt

1 teaspoon flavor extract of
 your choice
4 cups powdered sugar

Let your child mix the ingredients with a wooden spoon until the dough gets stiff, then knead it by hand until it's smooth. Roll bits of dough into balls and flatten them lightly with a fork. Place the candies on a wax-paper-lined baking sheet and refrigerate them for 30 minutes or until they're firm. Store them covered in the refrigerator.

Chocolate Basket

1¾ cups chocolate chips
⅓ cup light corn syrup
Easter treats

Melt the chocolate in a double boiler. Stir in the corn syrup. Spread the mixture in an 8-inch square about ⅜ inch thick on a piece of wax paper. Let it stand at room temperature for 2½ hours or until it's dry to the touch. Wrap it tightly in plastic wrap and let it stand overnight. Help your child shape the chocolate into a basket, then fill it with Easter treats. The basket can be stored in the refrigerator for up to 2 weeks.

Egg Decorating

For the following activities, use hard-boiled eggs. Set them on an upside down egg carton to dry. Store them in the refrigerator if you plan to eat them.

- Pour ½ cup of water into each of several saucepans (one for each color). Have your child add a different cut-up fruit, vegetable, or plant to each pan. (Try carrots, grass, blueberries, and coffee grounds.) Bring the water to a boil and simmer it until it turns the color you want. Strain and reserve the water. When it cools, soak the eggs in it.
- Have your child soak crepe paper in hot water in small containers (one for each color). Soak the eggs in the water.
- Measure ¼ teaspoon of food coloring into each of several small bowls (one for each color). Add ¾ cup of hot water and 1 tablespoon of white vinegar. Soak the eggs in the water.
- Grate crayon stubs. Fill a big glass jar with very hot water. Drop pinches of grated crayon in the water. When the crayon begins to melt, add an egg. Have your child twirl the egg in the water with a slotted spoon. The wax will make a design on the egg. Carefully remove the egg with the spoon.

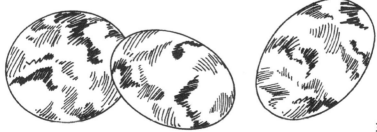

Easter Cookies

2 cups flour
½ teaspoon baking soda
Pinch of salt
1 cup sugar
½ cup butter

1 egg
2 teaspoons vanilla
1 teaspoon milk
⅓ cup pastel candy sprinkles

Have your child thoroughly mix the flour, baking soda, and salt while you beat the sugar and butter in a separate bowl. Let your child add the egg, vanilla, and milk to the sugar and butter, then beat the mixture until it's light and creamy. Let your child add the flour mixture and sprinkles and mix the dough with her hands until it's smooth.

Divide the dough in half and place it on a lightly floured surface. Let your child roll each piece of dough into a log about 1½ inches in diameter and 7 inches long. Wrap each log in plastic wrap and freeze it for 30 minutes or until it's firm enough to slice.

Preheat your oven to 400°F. Cut the logs into ¼-inch slices and place them on a baking sheet. Bake the cookies for 8–10 minutes or until they're light golden brown. This recipe makes about 50 cookies.

Bunny Game

This game is fun for two or more players.

Scissors
Pink, white, and black
  construction paper

Glue
Clear contact paper
Die

Cut one set of the following shapes from construction paper for each player: one white bunny head, two long pink and white ears, two black eyes, one black nose with whiskers, one smiling black mouth with two white teeth showing, and one black bow tie. To make the shapes durable, cover them with clear contact paper.

Have the players sit around a table or in a circle with all the bunny shapes in the center. The players take turns rolling a die. A player takes a specific shape for each number she rolls:

⚀	head shape	⚃	nose
⚁	one ear	⚄	mouth
⚂	one eye	⚅	bow tie

Each player may take only one head, two ears, two eyes, one nose, one mouth, and one bow tie.

For a competitive game, declare the first player to assemble a complete bunny face the winner. For a cooperative game, play until every player has assembled a complete bunny face.

Spring Tea

Elegant linens and tableware
Vase(s) and flowers
Balloons, streamers, ribbons, and bows
Special treats
Herbal tea or hot apple cider
Camera

Host a formal tea for your child and a few of her friends to celebrate the arrival of spring. Set a table indoors or out with elegant linens and tableware. Include a floral centerpiece or tie several small vases together with a ribbon and put a few big flowers in each. Decorate the room with balloons and streamers and the chairs with ribbons and bows. Ask the guests to dress up for the occasion. (If the kids don't own fancy clothes, dress up their outfits with items bought at a thrift shop.) Serve special treats like fancy sandwiches, chocolate-dipped strawberries, pastries, cookies, herbal tea, and hot apple cider. Take a photo of each guest. If you like, have the children make a simple craft or play a garden game like croquet.

Jellybean Toss

This game requires two or more players.

Jellybeans
One small container per child
Sheet or tablecloth
Large container
Tape, string, or chalk
Small prize (optional)

Distribute the jellybeans equally among the small containers. Lay a sheet or tablecloth on the floor or ground. Set a large container in the middle of the cloth and mark a line with tape, string, or chalk about five feet from the large container.

Give each player a container of jellybeans. Have the players take turns standing behind the line and tossing jellybeans at the large container. Allow the players four or five tosses per turn. Award a point for each jellybean that lands in the container.

The player who gets the most points is the winner. Give the winner a small prize if you like or let her keep all the jellybeans in the large container and on the sheet.

Confetti Egg Fight

Even though this game uses up lots of eggs, takes time to prepare, and leaves a big mess in our yard, I love it!

Eggs   *Confetti*
Skewer or large needle   *Glue*
Egg carton   *Tissue paper*
Funnel

Show your child how to poke a half-inch hole in the end of each egg, then twist the skewer or needle around inside the egg to break the yolk. Have your child drain the egg into a bowl and rinse the empty shell carefully with cool water. Set the shell hole side down in an egg carton to dry and save the contents of the egg for cooking or baking.

Use a funnel to fill the shell with confetti. Glue a small piece of tissue paper over the hole to seal it.

Give your child and her sibling(s) and/or friend(s) a supply of confetti eggs and let them have fun throwing the eggs at each other outdoors.

CANADA DAY (JULY 1)

Canada Day is Canada's birthday. It honors the anniversary of Canada's confederation in 1867. The celebration of Canada Day differs from family to family, but it usually includes a parade, a picnic or barbecue with family and friends, and fireworks at night.

Help your child understand why Canada celebrates this day and do a few simple things to begin building Canada Day traditions with your family. Your family's traditions will help your child feel proud of her country. (Even if you're not Canadian, your child is sure to enjoy learning about Canada and doing the crafts, games, and treats on the following pages.) Fly the Canadian flag and sing Canadian folksongs. Wear red and white clothes and decorate your house in red and white. Bake a birthday cake, light a few candles, and sing "Happy Birthday" to Canada.

Recommended Reading
Discovering Canada series by Robert Livesey
The Kids Book of Canada by Jock MacRae and Barbara
   Greenwood
*Wow, Canada! Exploring This Land from Coast to Coast to
   Coast* by Vivien Bowers

Water Play

- Fill four plastic bottles with water. Place a Ping-Pong ball on top of each bottle. Challenge your child to shoot the balls off the bottles with a squirt gun or hose.
- Soak sponges in water and throw them at each other.
- Play catch with water balloons.

Canada Day Cake

1 package white cake mix
One 3-ounce package
* vanilla pudding mix*
4 eggs
¼ cup vegetable oil
2 cups cold water

One 3-ounce package red
* Jell-O powder*
1 cup boiling water
White frosting
Scissors and cardboard
Red candy sprinkles

Preheat your oven to 350°F. Grease a 9-by-13-inch pan. Beat the mixes, eggs, oil, and 1 cup of water until smooth. Pour the batter into the pan and bake it for 45–50 minutes. Let the cake cool slightly. Dissolve the Jell-O in the boiling water. Mix in 1 cup of cold water. Let your child poke holes ½ inch apart all over the cake with a toothpick, then pour the Jell-O over the cake. Chill it for at least 2 hours. Frost the cake. Cut a maple leaf shape from cardboard. Set the leaf on the frosting and let your child shake the sprinkles on the cake. Remove the leaf to reveal a stenciled shape.

Canadian Flag

As you make this flag with your child, talk about its shapes and colors.

*One sheet each red and
    white construction
    paper (same size)
Scissors*

*Pencil and maple leaf
Glue
Tape and dowel (or clear
    contact paper)*

Fold the red paper into thirds along the long side, then unfold it. Cut along both folds to make three equal strips of red paper. Draw or trace a maple leaf onto one of the strips and cut it out. Lay the white paper on the table with a long side facing you. Glue one red strip onto the left side of the white paper and the other red strip onto the right side. Glue the maple leaf onto the middle of the white strip. Tape the flag to a dowel and wave it proudly or make a place mat by covering the flag with clear contact paper.

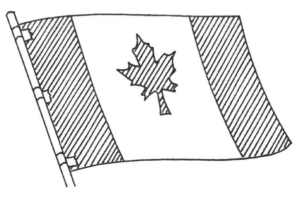

Maple Syrup

1 cup sugar
½ cup water

1 teaspoon each vanilla and
maple flavorings

Cook the sugar and water in a small saucepan over medium heat. Do not stir; instead, gently shake the pan. When the sugar dissolves, turn off the heat and let your child stir in the vanilla and maple flavorings. Serve your syrup over ice cream for a delicious Canada Day dessert.

Popcorn Relay

Two empty wine or soda
bottles
Three large bowls

Unpopped popcorn kernels
Two equal-size measuring cups

Put each bottle in a separate large bowl and set the bowls on a table. Between the bowls set another large bowl filled with popcorn kernels. Set the measuring cups in the kernels. Divide the players into two teams. Have each team line up in front of a bottle. The first player on each team scoops up a cup of kernels and tries to pour as many as possible into the bottle. When the cup is empty, she passes it to the next person in line. Play continues in this way until one team fills its bottle and wins the game.

INDEPENDENCE DAY (JULY 4)

Independence Day celebrates the United States' adoption of the Declaration of Independence in 1776. This holiday is America's birthday. The celebration of Independence Day differs from family to family, but it usually includes a parade, a picnic or barbecue with family and friends, and fireworks at night.

Help your child understand why the United States celebrates this day and do a few simple things to begin building Independence Day traditions with your family. Your family's traditions will help your child feel proud of her country. (Even if you're not American, your child is sure to enjoy learning about the United States and doing the crafts, games, and treats on the following pages.) Fly the U.S. flag and sing American folksongs. Decorate and dress in red, white, and blue. Bake a birthday cake, light a few candles, and sing "Happy Birthday" to the United States.

Recommended Reading

Fireworks, Picnics, and Flags by James Cross Giblin
Sam the Minuteman by Nathaniel Benchley
The Star-Spangled Banner illustrated by Peter Spier
Why Don't You Get a Horse, Sam Adams? by Jean Fritz

Old Glory Cookies

½ cup soft butter
½ cup powdered sugar
¾ teaspoon vanilla

1 cup flour
Red and blue food coloring

Preheat your oven to 350°F. Beat the butter, sugar, and vanilla until the mixture is creamy. Beat in the flour to make a smooth dough. Divide the dough into 3 equal portions. Put each of 2 portions into a separate small bowl. Have your child add 5 drops of red food coloring to one and 5 drops of blue food coloring to the other, then work the food coloring into the dough with a fork until it's evenly blended. Add more food coloring if you want deeper colors.

Have your child divide each portion of dough into 3 pieces and roll each piece into a ball. Then help her flatten the balls and stack them, alternating colors. Roll the dough into a log 8 inches long. Use a sharp knife to slice the log into ¼-inch-thick slices. (If the log is too soft, refrigerate it for about 30 minutes). Bake the cookies on ungreased baking sheets for about 10 minutes.

Pie à la Mud

This cold, chocolaty pie is perfect for a summer celebration.

6 tablespoons melted butter
2 cups chocolate cookie crumbs
1 quart (or more) chocolate ice cream, softened
½ cup chocolate fudge topping
½ cup chocolate chips, M&M's, crushed candy bar, or miniature marshmallows
1 cup whipping cream
¼ cup powdered hot cocoa mix

Have your child mix the butter with 1½ cups of cookie crumbs and press them into a 9-inch pie pan. Freeze the piecrust for 20 minutes. Spread half the ice cream on the bottom of the chilled crust. Let your child dig 8 holes in the ice cream and fill each with a tablespoon of fudge. Return the pan to the freezer for 10 minutes or until the fudge is firm. Stir the chocolate chips, candy, or marshmallows into the remaining ice cream and spread it over the pie. Return the pie to the freezer.

Beat the cream with an electric mixer until it thickens. Add the cocoa mix and beat it for 2 more minutes or until it's stiff. Spread the whipped topping evenly over the pie. Sprinkle it with the remaining cookie crumbs, then cover the pie with plastic wrap and freeze it for at least 3 hours. This pie serves 6–8 people.

Fruit Kebabs

Apples or bananas, cut in chunks
Lemon juice
Strawberries or pitted cherries
Blueberries
Wooden skewers

Sprinkle the apple or banana chunks with lemon juice to keep them from turning brown. Let your child arrange the fruit on wooden skewers in a red, white, and blue pattern. Serve the skewers with fruit dip. (See page 118.)

Patriotic T-Shirts

Paintbrush
Red and blue fabric paint
White T-shirt

Scissors
Red and blue plastic pony beads

Let your child paint a phrase like *Happy Independence Day!* or a picture of a flag or fireworks on the shirt.

Cut a fringe around the bottom of the shirt. Have your child thread red and blue beads on each strip. Tie an overhand knot at the bottom of each strip to secure the beads.

Frisbee Golf

Boxes, sticks, rocks, and so on
Markers or index cards
One Frisbee or gallon ice cream pail lid per player
Pen or pencil
Paper

Set up a Frisbee golf course using boxes, sticks, rocks, and so on as "holes." Number the holes consecutively by writing on them or attaching numbered index cards to them. Number each Frisbee as well and give one to each player.

Have the players take turns throwing their Frisbees at the first hole. Tell the players whether their Frisbees must land in the hole (if it's a box) or on it (if it's a stick or rock). Count and record how many throws it takes each player to get her Frisbee to the hole. When all the players have completed the first hole, move on to the second. Continue playing this way until all the players have completed the course. The player with the lowest score at the end of the course is the winner.

HALLOWEEN (OCTOBER 31)

Halloween began in ancient times, and there is great debate over the origins of various aspects of the celebration. One thing is certain, however: People in Europe and North America have celebrated Halloween for many centuries.

If any of the stories, imagery, and/or customs surrounding Halloween bother you, you can still enjoy the holiday by focusing on its seasonal aspects. Many churches and community centers host fall carnivals or Halloween parties where children can play games, eat food, and have fun together while avoiding the dangers associated with trick-or-treating. If you want to have a small Halloween party yourself, encourage guests to dress in fun (not frightening) costumes. Make simple crafts, play a few games together, then decorate and eat some Halloween cookies, cupcakes, or other treats.

Recommended Reading

It's Halloween by Jack Prelutsky
Halloween Is... by Gail Gibbons
The Witch Family by Eleanor Estes

Spider Bread

1 package active dry yeast
1 cup warm water
⅓ cup dry powdered milk
¼ cup sugar
¼ cup softened margarine

1 teaspoon salt
1 egg
3½ cups flour
Milk

In a large bowl, dissolve the yeast in ¼ cup of warm water. Mix in the remaining water and other ingredients except the milk until the dough is smooth. Cover the dough and let it rise in a warm place for 1 hour. Stir the dough. Cover it and let it rise again for 30 minutes. Divide the dough into 6 pieces. Each piece will make one spider.

For each spider, have your child roll half a piece of dough into a ball shaped body. Set it on a greased baking sheet. Have your child make eyes and legs with the rest of the dough and press or pinch them onto the body. Brush the spiders with milk. Preheat your oven to 400°F. Let the spiders rise for 20 minutes, then bake them for 12–15 minutes.

Pumpkin Cookies

These are ideal for pumpkin pie lovers!

½ cup softened margarine
¾ cup brown sugar
1 egg
1 teaspoon vanilla extract
1 cup canned pumpkin
2 cups flour

1 teaspoon baking soda
1 teaspoon ground cinnamon
1 teaspoon ground nutmeg
½ teaspoon ground ginger
1 cup raisins (optional)

Preheat your oven to 350°F.

Help your child beat the margarine and sugar with an electric mixer in a large bowl until the mixture is smooth. Beat in the egg, vanilla, and pumpkin until the batter is smooth. Add the remaining ingredients and stir them just until they're mixed.

Let your child drop the batter onto greased baking sheets with a spoon. Space the cookies about 1 inch apart. Bake them for 15 minutes. Remove them from the baking sheets and let them cool on a wire rack.

This recipe makes about 3 dozen cookies.

Pumpkin Punch

1 cup canned pumpkin
1 cup brown sugar
1 teaspoon ground cinnamon
½ teaspoon each ground
  ginger and nutmeg

½ cup orange juice
4 cups vanilla ice cream
Cleaned-out pumpkin shell
  (optional)

Help your child mix all the ingredients in a blender until the mixture is smooth. Serve the punch immediately. If you like, pour it into a cleaned-out pumpkin shell.

Pumpkin-Painting Party

Invite your child's friends over for a pumpkin-painting party. Tell the kids to wear old clothing or provide an art smock or old T-shirt for each child.

One small pumpkin per child
Permanent markers or paintbrushes and acrylic paints
Camera

Give each child a pumpkin and markers or a paintbrush and paints in several colors. Display the finished pumpkins, photograph them, then let each child take her creation home.

Scarecrow Contest

Old clothing
Prize (optional)

Hold a scarecrow contest with the families in your neighborhood. Provide old clothing and have the children dress up like
scarecrows. Decide ahead of time how the winner will be chosen: Perhaps you'll appoint several judges, or maybe each par-
ticipant will vote for her favorite scarecrow. If you like, before
the contest have each family contribute a few dollars toward
the purchase of a prize for the winner.

Halloween Whatsit

Marker
Several sheets of paper
Hat, box, or other container

Write a different Halloween word on each sheet of paper. Fold each sheet several times to conceal the word on it. Put all the folded sheets of paper in a container.

Choose one player to be the guesser. The guesser stands at the front of the room facing the other players; the rest of the players sit facing the guesser. The guesser closes her eyes, picks a sheet of paper from the container, and hands it to you. You stand behind the child, unfold the paper, and hold it up so the seated players can read the word, but the guesser can't. The guesser may open her eyes but may not look at the word.

The guesser then tries to guess the word by asking only yes-or-no questions. For example, if the word is *pumpkin*, the guesser may ask, "Is it something to eat?" but she may not ask, "What color is it?" The guesser may ask up to twelve questions before she makes a guess. If she guesses correctly, she gets to try guessing another word. If she guesses incorrectly, choose another player to be the guesser and start over with a new word. Continue playing until each child has had a turn as the guesser.

THANKSGIVING (DATE VARIES)

The first Thanksgiving celebration was held by the Pilgrims after their first harvest in 1621. Although many of the original settlers died that first year, the remaining Pilgrims were grateful for the abundance of their harvest and invited their Native American neighbors to join in their three-day feast.

Thanksgiving celebrations today usually include a huge family meal of roast turkey with all the trimmings. The sheer abundance of food on the table makes this an excellent time to encourage a spirit of thankfulness in your child. Talk with your child about things for which you both are thankful.

You can also use Thanksgiving to encourage a giving spirit in your child and make a positive impact on your community. Donate canned food to a food bank. Set aside good, usable clothing and toys and take them to a local relief agency. Bake a plate of cookies or other treats for homebound friends or community workers. Invite someone who is alone to share your Thanksgiving celebration. Your child will learn just how good it can feel to share her blessings with others!

Recommended Reading
A Pioneer Thanksgiving by Barbara Greenwood
The Thanksgiving Story by Alice Dalgliesh
Turkeys, Pilgrims, and Indian Corn: The Story of the Thanksgiving Symbols by Edna Barth

Cranberry Shapes

Canned jellied cranberry sauce
Small cookie cutters in Thanksgiving shapes

Open the can and remove the contents in one piece. Cut it into slices ¼ to ½ inch thick. Let your child cut shapes from the slices with cookie cutters and arrange the shapes on a plate. Serve the cranberry shapes at Thanksgiving dinner. Serve the scraps with the next day's leftovers.

Hot Cranberry Punch

½ cup brown sugar
4 cups water
½ teaspoon each ground
cinnamon, allspice, cloves,
and nutmeg

Two 16-ounce cans jellied
cranberry sauce
4 cups unsweetened
pineapple juice

Have your child mix the sugar, 1 cup of water, and spices in a large saucepan. Bring the mixture to a boil, then reduce the heat. Simmer the mixture over medium heat until the sugar dissolves. Turn off the heat and whisk in the cranberry sauce. Have your child stir in the rest of the water and the juice. Reheat the punch before serving it. This recipe makes 2 quarts of punch.

Turkey Treats

One 15-ounce package
  prepared piecrusts
Turkey-shaped cookie cutter

½ cup sugar
2 tablespoons cinnamon

Preheat your oven to 450°F. Unfold the piecrusts on wax paper. Let your child cut shapes from the pastry with the cookie cutter. Mix the sugar and cinnamon and sprinkle the mixture over the shapes. Transfer them to an ungreased baking sheet and bake them for 8–10 minutes. Remove them from the baking sheet and let them cool on a wire rack. This recipe makes about 16 turkey treats.

Thanksgiving Journal

Pen
Blank journal or notebook

Camera

Sometime on Thanksgiving Day, have each family member record what she's thankful for in the journal or notebook. If you like, describe your celebration, the names of guests, the foods you ate, and so on. Take a photo of everyone at the dinner table and glue it into your memory book. Bring out your journal each Thanksgiving. Have fun recalling past celebrations and adding new material.

Pilgrim Hats

Utility knife
10-ounce paper cups
Scissors
Black and white paper
Glue

Any circular item about 4
  inches in diameter
Pen, pencil, or marker
Popcorn, candy, or other
  treats

For each hat, cut the bottom out of a cup with a utility knife. Cut black paper to fit around the outside of the cup, then glue it in place. Have your child trace a 4-inch circle on black paper. Cut the circle out, then glue it onto the rim of the cup to make the hat's brim. Turn the hat brim side down. Cut a strip of white paper ½ inch wide and long enough to wrap around the cup at the brim. If you like, write the name of a dinner guest on the strip of white paper. Glue the strip in place just above the brim.

Fill each hat with treats and place it at a place setting.

Alphabet Game

Marker
26 index cards

Write each letter of the alphabet on a separate index card. (If you like, omit the tough letters like *Q*, *X*, and *Z*.) Shuffle the cards.

Choose one player to be the caller. The caller chooses a card and holds it up or announces the letter. The first player to call out a Thanksgiving word that begins with that letter (for example, *turkey* for the letter *T* or *pumpkin* for the letter *P*) wins the card. Continue playing this way until all the cards have been won. The winner is the player who has the most cards at the end of the game.

Variation
Award a small treat, toy, or coin as each item is named and shuffle the card back into the deck. If a letter comes up more than once, players must come up with a different word each time.

HANUKKAH (DATES VARY)

Hanukkah, the most joyous and festive of Jewish holidays, lasts eight days and takes place in December—sometimes early and sometimes late in the month.

The Hebrew word *hanukkah* means "dedication." Hanukkah was first celebrated more than two thousand years ago. It commemorates a time when the temple in Jerusalem had been restored and was about to be rededicated. Only one day's supply of oil for the holy lamps was found, but the lamps miraculously burned for eight days! This is why Hanukkah is also called the Festival of Lights and why the main focus of the celebration is the lighting of candles. A menorah, a special nine-branch candleholder, is used each day throughout the celebration.

Every year, families gather to light the Hanukkah menorah, remember their ancestors' historic struggle for religious freedom, recite prayers of thanks, exchange gifts, eat special foods, play games, and retell the story of Hanukkah.

Recommended Reading
The Golem's Latkes by Eric A. Kimmel
An Adventure in Latkaland: A Hanukkah Story by Karen Fisman
Chanukah Lights Everywhere by Michael J. Rosen

Patchwork Star of David

Scissors
Cardboard
Pencil

Fabric scraps in contrasting
  colors
Glue
Ribbon or trim (optional)

Cut a triangle from the cardboard. The triangle should have 3 equal sides, each about 1½ inches long. Trace the triangle on fabric scraps and cut out 12 triangles.

On a piece of cardboard, have your child arrange 6 of the fabric triangles to form the points of a Star of David. (The bases of the triangles join to form an empty hexagon in the middle.) Glue the triangles in place. Fill in the middle hexagon with the remaining fabric triangles and glue them in place.

Carefully cut around the outline of the star. If you like, glue a length of ribbon or trim along each side of the middle hexagon. Glue a small loop of ribbon onto the back of the star for hanging.

Cheese Fritters

Because oil is an important part of the Hanukkah story, eating foods cooked in oil is customary during Hanukkah. Hot oil can be quite hazardous, so insist on frying these fritters yourself while your child is occupied elsewhere. (For safety's sake, use a sealed deep fryer if possible.) Your child will enjoy helping you make the batter and sprinkling the fritters with powdered sugar.

1 cup drained cottage
  cheese
1 egg
¼ cup light cream
1 cup all-purpose flour
1¾ teaspoons baking
  powder

¼ teaspoon salt
2 tablespoons white sugar
1 teaspoon ground nutmeg
Vegetable oil
Powdered sugar
Jam

Beat the cottage cheese and egg in a medium bowl. Stir in the cream, flour, baking powder, salt, sugar and nutmeg until the ingredients are just mixed.

Fill a deep fryer or pot with 2 inches of oil. Heat the oil to 375°F. Drop the batter by rounded tablespoons into the oil. Fry the fritters for 3–4 minutes or until they're golden brown on all sides. Drain the fritters on paper towels and sprinkle them with powdered sugar. Serve them hot with jam on the side. This recipe makes 10 fritters.

Sufganiyot

Hot oil is hazardous, so fry these doughnuts yourself while your child is busy elsewhere. (Use a sealed deep fryer if possible.) Your child will enjoy helping you make the dough and rolling the doughnuts in powdered sugar.

2½ cups flour
2 cups hot milk
2 ounces active dry yeast
¼ cup lukewarm milk
2 eggs and 1 extra yolk
⅔ cup granulated sugar

1 teaspoon vanilla
1 teaspoon lemon rind
½ cup butter
¼ cup jam
Vegetable oil
Powdered sugar

Sift 1 cup of flour into the hot milk, beat the mixture until it's smooth, then let it cool. Dissolve the yeast in the lukewarm milk. Mix the yeast mixture into the flour mixture and let it sit for about 30 minutes. Mix the eggs, sugar, vanilla, and lemon rind into the dough. Stir in the butter and the remaining flour. Knead the dough well. Cover it with a damp towel and set it in a warm place to rise until it doubles in size (about 45 minutes). Roll the dough into 2-inch balls. If you like, use a cake decorator to insert 1 teaspoon of jam into each doughnut. Let the doughnuts rise again for about 30 minutes. Fill a deep fryer or pot with 2 inches of oil. Heat the oil to 375°F. Fry the doughnuts in the oil until they're brown on both sides. Drain them on paper towels and roll them in powdered sugar. This recipe makes 12 doughnuts.

Dreidel

A dreidel is a small spinning top used to play Hanukkah games. Follow these directions to make your own dreidel. Dreidel games appear on the next page.

*Single-serving milk or
    juice carton
Tape
Plain paper*

*Pen or marker
Scissors
¼-inch dowel or unsharpened
    pencil*

Flatten the top of the carton and tape it down securely. Cover the carton with plain paper. On each side, write one of the letters *N, G, H,* and *S* or the following Hebrew characters:

Shin   Hay   Gimel   Noon
שׁ   ה   ג   נ

These characters are the first letters in the four words of the Hebrew message *nes gadol hayah sham,* which means "A great miracle happened there." (Hebrew characters are read from right to left.)

    Poke a small hole in the centers of the top and bottom of the carton and push the dowel or pencil through both holes to make a spinning top.

Dreidel Games

Dreidel (page 381)
Pennies, dry beans, raisins, or other tokens

Distribute the tokens evenly among the players. Each player puts one token into the center, making a pile called the pot. The players take turns spinning the dreidel. The letter that lands faceup determines what the player does:

נ or *N:* The player does nothing.

ג or *G:* The player takes the pot, and everyone puts in one more token before the next player spins.

ה or *H:* The player takes half the pot.

ש or *S:* The player puts one token in the pot.

Whenever the pot is empty or contains only one token, every player puts in one token before the next player spins. The game is over when one player has won all the tokens and everyone else has nothing.

Variation
Hebrew characters also have number values. נ is fifty, ג is three, ה is five, and ש is three hundred. When a player spins the dreidel, she wins the number of points corresponding to the Hebrew letter that lands faceup.

CHRISTMAS (DECEMBER 25)

Christmas is a time when Christians celebrate the birth of Jesus Christ. For some, Christmas means the arrival of Santa Claus, Father Christmas, Père Noël, or Saint Nicholas. Christmas celebrations usually emphasize family togetherness, thoughtful and loving acts, and good food.

But Christmas often brings more than just peace, joy, love, and goodwill. For adults, Christmas can be frenzied, stressful, and financially demanding. Unrealistic expectations can make it hard to truly enjoy the season. Add too many late nights and too much rich food, and it's no wonder that we often breathe a sigh of relief when Christmas is over!

The best way to make the most of your Christmas is to forget what everyone else is doing and concentrate on what matters most to your family. Spend your time, money, and energy on activities that build or uphold family traditions and make memories for your child. Don't forget simple pleasures like reading, singing carols, making crafts, baking cookies, taking walks, and sipping hot chocolate together. Your child needs your time and attention more than anything. She'll soon forget toys and other things, but she won't forget the memories you've made together.

Recommended Reading
The Best Christmas Pageant Ever by Barbara Robinson
The Family under the Bridge by Natalie Savage Carlson
The Gift of the Magi by O. Henry
The Little Match Girl by Hans Christian Andersen

Candy Advent Calendar

Ornamental frosting (page 409)
Matte board, poster board, or heavy cardboard
Markers, stickers, rubber stamps, or old Christmas cards
Plastic knife
Small bowl
Wrapped Christmas candy
Scissors
Ribbon

Make a batch of ornamental frosting. Draw an Advent calendar for your child on a sheet of matte board, poster board, or cardboard.

Have your child decorate her calendar with drawings, stickers, rubber stamps, or pictures cut from old Christmas cards. Then give your child a plastic knife and a small bowl of frosting. Let her spread frosting on pieces of wrapped candy and stick one candy to each space on the calendar. Lay the calendar flat until the frosting sets, then poke a hole in the top and tie a loop of ribbon to it for hanging.

Hang the calendar up and let your child remove a candy each day of Advent as a tasty reminder of the number of days until Christmas.

Christmas Card Magnets

Scissors
Old Christmas cards
Self-adhesive magnetic strip

Help your child cut images from old Christmas cards. Cut small pieces of magnetic strip and attach one to the back of each cutout. Use the magnets to decorate your refrigerator or bring them with a baking sheet when you're traveling.

Cinnamon Ornament

Glue gun
6–7 cinnamon sticks
2 feet red ribbon
Scissors
Small sprig of holly or other greenery

Glue 2 cinnamon sticks together. Glue the remaining cinnamon sticks one at a time to make a little bundle.

Let your child knot the ribbon around the middle of the bundle and tie the ends of the ribbon into a loop for hanging. Trim the ends if necessary. Tuck the sprig of holly or other greenery under the ribbon knot.

Strawberry Ornament

*Large whole walnuts in the
  shell
Paintbrushes
Red and black acrylic paint
Scissors
Ruler*

*Green felt
4 inches thin gold cord or
  ribbon
Glue gun
Magnet (optional)*

Have your child paint a walnut red. When the paint is dry, use a very fine brush to paint tiny black dots all over the walnut. Cut a 1½-inch square of green felt. Then cut a 4-pointed star from the felt. Poke a small hole in the center of the star. Glue the ends of the cord or ribbon onto one end of the walnut shell to make a hanging loop. Slip the felt star over the loop and glue it onto the walnut. Voilà—a strawberry!

Variation
Omit the cord or ribbon and glue a small magnet onto one side of the walnut.

Reader's Digest
Christmas Tree

Old copy of Reader's Digest   *Green, gold, silver, or white*
Tape or stapler   *spray paint*

Beginning with the first page of the magazine, fold down the top corner so the top edge meets the binding. Sharply crease the fold. Let your child fold all the remaining pages in the same way. Fold the front and back covers last. Tape or staple them together so the pages fan out to make a tree shape. Spray-paint the tree.

Chocolate Mints

8 ounces white or semisweet baking chocolate
1 cup crushed peppermint candy canes

Lightly grease a large, shallow pan. Break the chocolate into small pieces and heat it in a double boiler until it's almost melted. Turn off the heat and stir it until it's melted. Let your child stir in the candy canes and spread the mixture in the pan. Refrigerate it for 30 minutes or until it's hard. Break the chocolate into small pieces and store it covered in the refrigerator. Fill a new coffee mug with chocolate mints and wrap it with cellophane and ribbon for a quick, easy, and delicious gift for chocolate lovers.

Hot Cocoa Mix

1 cup cocoa powder
2½ cups powdered sugar

2 cups dry coffee creamer
1 cup nonfat milk powder

Have your child mix all the ingredients in a large bowl. Store the mix in a Ziploc bag, Christmas tins, or pretty canning jars. Cut a circle of Christmas fabric and tie it over a jar lid with ribbon. If you're giving the mix as a gift, attach a gift tag or card with serving instructions: "To serve, put 3 tablespoons of mix in a mug. Stir in ¾ cup boiling water."

Glazed Spiced Nuts

1 egg white, slightly beaten mon
¼ cup sugar

1 tablespoon ground cinnamon
2 cups pecan or walnut halves

Preheat your oven to 300°F. Have your child mix the egg, sugar, and cinnamon well. Stir in the nuts until they're completely coated. Spread the nuts on an ungreased baking sheet, separating them to prevent clumps. Bake the nuts for 20 minutes or until they're light brown. If you like, package the nuts
in Christmas tins or pretty canning jars. Cut a circle of Christmas fabric and tie it over a jar lid with ribbon.

Ginger Crinkles

1 cup soft butter
1¾ cups sugar
1 large egg
2 tablespoons dark corn
  syrup
½ cup mild molasses
3 cups flour

2 teaspoons baking soda
2 teaspoons ground cinnamon
1 teaspoon ground ginger
¼ teaspoon ground cloves
½ teaspoon salt
White chocolate (optional)

Preheat your oven to 375°F.

Help your child beat the butter, 1½ cups sugar, egg, corn syrup, and molasses with an electric mixer on low speed until they're blended. Then beat them on medium speed until the mixture is smooth.

Have your child stir in the flour, baking soda, cinnamon, ginger, cloves, and salt until they're moistened, then roll the dough into 1½-inch balls.

Put the remaining sugar in a small bowl. Let your child roll the balls in the sugar one at a time until they're coated. Bake them on ungreased baking sheets for 12–14 minutes. (To make extra special cookies, dip the cookies in melted white chocolate.)

Store the cookies in a covered container. This recipe makes about 3 dozen cookies.

Caramel Cinnamon Rolls

Our Christmas morning wouldn't be complete without cinnamon rolls. If you like, you can make and freeze these ahead of time, then take them out to thaw on Christmas Eve and heat them up on Christmas morning.

½ cup brown sugar, packed
⅓ cup whipping cream
¼ cup chopped pecans
2 tablespoons granulated sugar
1 teaspoon ground cinnamon
One 11-ounce can bread stick dough

Preheat your oven to 350°F. Let your child mix the brown sugar and cream in an 8-inch round cake pan, then sprinkle the mixture with pecans and set it aside.

Mix the granulated sugar and cinnamon. Open the can and unroll the dough, but don't separate it into bread sticks. Have your child sprinkle the cinnamon-sugar mixture on it, then roll it up, starting at one of the short ends. Use a knife to slice the rolled-up dough at the cut marks. Lay the slices on top of the sauce in the pan.

Bake the rolls for 25 minutes or until they're golden brown. Let them cool for 1 minute, then turn the pan upside down onto a plate. Let the pan sit on top of the rolls for 1 minute to let the sauce drizzle over the rolls, then remove the pan. This recipe makes 6 rolls.

Beeswax Candle

Sheet of beeswax   *Utility knife*
Newspaper and wax paper   *Scissors*
Yardstick   *Candlewick*

Place the beeswax on newspaper covered with wax paper. Lay the yardstick so it bisects the wax diagonally. Cut the wax in half along the yardstick with a utility knife. Set aside half the wax. Each wax triangle will make 1 candle.

Turn the paper so the shortest edge of the wax triangle is near you. Cut a length of candlewick 2 inches longer than this edge. Lay the wick along this edge so a little wick sticks out beyond each end. Starting at this edge, help your child roll up the wax and press it into the wick. Work slowly so the warmth of her hands softens the wax. Continue rolling the wax, trying to keep the perpendicular edge (which will be the bottom of the candle) even. When you've finished, press the end of the wax triangle firmly into the candle. If the bottom of the candle is uneven, tap it gently on your work surface. Trim the wick to ½ inch at the top of the candle and cut off the wick at the bottom.

Balloon Game

This game helps use up extra energy indoors.

Scissors
Paper
Pen or pencil
Red and green balloons
Small candies or other prizes

Cut small strips of paper. On each strip write instructions like *sing a Christmas carol, jump up and down twenty-five times,* or *recite the first verse of "'Twas the Night before Christmas."* If you like, you can also write jokes, riddles, and tongue twisters. Roll up the strips and insert each into a balloon. Insert small candies or other prizes into other balloons. Blow up the balloons, tie the ends, and put them on the floor all around your home.

　　Have your child (or any Christmas guest) sit on the balloons and try to pop as many as she can, collecting the prizes and paper strips from the balloons as she pops them. When all the balloons have been popped, have the player(s) do the stunts (or tell the jokes, riddles, and tongue twisters) written on the strips of paper.

KWANZAA (DECEMBER 26–JANUARY 1)

Kwanzaa is a seven-day African-American cultural celebration. The Swahili word *kwanzaa* means "first fruit of the harvest," and the holiday is based on the traditional African winter harvest festival. During this time, African Americans reflect upon the year that's ending and celebrate their African heritage.

Kwanzaa begins the day after Christmas, but the two celebrations are very different. Kwanzaa celebrates the harvest and a way of life handed down by ancestors and parents. Special handmade gifts or educational games and books are exchanged, but Kwanzaa emphasizes values rather than gifts. Each day of the Kwanzaa week celebrates one of seven principles or values. These are unity, self-determination, collective work and responsibility, cooperative economics, purpose, creativity, and faith.

Recommended Reading
Celebrate Kwanzaa: With Candles, Community, and the Fruits of the Harvest by Carolyn B. Otto
The Story of Kwanzaa by Donna L. Washington

Kwanzaa Necklace

One of the symbols of Kwanzaa is *zawadi,* or gifts. A hand-made gift like this necklace is the most treasured.

1 cup flour
½ cup salt
¼ cup water
1 tablespoon oil
Toothpick

Acrylic paints
Clear acrylic spray
Fishing line, beading thread,
    or thin elastic cord

Help your child mix the flour, salt, water, and oil to make a smooth clay. Roll the clay into small beads. Poke a hole through each bead with a toothpick. Let the beads air-dry or bake them on a baking sheet at 350°F for 10 minutes.

Have your child paint the beads in the Kwanzaa colors of red, green, and black. Or if she likes, she can paint the beads to look like the hides of African animals: white with black stripes for a zebra, orange with black spots for a cheetah, and so on. Finish the beads with clear acrylic spray. String the beads on fishing line, beading thread, or thin elastic cord to make a necklace.

Kwanzaa Place Mat

Another Kwanzaa symbol is the *mkeka,* the mat upon which the other symbols are placed. Be sure to use a bold, expressive pattern and bright colors when you design your place mat. *(Kwanzaa Crafts* by Judith Hoffman Corwin contains pages of beautiful patterns you can copy.)

Scissors
White muslin
Ruler
Markers
White or black construction paper or poster board
Brightly colored paper (optional)
Glue
Clear contact paper

- To make a fabric mat, cut a piece of muslin about 12 by 18 inches. Have your child use markers to draw bold geometric patterns on the muslin.
- To make a paper mat, have your child draw bold geometric patterns on a sheet of white construction paper or poster board. Or if you like, have her cut geometric shapes from brightly colored paper and glue them onto the mat. For a dramatic effect, glue the shapes onto a black mat. Cover the place mat with clear contact paper.

Corn Muffins

Vibunzi, or dry ears of corn, are another symbol of Kwanzaa. They represent children and hope for the future. These delicious corn muffins are easy to make and taste great served with bacon, ham, chicken, or soup.

1 cup cornmeal
2 teaspoons baking powder
½ teaspoon baking soda
1 teaspoon salt
2 eggs
¼ cup corn oil
1 cup sour cream
1 cup creamed corn

Preheat your oven to 400°F. Grease a muffin pan.

In a large bowl, have your child mix the cornmeal, baking powder, baking soda, and salt. Stir in the eggs, oil, sour cream, and creamed corn until the ingredients are well mixed.

Spoon the batter into the pan. Bake the muffins for 20 minutes. Remove them from the pan and let them cool on a wire rack. This recipe makes about 10 medium muffins.

Variation
Bake the batter in a greased loaf pan instead. When the loaf of corn bread is cool, use a knife to slice it.

Peanut Cookies

George Washington Carver was a famous African-American scientist who developed many uses for the peanut. One of my favorite ways to use peanuts is in these delicious cookies.

1 cup peanut butter
1 cup butter
¾ cup brown sugar
¾ cup white sugar
2 eggs
2½ cups whole-wheat flour
2 teaspoons baking soda
1 cup chopped peanuts

Preheat your oven to 350°F.

Help your child cream the peanut butter, butter, and sugars with an electric mixer, then beat in the eggs. Have her mix the flour and baking soda in a separate bowl and gradually beat them into the creamed mixture. Stir in the peanuts just until they're blended.

Let your child roll the dough into walnut-size balls and place them on greased baking sheets. Flatten the balls with a fork. Bake the cookies for about 15 minutes.

This recipe makes about 6 dozen cookies.

Kwanzaa Brainteasers

Education is an important part of Kwanzaa. Here are some problems that will test your child's brainpower!

- One day Josh was running home with ten rocks in his pocket. As he ran, two rocks fell out, but he found three more and put those in his pocket. As he continued on his way, four more rocks fell out, but just before he got home, he found another rock and put that in his pocket. How many rocks did he have in his pocket when he got home? (Answer: eight.)

- Emily has fewer than twenty books. When she puts them in piles of two, she has one left. When she puts them in piles of three, she has none left. When she puts them in piles of four, she has three left. How many books does Emily have? (Answer: fifteen.)

- A hamburger and a soda cost one dollar and seventy-five cents. Two hamburgers and a soda cost three dollars. How much does a soda cost? (Answer: fifty cents.)

- When two people shake hands, there's one handshake between them. When three people shake hands, how many handshakes will there be? (Answer: three.) What about when four people shake hands? (Answer: six.) Five people? (Answer: ten.)

- Old McDonald raises chickens and pigs. The animals have a total of ten heads and twenty-eight feet. How many chickens and how many pigs does Old McDonald have? (Answer: six chickens and four pigs.)

APPENDIX A
Basic Craft Recipes

Children begin to develop creative skills at a very early age. Most don't care as much about what they make as about the process of working with materials of many different colors and textures. Whether it's the process or the product that interests your child, the craft materials in this appendix are essential for his artwork. On the following pages you'll find easy recipes for paint, glue, paste, modeling compounds, and more.

PAINT

Each of the following recipes will produce a good-quality paint for your child's use. The ingredients and preparation vary from recipe to recipe, so choose one that best suits the supplies and time you have available.

When mixing paint, keep in mind the age of your young artist. As a general rule, younger children require thicker paint and brushes. Paint should always be stored in covered containers. Small plastic spillproof paint containers are available at art supply stores. Each comes with an airtight lid, holds brushes upright without tipping, and is well worth the purchase price of several dollars.

Flour-Based Poster Paint

¼ cup flour	*3 tablespoons powdered tempera*
Saucepan	*paint per container*
1 cup water	*2 tablespoons water per container*
Small jars or plastic containers	*½ teaspoon liquid starch or liquid*
	detergent per container (optional)

Measure the flour into a saucepan. Slowly add 1 cup of water while stirring the mixture to make a smooth paste. Heat the paste, stirring constantly, until it begins to thicken. Let it cool. Measure ¼ cup of the paste into each container. Add 3 tablespoons of powdered tempera paint and 2 tablespoons of water to each container. If you like, add liquid starch for a matte finish or liquid detergent for a glossy finish.

Cornstarch Paint

½ cup cornstarch
Medium saucepan
½ cup cold water
4 cups boiling water

Small jars or plastic containers
1 teaspoon powdered tempera paint
or 1 tablespoon liquid tempera
paint per container

Measure the cornstarch into a saucepan. Add the cold water and stir the mixture to make a smooth, thick paste. Stir in the boiling water. Place the saucepan over medium-low heat and stir the paste until it's boiling. Boil the paste for 1 minute, then remove it from the heat and let it cool. Spoon about ½ cup of the paste into each container. Stir 1 teaspoon of powdered tempera paint or 1 tablespoon of liquid tempera paint into each container, using a different container for each color. (Use more paint for a more intense color.) If the paint is too thick, stir in 1 teaspoon of water at a time until the desired consistency is achieved. Cover the containers and refrigerate them for storage.

Detergent Poster Paint

Small jars or plastic containers
1 tablespoon clear liquid
detergent per container

2 teaspoons powdered tempera
paint per container

In each container, mix 1 tablespoon of detergent and 2 teaspoons of powdered paint. Use a different container for each color.

Edible Egg Yolk Paint

Small jars or plastic containers
1 egg yolk per container

¼ teaspoon water per container
Food coloring

In each container, mix 1 egg yolk with ¼ teaspoon of water and many drops of food coloring. Use a paintbrush to apply paint to freshly baked cookies. Return cookies to the warm oven until the paint hardens.

Cornstarch Finger Paint

3 tablespoons sugar
½ cup cornstarch
Medium saucepan
2 cups cold water

Muffin pan or small cups
Food coloring
Soap flakes or liquid detergent

Mix the sugar and cornstarch in a saucepan. Turn the heat on low, add the water, and stir the mixture constantly until it's thick. Remove it from the heat. Spoon the mixture into 4–5 muffin pan sections or small cups. Add a few drops of food coloring and a pinch of soap flakes or a drop of liquid detergent to each cup. Stir the paint and let it cool before use. Cover the paint and refrigerate it for storage.

Flour Finger Paint

1 cup flour
2 tablespoons salt
Saucepan
1½ cups cold water

Wire whisk or eggbeater
1¼ cups hot water
Food coloring or powdered tempera
  paint

Mix the flour and salt in a saucepan. Beat in the cold water until the mixture is smooth. Mix in the hot water and boil the mixture until it's thick, then beat it again until it's smooth. Tint the paint however you like with food coloring or powdered tempera paint. Cover the paint and refrigerate it for storage.

PLAY DOUGH

Each of the following recipes produces a good-quality play dough. Some require cooking and some don't; some are meant to be eaten and some aren't. Choose the recipe that best suits your needs and the ingredients you have on hand. Store play dough in a covered container or Ziploc bag. If it sweats a little, just add more flour. For sensory variety, warm or chill the play dough before use.

Oatmeal Play Dough

Your child will be able to make this play dough with little help, but it doesn't last as long as cooked play dough. This play dough isn't meant to be eaten, but it won't hurt a child who decides to taste it.

1 part flour   *2 parts oatmeal*
1 part water   *Bowl*

Place all the ingredients in a bowl; mix them well and knead the dough until it's smooth. Cover the play dough and refrigerate it for storage.

Uncooked Play Dough

Bowl   *Tempera paint or food coloring*
1 cup cold water   *3 cups flour*
1 cup salt   *2 tablespoons cornstarch*
2 teaspoons vegetable oil

In a bowl, mix the water, salt, oil, and enough tempera paint or food coloring to make a brightly colored mixture. Gradually blend in the flour and cornstarch until the mixture has the consistency of bread dough.

Peanut Butter Play Dough

2 cups peanut butter
6 tablespoons honey
Nonfat dry milk or milk
  plus flour
Bowl

Cocoa or carob powder (optional)
Edible decorations like chocolate
  chips, raisins, candy sprinkles,
  and colored sugar

Mix the first 3 ingredients in a bowl, using enough dry milk or milk plus flour to give the mixture the consistency of bread dough. Flavor the dough with cocoa or carob powder if you like. Shape the dough, decorate it with edible treats, and eat your artwork!

Salt Play Dough

1 cup salt
1 cup water

½ cup plus additional flour
Saucepan

Mix the salt, water, and ½ cup of flour in a saucepan. Stir and cook the mixture over medium heat. Remove it from the heat when it's thick and rubbery. As the mixture cools, knead in enough additional flour to make the dough workable.

Colored Play Dough

Cream of tartar makes this play dough last 6 months or longer, so resist the temptation to omit this ingredient if you don't have it on hand.

1 cup water
1 tablespoon vegetable oil
½ cup salt
1 tablespoon cream of tartar

Food coloring
Saucepan
1 cup flour

Mix the water, oil, salt, cream of tartar, and a few drops of food coloring in a saucepan and heat the mixture until it's warm. Remove the mixture from the heat and stir in the flour. Knead the dough until it's smooth.

403

Kool-Aid Play Dough

This dough will last 2 months or longer.

½ cup salt
2 cups water
Saucepan
Food coloring, powdered tempera
* paint, or Kool-Aid powder*

2 tablespoons vegetable oil
2 cups sifted flour
2 tablespoons alum

Mix the salt and water in a saucepan and boil the mixture until the salt dissolves. Remove the mixture from the heat and tint it with food coloring, powdered tempera paint, or Kool-Aid powder. Add the oil, flour, and alum. Knead the dough until it's smooth.

CLAY

Use the following recipes to make clay that can be rolled or shaped into sculptures. Some clays should be dried overnight, while others are best baked in an oven. When hard, sculptures can be decorated with paint, markers, and/or glitter and preserved with shellac, acrylic spray, or clear nail polish. Store leftover clay in a covered container or Ziploc bag. Please note that none of these clays is edible.

Modeling Clay

2 cups salt
⅔ cup water
Saucepan

1 cup cornstarch
½ cup cold water

Stir the salt and ⅔ cup of water in a saucepan over heat for 4–5 minutes. Remove the mixture from the heat. Blend in the cornstarch and cold water until the mixture is smooth. Return it to the heat and cook it until it's thick. Let the clay cool, then shape it however you like. Let your sculpture dry overnight before decorating and finishing it.

Baker's Clay

4 cups flour
1 cup salt
1 teaspoon alum
1½ cups water
Large bowl

Food coloring (optional)
Rolling pin, cookie cutters, drinking
   straw, and fine wire (optional)
Baking sheet
Fine sandpaper

Preheat your oven to 250°F. Mix the flour, salt, alum, and water in a bowl. If the clay is too dry, knead in another tablespoon of water. If you like, tint the clay by dividing it and kneading a few drops of food coloring into each portion. Shape the clay however you like. To make hanging ornaments, roll or mold the clay as follows, then attach a loop of fine wire to each ornament.

- **To roll:** Roll the clay ⅛ inch thick on a lightly floured surface. Cut it with cookie cutters dipped in flour. Make a hole for hanging the ornament by dipping the end of a drinking straw in flour and using the straw to cut a tiny hole ¼ inch from the ornament's edge. You can also use the straw to cut out clay dots for press-on decorations.
- **To mold:** Shape the clay into flowers, fruits, animals, and so on. The figures should be no more than ½ inch thick.

Bake your sculpture(s) on an ungreased baking sheet for about 30 minutes. Turn and bake them for another 90 minutes until they're hard and dry. Remove them from the oven and let them cool, then smooth them with fine sandpaper before decorating and finishing them.

No-Bake Craft Clay

Food coloring (optional)
1¼ cups cold water
1 cup cornstarch
2 cups baking soda

Saucepan
Plate
Damp cloth

If you want tinted clay, mix a few drops of food coloring into the water. Then mix the water, cornstarch, and baking soda in a saucepan over medium heat for about 4 minutes until the mixture has the consistency of moist mashed potatoes. Remove the mixture from the heat, turn it onto a plate, and cover it with a damp cloth until it's cool. Knead the clay until it's smooth, then shape it however you like. Let your sculpture dry overnight before decorating and finishing it.

No-Bake Cookie Clay

2 cups salt
⅔ cup water
Medium saucepan
1 cup cornstarch

½ cup cold water
Rolling pin, cookie cutter, drinking
straw, and fine wire (optional)

Mix the salt and ⅔ cup of water in a medium saucepan and boil the mixture until the salt dissolves. Remove it from the heat. Stir in the cornstarch and cold water. If the mixture doesn't thicken right away, heat and stir it until it does, then let it cool. Shape the clay however you like. To make hanging ornaments, follow the instructions on page 405. Let your sculpture(s) dry overnight before decorating and finishing them.

GLUE AND PASTE

The following recipes use a variety of ingredients, and the resulting glues and pastes have a variety of uses. Choose the one that best suits your project. For fun, add food coloring to glue or paste before using it. Cover and refrigerate all glues and pastes for storage.

Glue

¾ cup water
2 tablespoons corn syrup
1 teaspoon white vinegar
Small saucepan

Small bowl
2 tablespoons cornstarch
¾ cup cold water

Mix ¾ cup of water, corn syrup, and vinegar in a saucepan. Bring the mixture to a full rolling boil. In a small bowl, mix the cornstarch and cold water. Stir this mixture slowly into the hot mixture until it begins to boil again. Boil the mixture for 1 minute, then remove it from the heat. When it's cooled slightly, pour it into another container and let it stand overnight before you use it.

Homemade Paste

This wet, messy paste takes a while to dry.

⅛ cup flour   *Cold water*
Saucepan

Measure the flour into a saucepan. Stir in the water until the mixture is as thick as cream. Simmer the mixture, stirring constantly, for 5 minutes. Remove it from the heat and let it cool before you use it.

Papier-Mâché Paste

6 cups water   *¼ cup flour*
Saucepan   *Small bowl*

Lightly boil 5 cups of water in a saucepan. Measure the flour into a small bowl. Stir in 1 cup of water to make a runny mixture. Stir this mixture into the boiling water. Stir and gently boil the paste for 2–3 minutes. Let it cool before you use it.

No-Cook Paste

Water   *Bowl*
½ cup flour   *Salt*

Gradually mix water into the flour until the mixture is gooey. Stir in a pinch of salt.

OTHER CRAFT RECIPES

Use the following recipes to make interesting supplies for use in various arts-and-crafts projects.

Colorful Creative Salt

Use this salt as you would use glitter.

Small bowl	*½ cup salt*
5–6 drops food coloring	*Microwave or wax paper*

In a small bowl, stir the food coloring into the salt. Microwave the mixture for 1–2 minutes or spread it on wax paper and let it air-dry. Store the salt in an airtight container.

Dyed Pasta

½ cup rubbing alcohol	*Dry pasta*
Food coloring	*Newspaper and wax paper*
Small bowl	

Mix the alcohol and food coloring in a small bowl. Add small amounts of dry pasta to the liquid and mix it gently. The larger the pasta, the longer it will take to absorb the color. Dry the dyed pasta on newspaper covered with wax paper.

Dyed Eggs

Small bowls	*¾ cup hot water per bowl*
¼ teaspoon food coloring	*1 tablespoon white vinegar per bowl*
* per bowl*	*Hard-boiled eggs*

In each bowl, mix ¼ teaspoon food coloring, ¾ cup hot water, and 1 tablespoon white vinegar. Use a different bowl for each color. Soak hard-boiled eggs in the dyes. The longer you soak an egg, the more intense its color will be.

Ornamental Frosting

This frosting is an edible glue; use it for gingerbread houses or other food art. It can be made several hours or a day before you use it.

Electric mixer or eggbeater   *Bowl*
3 egg whites   *4 cups powdered sugar*
1 teaspoon cream of tartar

Beat the egg whites and cream of tartar in a bowl until stiff peaks form. Add the powdered sugar and continue beating the frosting until it's thick and holds its shape. Cover the frosting with a damp cloth when you're not using it. Store it in an airtight container in the refrigerator.

APPENDIX B
Crazy Can Activities

The following activities are suitable for a crazy can. (See page 11.) These activities require no special materials, need no time-consuming preparation or cleanup, and above all, demand minimal adult participation. Some require a little planning (for example, preparing lists in advance for the scavenger hunt). These activities will provide you with an instant remedy when things start to get crazy, or when there's just "nothing to do." The number following each activity refers to the page on which that activity is found.

APPENDIX C
Making Books with Children

Creating books with your child is fun to do and can be as simple or complex as you wish. Some home-schoolers spend weeks creating professional-looking bound books, but the process needn't be time consuming. If you like, you can simply staple sheets of paper inside a construction paper cover or use a small notebook, scrapbook, photo album, or three-ring binder with plastic sleeves. Print the story your child dictates (or let him print it himself) at the bottom of each page, then let your child illustrate the pages with his own artwork, photos, or pictures cut from magazines.

Making a bound book with your child takes a little more time, but the quality of the finished book makes it well worth the effort. The following instructions were adapted from the book *Parents Are Teachers, Too* by Claudia Jones.

Scissors
1 sheet construction paper
Up to 8 sheets plain white paper
  (8½ by 11 inches)
Sewing machine or needle and
  thread
Utility knife

Cardboard or matte board
Nonstretch fabric (at least 14 by 9
  inches)
Paintbrush
White glue thinned with water
Wax paper
Several heavy books

1. Cut the construction paper to 8½ by 11 inches. Stack up to 8 sheets of plain paper on top of the construction paper. Fold the whole stack in half, with the construction paper on the outside. Stitch along the fold with a sewing machine or needle and thread.

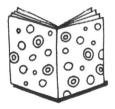

2. Use a utility knife or scissors to cut 2 pieces of cardboard or matte board each measuring 5½ by 6¾ inches. Lay the 2 pieces side by side about ¼ inch apart on the wrong side of a piece of non-stretch fabric. Trim the fabric, leaving a 1-inch border on all sides of the cardboard or matte board.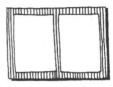

3. Paint a layer of watery white glue on 1 side of each piece of cardboard or matte board. Place the pieces of cardboard or matte board back in position (glue side down) on the fabric and press on them to glue them onto the fabric.

4. Brush glue on the 1-inch fabric border, then fold the fabric over onto the cardboard. Smooth out the edges of the fabric as best you can, but don't worry about them too much, as they will be covered up in the next step.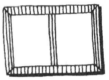

5. Open the paper booklet you made in step 1. Paint the entire outside surface of the construction paper cover with glue. Press the gluey construction paper onto the inside of the fabric-covered cardboard cover.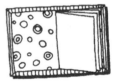

6. Place wax paper inside the front and back covers. Close the book and place more wax paper around the outside of the book. Then place it under a stack of heavy books so it will dry flat.

Illustrations for Appendix C by Terri Moll

412

APPENDIX D
Best Books for Children

The books listed on the following pages are suitable for children from six to ten years old, and many are loved by older children, too. This list includes a variety of books: picture books, books for beginning readers, chapter books, and novels. Your child will likely enjoy reading some of the books by himself, and he'll enjoy hearing others read aloud.

Keep in mind that this appendix is by no means a complete guide to the best authors and books for young children. An author listed may have written many titles, of which only one or two are noted. Other authors who have written excellent books are not listed at all. The purpose of this appendix is simply to suggest books you and your child may enjoy.

The books on this list are often recommended by experts in the field of children's literature. Our family has enjoyed many of them over the years, but that doesn't guarantee that your child will. The best way to determine what books your child will enjoy is to read children's books—lots of them. Read award-winners and award-losers. (Some of the best-loved books are runners-up!) Read books about children's books, too. In Appendix E (page 418) I've listed my favorite such books—ones that I've relied on for many years.

Give your child high-quality books for his birthday and other special occasions. Visit your local bookstore and browse the shelves of the children's section. But be cautious when asking for recommendations. Many clerks aren't knowledgeable about children's books, and they may simply recommend what everyone else is buying. That's not necessarily a bad thing, but bear in mind that today's buying trends tend to be based more on advertising and popular culture than on quality.

The librarians in the children's room of your library are excellent sources of information. They can usually make suggestions tailored to your child's reading ability and interests. The most popular books are usually checked out as soon as they are returned, so reserve them ahead of time if you can. If you have a computer with Internet access, you may be able to reserve books from home—a lifesaver for those who visit the library with small children! Alternatively, you could schedule an afternoon or evening to visit the library without children in tow and spend some time getting to know the best in old and new children's books.

Aesop
Aesop's Fables

Allard, Harry
Miss Nelson Is Missing!
The Stupids Step Out

Andersen, Hans Christian
The Little Match Girl

Atwater, Richard and Florence
Mr. Popper's Penguins

Babbitt, Natalie
Tuck Everlasting

Banks, Lynne Reid
The Indian in the Cupboard

Bemelmans, Ludwig
Madeline series

Brenner, Barbara
Wagon Wheels

Brink, Carol Ryrie
Caddie Woodlawn

Brunhoff, Jean de
The Story of Babar

Bulla, Clyde Robert
The Chalk Box Kid

Burningham, John
Borka
Harquin
Mr. Gumpy's Outing

Burton, Virginia Lee
Mike Mulligan and His Steam Shovel
The Little House

Byars, Betsy
The Summer of the Swans

Carlson, Natalie Savage
The Family under the Bridge

Cleary, Beverly
Ramona the Pest

Coerr, Eleanor
Sadako and the Thousand Paper Cranes

Cohen, Barbara
Molly's Pilgrim

D'Aulaire, Ingri and Edgar
D'Aulaires' Book of Greek Myths

Dahl, Roald
Charlie and the Chocolate Factory

Dalgliesh, Alice
  The Bears on Hemlock Mountain
  The Courage of Sarah Noble

dePaola, Tomie
  26 Fairmount Avenue

Estes, Eleanor
  The Hundred Dresses

Gardiner, John Reynolds
  Stone Fox

Gipson, Fred
  Old Yeller

Godden, Rumer
  The Mousewife

Grahame, Kenneth
  The Reluctant Dragon

Haywood, Carolyn
  "B" Is for Betsy
  Little Eddie

Henry, Marguerite
  Five O'clock Charlie

Henry, O.
  The Gift of the Magi

Holling, Holling Clancy
  Paddle-to-the-Sea

Isadora, Rachel
  Ben's Trumpet

Johnson, Crockett
  Ellen's Lion

Kinney, Jeff
  Diary of a Wimpy Kid

Lewis, C. S.
  *The Lion, the Witch and the
  Wardrobe* (and other books in
  the Chronicles of Narnia series)

Lindgren, Astrid
  Pippi Longstocking

Lobel, Arnold
  Frog and Toad Together

Lowry, Lois
  The Giver

Mills, Lauren
  The Rag Coat

Milne, A. A.
  The House at Pooh Corner
  Now We Are Six
  When We Were Very Young
  Winnie-the-Pooh

Minarik, Else Holmelund
  Little Bear

Mosel, Arlene
  The Funny Little Woman
  Tikki Tikki Tembo

Mowat, Farley
  Owls in the Family
  Two against the North (or *Lost in
  the Barrens*)

Munsch, Robert
Love You Forever
The Paper Bag Princess

Naylor, Phyllis Reynolds
Shiloh

Newberry, Clare Turlay
Marshmallow

Numeroff, Laura Joffe
If You Give a Mouse a Cookie

Parish, Peggy
Amelia Bedelia

Perrault, Charles
Cinderella

Polacco, Patricia
Just Plain Fancy

Potter, Beatrix
The Tale of Peter Rabbit

Rawls, Wilson
Where the Red Fern Grows

Rey, H. A.
Curious George series

Robinson, Barbara
The Best Christmas Pageant Ever

Rowling, J.K.
Harry Potter and the Sorcerer's Stone

Selden, George
The Cricket in Times Square

Sendak, Maurice
Where the Wild Things Are

Seuss, Dr.
The Cat in the Hat
The 500 Hats of Bartholomew Cubbins
Green Eggs and Ham

Sobol, Donald
Encyclopedia Brown series

Sorensen, Virginia
Miracles on Maple Hill

Speare, Elizabeth George
The Sign of the Beaver

Sperry, Armstrong
Call It Courage

Steig, William
The Amazing Bone
Brave Irene
Sylvester and the Magic Pebble

Stevenson, Robert Louis
A Child's Garden of Verses

Taylor, Mildred D.
Song of the Trees

Waber, Bernard
Lyle, Lyle, Crocodile
The House on East 88th Street

White, E. B.
Charlotte's Web
Stuart Little
The Trumpet of the Swan

Wilder, Laura Ingalls
Little House in the Big Woods
(and other books in the Little
House series)

Williams, Margery
The Velveteen Rabbit

Yolen, Jane
Owl Moon

Zion, Gene
Harry the Dirty Dog

APPENDIX E
Resources for Parents

The games, activities, and information that make up *The Children's Busy Book* are gleaned from years of parenting experience as well as from friends, family members, and other books and resources. The following titles will help you plan activities and find the best, most practical ideas and information.

Atwood, Lisa. *The Cookbook for Kids.* Weldon Owen, 2011.

Beginning American Sign Language VideoCourse. Sign Enhancers, 1992.

Benchley, Nathaniel. *Sam the Minuteman.* HarperCollins, 1987.

Bennett, Steve and Ruth. *365 TV-Free Activities You Can Do with Your Child.* Bob Adams, 1991.

Bledsoe, Karen E. *Hanukkah Crafts.* Enslow Elementary, 2004.

Block, Stanley. *Marble Mania.* Schiffer Publishing, 2011.

Bornstein, Harry and Karen L. Saulnier. *Nursery Rhymes from Mother Goose.* Gallaudet University Press, 1992.

Choron, Sandra and Harry. *The All-New Book of Lists for Kids.* Mariner Books, 2002.

Cole, Joanna. *Anna Banana.* HarperCollins, 1989.

Corwin, Judith Hoffman. *Kwanzaa Crafts.* Franklin Watts, 1995.

The Complete Book of Arts & Crafts. American Education Publishing, 2000.

Crocker, Betty. *Betty Crocker's Kids Cook!* Betty Crocker, 2007.

Dalgliesh, Alice. *The Thanksgiving Story.* Atheneum Books for Young Readers, 1988.

d'Aulaire, Ingri and Edgar. *Benjamin Franklin.* Beautiful Feet Books, 1998.

DePaola, Tomie. *Patrick: Patron Saint of Ireland.* Holiday House, 1994.

Ellison, Sheila and Judith Gray. *365 Foods Kids Love to Eat.* Sourcebooks, 2005.

Ellison, Sheila and Judith Gray. *365 Smart Afterschool Activities.* Sourcebooks, 2005.

Englehart, Steve. *Easter Parade.* Avon Books, 1995.

Fisman, Karen. *An Adventure in Latkaland: A Hanukkah Story.* Jora Books, 2010.

Freedman, Russell. *Out of Darkness: The Story of Louis Braille.* Houghton Mifflin Company, 1997.

Fritz, Jean. *Why Don't You Get a Horse, Sam Adams?* Puffin, 1996.

Gans, Roma. *Let's Go Rock Collecting.* HarperCollins, 1997.

Gibbons, Gail. *Easter.* Holiday House, 1991.

Gibbons, Gail. *Halloween Is....* Holiday House, 2003.

Gibbons, Gail. *St. Patrick's Day.* Holiday House, 1994.

Gibbons, Gail. *Thanksgiving Is....* Holiday House, 2005.

Golick, Margie. *Wacky Word Games.* Pembroke Publishing, 1995.

Gould, Toni S. *Get Ready to Read.* Walker Publishing, 1991.

Hablitzel, Marie and Kim Stitzer. Draw-Write-Now series. Barker Creek Publishing, 1995–2000.

Hanson, Lisa and Heather Kempskie. *The Siblings' Busy Book.* Meadowbrook Press, 2008.

Hirsch, E. D. *What Your 1st Grader Needs to Know.* Delta, 1998.

Hirsch, E. D. *What Your 2nd Grader Needs to Know.* Delta, 1999.

Hirsch, E. D. *What Your 3rd Grader Needs to Know.* Delta, 2002.

Hunt, Gladys. *Honey for a Child's Heart.* Zondervan Books, 2002.

Isaac, Dawn. *Garden Crafts for Children.* CICO Books, 2012.

Johnson, June. *838 Ways to Amuse a Child.* Gramercy Publishing, 1997.

Jones, Claudia. *More Parents Are Teachers, Too.* Williamson Publishing, 1990.

Jones, Claudia. *Parents Are Teachers, Too.* Williamson Publishing, 1988.

Kelly, Marguerite and Elia Parsons. *The Mother's Almanac.* Doubleday, 1975.

Kenda, Margaret and Phyllis S. Williams. *Science Wizardry for Kids.* Barron's, 1992.

Kimmel, Eric A. *The Golem's Latkes.* Amazon Children's Publishing, 2011.

Kite, L. Patricia. *Gardening Wizardry for Kids.* Barron's, 1995.

Kranowitz, Carol Stock. *101 Activities for Kids in Tight Spaces.* St. Martin's Press, 1995.

Lankford, Mary D. *Hopscotch around the World.* HarperCollins, 1996.

Lasky, Kathryn. *The Librarian Who Measured the Earth.* Little, Brown and Company, 1994.

LeBaron, Marie. *Make and Takes for Kids: 50 Crafts Throughout the Year.* Wiley, 2011.

Levine, Mark. *Story of the Orchestra: Listen While You Learn About the Instruments, the Music and the Composers Who Wrote the Music!* Black Dog & Leventhal Publishers, 2000.

Lewis, Amanda. *Making Memory Books.* Kids Can Press, 1999.

Macaulay, David. *The New Way Things Work.* Houghton Mifflin, 1998.

Martha Stewart's Handmade Holiday Crafts: 225 Inspired Projects for Year-Round Celebrations. Potter Craft, 2011.

Morris, Karyn. *The Kids Can Press Jumbo Book of Gardening.* Kids Can Press, 2000.

National Audobon Society. *The National Audubon Society Pocket Guide to Familiar Rocks and Minerals.* Knopf, 1988.

Nissenberg, Sandra K. *The Everything Kids' Cookbook*. Adams Media, 2008.

Nye, Bill. *Bill Nye the Science Guy's Big Blast of Science*. Basic Books, 1993.

Otto, Carolyn B. *Celebrate Kwanzaa: With Candles, Community, and the Fruits of the Harvest*. National Geographic Children's Books, 2008.

Paré, Jean. *Company's Coming Kids' Healthy Cooking*. Company's Coming Publishing, 2006.

Peel, Kathy. *The Family Manager's Guide to Summer Survival*. Fair Winds Press, 2006.

Pellant, Chris. *The Best Book of Fossils, Rocks & Minerals*. Kingfisher, 2007.

Perry, Susan K. *Playing Smart*. Free Spirit Publishing, 1990.

Prelutsky, Jack. *It's Valentine's Day*. HarperTrophy, 1996.

Riekehof, Lottie L. *The Joy of Signing*. Gospel Publishing House, 1987.

Ross, Kathy. *More of the Best Holiday Crafts Ever!*. 21st Century, 2003.

Rusackas, Francesca. *60 Super Simple Friendship Crafts*. Lowell House Juvenile, 1999.

Sadler, Judy Ann. *The New Jumbo Book of Easy Crafts*. Kids Can Press, 2009.

Schuman, Jo Miles. *Art from Many Hands*. Prentice-Hall, 2003.

Schwake, Susan and Rainer. *Art Lab for Kids*. Quarry Books, 2012.

Sheinwold, Alfred. *101 Best Family Card Games*. Sterling Publishing, 1992.

Sieber, Arlyn G. *A Kid's Guide to Collecting Coins*. Krause Publications, 2011.

Smedley, Wendy. *Start Scrapbooking: Your Essential Book to Recording Memories*. Memory Makers, 2010.

Spier, Peter. *The Star-Spangled Banner*. Dragonfly Books, 1992.

Stenmark, Jean Kerr, Virginia Thompson, and Ruth Cossey. *Family Math*. Lawrence Hall of Science, 1986.

Toone, Matthew. *Great Games! 175 Games & Activities for Families, Groups, & Children!* Mullerhaus Publishing, 2009.

Trelease, Jim. *The Read-Aloud Handbook, 6th Edition*. Penguin Books, 2006.

Warner, Penny. *Kids' Holiday Fun!* Meadowbrook Press, 1994.

Warner, Penny. *Kids' Party Games and Activities*. Meadowbrook Press, 2012.

Washington, Donna L. and Stephen Taylor. *The Story of Kwanzaa*. HarperCollins, 1997.

Wilson, Mimi and Mary Beth Lagerborg. *Once-a-Month Cooking: A Proven System for Spending Less Time in the Kitchen and Enjoying Delicious, Homemade Meals Every Day*. St. Martin's Griffin, 2007.

Woram, Catherine. *Paper Scissors Glue: 45 Fun and Creative Papercraft Projects for Kids*. Ryland Peters & Small, 2010.

The United States General Services Administration makes available many free and low-cost federal publications of consumer interest, including many on learning activities and parenting. If you would like a free copy of the Consumer Information Catalog, you can download or order a copy online at www.publications.usa.gov/USAPubs.php.

Index

A

Accordion, 40
Aces Up, 41
Act It Out, 249
Action Jumping, 163
Address Book, 216
All By Myself, 20
All-Purpose Bubble Solution, 133
Alphabet Cookies, 105
Alphabet Game, 376
Amazing Inflating Balloon, 232
American Sign Language, 33
Anagrams, 201
Another Kind of Alphabet, 32
Apples of Gold, 253
Applesauce-Oatmeal Muffins, 104
Art Book, 246
Artist of the Month, 248
Arts and Crafts, 277

B

Backwords, 207
Baked Apple Crisp, 102
Baked Fish, 95
Baker's Box, 8
Baker's Clay, 405
Balloon Game, 392
Basic Craft Recipes, 399
Basic Hopscotch, 148

Basics, The, 1
Battleships, 183
Beanbag Race, 72
Beanbag Throw, 70
Beeswax Candle, 391
Best Books for Children, 413
Best Chocolate Chip Cookies in the
    World, 106
Bird's Nest Pie, 98
Blind Penny Hunt, 75
Blueberry Dessert Cake, 111
Bombers, 156
Book of Lists, 275
Book of Me, 273
Books, Books, Books, 314
Bounce Eye, 158
Bouncy Bubble Solution, 134
Bowling, 155
Braille, 34
Brainstorming, 190
Breakfast in the Park, 131
Bubble, Bubble, 132
Bubble Contest, 137
Bubble Doughnut, 138
Bubble Fun, 136
Bubble Solution, 133
Budding Author, 316
Bunny Game, 353
Busy bag, 12
Busy box, 8

G

H

I

J

Notes _____

Notes _____

Notes _____

_____

_____

_____

_____

_____

_____

_____

_____

_____

_____

_____

_____

_____

_____

_____

_____

Notes

Also from Meadowbrook Press

✦ *Busy Books*
The Toddler's Busy Book and *The Preschooler's Busy Book* each contain 365 activities (one for each day of the year) for your children using items found around the home. These books offer parents and child-care providers fun reading, math, and science activities that will stimulate a child's natural curiosity. They also provide great activities for indoor play during even the longest stretches of bad weather! Both show you how to save money by making your own paints, play dough, craft clays, glue, paste, and other arts-and-crafts supplies.

✦ *Play and Learn*
Baby Play and Learn and *Preschooler Play and Learn*, from child-development expert Penny Warner, offer ideas for games and activities that will provide hours of developmental learning opportunities and fun for babies and young children. Each book contains step-by-step instructions, illustrations, and bulleted lists of skills your child will learn through play activities.

✦ *Discipline without Shouting or Spanking*
The most practical guide to discipline available, this newly revised book provides proven methods for handling the 30 most common forms of childhood misbehavior, from temper tantrums to sibling rivalry.

✦ *Kids Pick the Funniest Poems*
Three hundred elementary-school kids will tell you that this book contains the funniest poems for kids—because they picked them! This book is guaranteed to please children ages 6–12!

We offer many more titles written to delight, inform, and entertain. To browse our full selection of titles, visit our web site at:

www.meadowbrookpress.com

For quantity discounts, please call: 1-800-338-2232